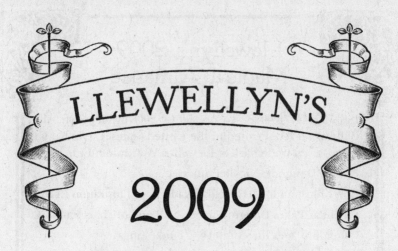

LLEWELLYN'S

2009

Magical Almanac

D1010236

Featuring

A. C. Fisher Aldag, Elizabeth Barrette, Nancy V. Bennett,
Boudica, Calantirniel, Dallas Jennifer Cobb,
Sally Cragin, Raven Digitalis, Ellen Dugan, Sybil Fogg,
Lily Gardner, Abel R. Gomez, Magenta Griffith,
Elizabeth Hazel, James Kambos, Estha McNevin,
Mickie Mueller, Sharynne MacLeod NicMhacha,
Paniteowl, Janina Renée, Laurel Reufner, K. D. Spitzer,
Abby Willowroot, Gail Wood, and Winter Wren

Llewellyn's 2009 Magical Almanac

ISBN 978-0-7387-0722-8. Copyright © 2008 by Llewellyn. All rights reserved. Printed in the United States. Llewellyn is a registered trademark of Llewellyn Worldwide, Ltd.

Editor/Designer: Nicole Edman

Cover Illustration: © Grizelda Holderness/Illustration LTD.

Calendar Pages Design: Andrea Neff and Michael Fallon

Calendar Pages Illustrations: © Fiona King

Interior Illustrations © Melissa Gay, pages 16, 19, 45, 48, 59, 62, 87, 92, 137, 268, 289, 294, 317, 319, 322, 324; © Carol Coogan, pages 13, 29, 76, 81, 85, 102, 105, 130, 133, 221, 233, 236, 260, 262, 265, 285, 304, 308, 310, 344; © David Wallace, pages 22, 25, 52, 94, 97, 124, 143, 146, 224, 226, 241, 245, 298, 326, 330, 350, 353; © Mickie Mueller, pages 37, 70, 73, 116, 121, 152, 155, 250, 253, 313, 337.

Clip Art Illustrations: Dover Publications

Special thanks to Amber Wolfe for the use of daily color and incense correspondences. For more detailed information, please see *Personal Alchemy* by Amber Wolfe.

You can order Llewellyn annuals and books from *New Worlds*, Llewellyn's catalog. To request a free copy of the catalog, call toll-free 1-877-NEW-WRLD or visit our website at www.llewellyn.com.

Astrological calculations are performed by the Kepler 6 astrology software program, specially created for Llewellyn Publications and used with the kind permission of Cosmic Patterns Software, Inc., www.AstroSoftware.com.

Llewellyn Worldwide
Dept. 0-7387-0722-8
2143 Wooddale Drive
Woodbury, MN 55125

About the Authors

A. C. FISHER ALDAG, one of the founders of Caer na Donia y Llew and the Pagan Academy, lives in southwestern Michigan near the beautiful Big Lake with her husband, Dave, children Rhiannon and Brandyn, her mom, the "Witch Emeritus," and too many animals to count. Look for her at a Pagan festival near you!

ELIZABETH BARRETTE has been involved with the Pagan community for more than twenty years. She serves as the managing editor of *PanGaia* (www.pangaia.com) and the Dean of Studies at the Grey School of Wizardry (www.greyschool.com). Her book *Composing Magic: How to Create Magical Spells, Rituals, Blessings, Chants, and Prayers* came out from New Page Books in 2007. She lives in central Illinois and enjoys gardening for wildlife and stone magic. She has done much networking with Pagans in her area, including coffeehouse meetings and open sabbats. Her other writing fields include speculative fiction and gender studies. Visit her Live-Journal "The Wordsmith's Forge" at http://ysabetwordsmith .livejournal.com/

NANCY V. BENNETT is a writer of more than 300 articles, essays and poems. Her work has also been featured in *We'Moon*, *Silver Wheel*, and other Llewellyn publications. She does mainstream articles as well, normally centered around history or animals, two of her passions. She can be reached at nvbennett@shaw.ca. Currently, she is working on a collection of essays, spells, and poems from a Canadian Witch perspective.

BOUDICA is reviews editor and co-owner of *The Wiccan/Pagan Times* and owner of *The Zodiac Bistro*, both online publications. She is a high priestess with the Mystic Tradition Teaching Coven

of Pennsylvania, Ohio, New Jersey, New York, and Maryland, and is a guest speaker at many local Ohio and East Coast events. A former New Yorker, she now resides with her husband and three cats in Ohio.

CALANTIRNIEL has practiced many forms of natural spirituality since the early 1990s. She lives in Western Montana with her husband and teenage daughter, while her older son is in college. She is a professional astrologer, tarot card reader, dowser, and became a certified Master Herbalist in 2007. She has an organic garden, crochets professionally and is co-creating *Tië eldaliéva*, meaning the Elven Spiritual Path. Find out more by visiting http://www.myspace.com/aartiana

DALLAS JENNIFER COBB lives an enchanted life in a waterfront village in Canada. Forever scheming novel ways to pay the bills, she's freed up resources for what she loves most: family, gardens, fitness and fabulous food. When she's not running country roads or wandering the beach, she is writing and daydreaming. Contact her at jennifer.cobb@sympatico.ca

SALLY CRAGIN writes the astrological forecast, "Moon Signs" for the *Boston Phoenix*, which is syndicated throughout New England. She can also be heard on a variety of radio stations as "Symboline Dai." A regular arts reviewer and feature writer for the Boston Globe, she has edited *Button, New England's Tiniest Magazine of Poetry, Fiction and Gracious Living* since 1993. She also provides forecasts for clients which are "scary-accurate." More on all these projects at moonsigns.net

RAVEN DIGITALIS (Missoula, Montana) is a Neopagan Priest of the "disciplined eclectic" shadow magick tradition Opus Aima Obscuræ, and is a radio and club DJ of Gothic, EBM, and industrial music. He is also the author of *Goth Craft: The Magickal Side*

of Dark Culture, and *Shadow Magick Compendium*. With his Priestess, Estha, Raven holds community gatherings, tarot readings, and a variety of ritual services. From their home, the two also operate the metaphysical business Twigs and Brews, specializing in magickal and medicinal bath salts, herbal blends, essential oils, and incenses. Raven holds a degree in anthropology from the University of Montana, is an animal rights activist, and is a black-and-white photographic artist. www.ravendigitalis.com www.myspace.com/oakraven

ELLEN DUGAN, aka "The Garden Witch" is an award winning author and a psychic-clairvoyant. She has been a practicing Witch for over twenty-four years. Her Llewellyn book titles include: *Garden Witchery: Magick from the Ground Up, Elements of Witchcraft, Natural Magick for Teens, 7 Days of Magic: Spells, Charms & Correspondences for the Bewitching Week, Cottage Witchery: Natural Magick for Hearth and Home, Autumn Equinox: The Enchantment of Mabon, The Enchanted Cat: Feline Fascinations, Spells & Magick, Herb Magic for Beginners: Down-to-Earth Enchantments, Natural Witchery: Intuitive, Personal & Predictive Magick*, and *How to Enchant a Man: Spells to Bewitch, Bedazzle & Bequile*. When she's not keeping up with her family (two of the kids are in college now and the oldest is out on his own), Ellen likes to unwind by working in her perennial gardens at home with her husband. Ellen wholeheartedly encourages folks to personalize their spellcraft. To go outside and connect with the spiritual side of nature. To get their hands dirty and discover the wonder and magick of the natural world that surrounds them. Visit Ellen online at her webstite: www.geocities.com/edugan_gardenwitch

SYBIL FOGG has been a practicing witch for more than twenty years, as well as a freelance writer, mother, and belly dancer.

Sybil believes that all dancing is a form of worship and weaves movement throughout her rituals and spellcraft. Along with her husband, Drew, Sybil used henna magic to ease the discomfort and fear of preterm birth with her fourth child in 2005 and thus the inspiration for combining dance, henna art, and ceremony was born in the form of the dance troupe of Luna Wind. Sybil holds a BA in English and an MFA in Creative Writing. She is currently working on a collection of nonfiction short stories.

LILY GARDNER has been studying and collecting bits of folklore and myth since childhood. In addition to writing for Llewellyn, she has written several short stories, a murder mystery and is completing work on saint folklore. Lily has been practicing witchcraft in Portland, Oregon, for fifteen years.

ABEL R. GOMEZ lives in the California Bay area. He is an actor and writer with a deep interest in myth, ritual, and symbolism of global spiritual traditions. His work has appeared in a number of Neopagan publications, most notably *Copper-Moon*, an online magazine for young adult Witches. Abel can often be found recycling, saving animals, exploring esotericism, or doing the Time Warp.

MAGENTA GRIFFITH has been a Witch more than 30 years, a high priestess for nearly 20 years, and is a founding member of the coven Prodea which has been celebrating rituals since 1980. She presents classes and workshops at a variety of events around the Midwest. She shares her home with a black cat.

ELIZABETH HAZEL is the author of *Tarot Decoded*, and is a high priestess, mystic sorceress, tarotist, and astrologer. She writes the "Astro-Spell" column for *newWitch* magazine and "StarCrypt" for *Mysteries Magazine*, and is currently working on another book. She may be contacted at http://kozmic-kitchen.com

JAMES KAMBOS writes the monthly introductions for Llewellyn's *Witches' Spell-A-Day Almanac* as well as several of the spells. His interest in spellcrafting began in childhood as he watched his grandmother create spells based on Greek folk magic. He is a regular contributor to Llewellyn's annuals. When not writing, James also paints in the American primitive style. The beautiful Appalachian hill country of southern Ohio is the place he calls home.

ESTHA MCNEVIN (Missoula, Montana) is a Neopagan Priestess and is the head of the Opus Aima Obscurae tradition. She is passionate about fine art and ancient history, is an avid bookworm, and is co-owner of the metaphysical business Twigs and Brews, specializing in magickal and medicinal bath salts, herbal blends, essential oils, and incenses. In addition to hosting public rituals for the sabbats, Estha hosts personal women's divination rituals each Dark Moon and holds private spiritual consultations and tarot card readings for the community. www.myspace.com/twigsandbrews

MICKIE MUELLER is an award-winning Pagan Spiritual artist and the illustrator of *The Well Worn Path* and *The Hidden Path* tarot decks. Her magically infused art has been seen on magazine covers internationally and on the web. She enjoys writing and speaking on many topics of magic and art, and has contributed articles to various magazines as well as Llewellyn's periodicals. Mickie is an ordained Pagan minister and a reiki master/teacher. She encourages people to use their magic to enhance every aspect of their everyday lives. www.mickiemuellerart.com

SHARYNNE MACLEOD NICMHACHA is a Celtic priestess, scholar and bard of Scottish, Irish, and Welsh ancestry, a direct descendant of "Fairy Clan" MacLeod. She has studied Celtic languages and mythology through Harvard University, and has presented work

in Scotland, Ireland, and North America. Sharynne is also a professional singer and musician (The Moors, Devandaurae) as well as a published author (*Queen of the Night*).

PANITEOWL lives in the foothills of the Appalachians in northeast Pennsylvania, where she and her husband are in the process of developing a private retreat for spiritual awareness. Paniteowl is co-coordinator of two annual events in Virginia known as the Gathering of the Tribes. She is founder and elder high priestess of the Mystic Wicca tradition.

JANINA RENÉE is a scholar of folklore, psychology, medical anthropology, the material culture of magic, ritual studies, history, and literature. Her award-winning books include *Tarot Spells, Tarot Your Everyday Guide, Tarot for a New Generation,* and *By Candlelight: Rites for Celebration, Blessing and Prayer.* Janina continues to work on multiple book projects, with ongoing research projects exploring the ways folk magic and medicinal techniques can apply to modern problems, including the modulation of Asperger's Syndrome and other neurosensory processing problems.

LAUREL REUFNER lives in gorgeous Athens County, Ohio with her husband and two daughters. Attracted to topics of history and mythology, she is slowly working on her first book. You can check out her website at ww.spiritrealm.com/laurelreufner

K. D. SPITZER is a Witchy writer living in coastal New Hampshire. She walks a labyrinth every chance she gets, taking problems to its center and walking out with a peaceful heart. Sometimes she casts a spell in the heart of the labyrinth.

ABBY WILLOWROOT is an artist, writer, metalsmith, and Priestess of the Goddess. Her online goddess temple is the Spiral Goddess Grove. Serving the metaphysical community since 1967, Abby's

work reflects many diverse cultural and artistic influences. Nine of her pieces are in the Smithsonian's permanent collection. Creator of the Spiral Goddess, Abby's Goddess Art and Willowroot Wands have been featured in books and museum shows. Llewellyn regularly publishes articles by Ms. Willowroot.

GAIL WOOD has been a Witch and priestess for more than twenty years, practicing a shamanic path celebrating the Dark Moon. She is a teacher, tarot reader, and reiki master. She is the author of *Rituals of the Dark Moon: 13 Lunar Rites for a Magical Path*, *The Wild God: Meditations and Rituals on the Sacred Masculine*, and many articles in a variety of Pagan publications.

WINTER WREN is a long time magical practitioner and tarot professional. She is the former cohost of The Witching Hour on WONX radio. She founded the Temple of the Sacred Lady of Avalon in 1989. Her days consist of magick, tarot, art, writing, and education. She makes her home in southeastern Michigan, where she and her partner share their home with a merry band of Maine coon kitties.

Table of Contents

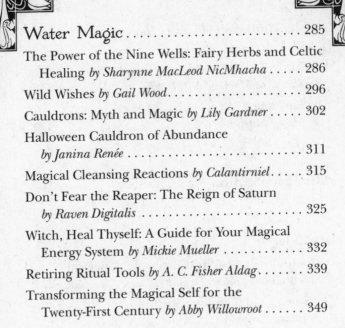

Water Magic

Earth Magic

Conjuring a Garden with Heart

by Ellen Dugan

He who would have beautiful roses in his garden
must have beautiful roses in his heart.
—Samuel Reynolds Hole

Whenever I teach a class on herbs and gardening, be it to magical folks or mundane, I typically get questions about how to create a mood or theme in a garden. The *ambiance* of a garden is everything. Even those of us who have been gardening for years realize that there is more to gardening than just sticking the plants in the ground; you want your garden to flow together and set an atmosphere or theme. For gardeners who are also magical practitioners, that theme is most likely going to be an enchanted one.

So, let's get motivated! What type of garden are you dreaming of? What would you do if you could just "go crazy" in the garden? Perhaps you'd plan a theme garden devoted to one specific deity, or design a faerie tale garden, or even a tranquil Feng Shui style of meditation garden. Maybe you wish to plant a bigger enchanted herb garden full of magical plants for spells and charms. Perhaps you would like to create a garden devoted to your favorite goddess. How about a handy kitchen Witch garden full of veggies and culinary herbs? The choice is completely yours.

No matter what magical mood you are trying to invoke in the Witch's garden, design and color will come into play. By applying these techniques and tweaking the design a bit further, you can conjure the atmosphere you want.

Make no mistake, the fastest way to turn a pedestrian flower bed into an enchanting garden is to get a little atmosphere going. There must be something here that captures people's imaginations and tugs at their heart. We make use of the basic elements of design not only to beautify but to increase our perception of the environment. This perception helps us to open up and receive the messages and secrets that are inherent in the natural and magical worlds.

The Enchanting Elements of Design

Creative design is what turns a collection of trees, herbs, perennials, and flowers into a garden. The clarity and color schemes found in your magical garden give focus to your goals and intentions. The complexity in your plant forms, including things such as texture and pattern, will make for a sensual garden that begs to be touched, sniffed, and enjoyed. Create a refuge, add a sense of mystery, and be conscious of the flow of energy when creating a magical garden.

The best gardens all share a few main qualities, even though the styles and themes may be radically different. These design qualities are: clarity, complexity, mystery, and refuge. Without these traits, a garden doesn't invite us in or enchant us.

Garden Design Qualities

Clarity – This defines the perimeter of the garden and the use of pathways. Where does the garden begin? Where does it lead, and where does it end? The clever use of a clearly defined entrance or threshold into the garden makes it special and welcomes you in. A good garden threshold area is like a welcoming embrace. The threshold into a garden is an in-between place that is full of possibilities and enchantment. In fact, a gate can be a symbol of a spiritual doorway or passage that separates one reality, or one world, from the next.

Once inside the garden you should be drawn along a pathway to its heart. The heart of the garden is a place you feel compelled to approach. It's fascinating and irresistible. Also, the heart of the garden defines its use. This is where your magical intentions are centered and where visitor's attentions will be focused.

Complexity – In the simplest terms, this is variety. You can achieve complexity with the magic of color. (Color in the garden will be discussed in our next section.) Now, it's true that color shouldn't be so overwhelming that the eye can't rest. However, keep in mind that even in a shady hosta garden, for example, there are dozens of varieties and shades of green available. All those hues of green can harmonize with each other beautifully. Anything from lime-green to blue-green to white stripes, edges, and yellow hues. Play on that, use your imagination and see what you can create.

Look at the pattern of the foliage, and the texture of leaf and flower. Pay attention to pattern and any symbolism that may be meaningful to you.

Mystery – Give your garden something that will inspire curiosity. Here you balance the known with the unexpected. The garden should captivate you and lure you in some subtle way—that tantalizing promise of *more*. For example, a path that turns the corner to an unexpected surprise. A hidden water feature that you can hear but have to search to find. Wind chimes that sings out in a breeze, hanging from a tall tree. A statue of a goddess or faerie tucked into a shady nook or grotto. A small, secret place to leave offerings to the elements and faeries of the garden. Mystery is vital in a magical garden because that feeling of stumbling upon a "secret garden" is a delicious one. Use your imagination and see what you can do to add some mystery magic to the garden.

Refuge – The final quality for an enchanting garden is refuge. This is best described as a feeling of welcome relaxation and reflection. In other words, a place where you can "sit a spell." Your garden should include a place to sit and relax. This can be as simple as a concrete or wooden bench, a tire swing, a boulder, a glider, or a curvy metal chair. Wherever you choose to make your refuge, offer some type of seating. And make the area special. In my garden, this area is under the rose arbor. Tucked underneath is a small bistro table and chair set. It's shady, private, and, when the roses bloom in May, filled with wall-to-wall hot-pink roses. Incorporating a resting place into your garden offers a chance to relax, to contemplate, and to enjoy. Or, perhaps even a serene spot to work a spell or two.

Color Magic in the Garden

Working successfully with color in the garden is one of the more important lessons that I have taught to Master Gardener interns over the year. It is necessary knowledge for budding landscape and magical garden designers, too. That being said, you'll need to ask yourself a few questions before deciding on your color scheme. These questions are: do you prefer the subtle blending of colors that complement each other or do you prefer contrasting colors? Magical gardeners can certainly apply these basic principles in the choices of the colors of their plants to absolutely charming effects. And, do you have a favorite color that you'd like to see dominant in the garden all year or would you like to see diverse colors all working together?

If you think color is not important in the garden, think again. The clever use of color can set the mood, and color can warm up a shady spot or cool down a sunny one. Color is often used to create a specific atmosphere in the garden. It can draw attention to a particular feature, create the impression of spaciousness, or help make a large area seem cozier. The trick is to learn which colors harmonize or work well together and how to identify them. Here are a few color schemes for you to peruse and consider.

Complementary colors – You remember your complementary colors from elementary school, don't you? These pairs of colors are directly opposite from each other on the color wheel. They are the tried and true color combinations. Examples include red and green, blue and orange, and yellow and purple.

Analogous colors – Also called "harmonious colors." These are colors that are next to each other on the color wheel, e.g., the warm tones of yellow, yellow-orange, and orange. Or the cooler hues of lavender, blue, and cool pink. These color combinations appeal to many people and are a lovely way to make a flower bed to flow together with a sense of unity.

Monochromatic colors – Sometimes referred to as "single-color gardens." This is the simplest kind of color scheme and one of the easiest for novice gardeners to work with. This type of color scheme is built on varying shades of one basic color. For example, the lighter and darker shades of red, such as medium pink, pale pink, purple, and reddish-purple. These single-color gardens give a sense of openness and space to even the smallest of gardens.

Monochromatic colors can really make a shady garden pop. Imagine an all-white garden tucked in a shady spot. You could turn it into a Moon goddess garden if you wanted. Imagine how gorgeous a creamy-white hydrangea, white-edged hostas, and white impatiens would look there. Each would play well off the other and show to their best advantage. With a monochromatic garden, the plant's form and texture will take center stage.

Bright Colors – The warm, vibrant colors—red, hot orange, and bright yellow—draw attention and make large areas seem smaller and cozier. They create the illusion of warmth, invoke the element of fire, and cast a festive atmosphere.

Neutral colors – Neutrals are the blending colors in the garden: gray, silver, and white. Also, true green may also be used as a neutral feature in the garden. Neutral colors tone down the effects of sharply contrasting or clashing colors, which may seem harsh to the eye if placed next to each other. Want an example? Let's say you have orange nasturtiums and purple pansies side by side. They will clash. Tuck in some silver dusty miller and it softens the look so the colors don't seem as visually jarring.

Dark Colors – Colors such as purples and blues will create an impression of more space. These are soothing, calming colors that invoke the element of water. Plus, dark colors will weave the illusion of coolness in hot, full Sun gardens, no matter how high the temperature rises.

Pastel Colors – These soft shades of white, pale yellow, and pink will stand out in twilight gardens and shady areas. You may employ these colors to invoke the element of air. Keep in mind that these colors will light up during twilight and are good color choices if you are most able to enjoy the evening hours in the garden. Consider pastels if you are planning a witchy nighttime garden.

Seasonal and Multiseason Color – Part of the fun of choosing colors for your magical garden is deciding when those colors will appear. Remember to choose plants for all of the seasons. Select plants for spring, summer, and the fall months and make a plan for a little bit of winter interest. This way your garden shifts seamlessly from one season to the next.

Those Enchanting Elements of Design

No matter if you are designing a kitchen Witch garden, a formal knot garden, tending magical herbs in simple raised beds, planting a flowing cottage-style garden, or creating a serene and stylish oriental garden, you'll enjoy better results if you incorporate the design tips that we have covered here. Don't forget to look at your magical garden with an eye toward design. Pay attention to your feelings and work on improving the mood and the overall aura or atmosphere in your landscape.

Have fun incorporating these practical ideas and tips into your magical garden with heart. Dare to turn a simple garden into one that inspires you spiritually and transforms your dreams into something spectacular.

For Further Study:

Dugan, Ellen. A Garden Witch's Herbal. Woodbury, MN: Llewellyn Worldwide, forthcoming.

Magic In Your Cupboard

by James Kambos

Centuries ago, the kitchen wasn't just a place to prepare food, it was also the center for both magical and healing activities. The herbalist, Witch, or Wise Ones of long ago knew that ordinary cooking ingredients, foods, and kitchen utensils could be used to create powerful magic. Spices, herbs, berries, and roots were just a few of the ingredients used by the village Wise One to heal or work magic.

The knowledge and magical lore possessed by these healers/magicians was highly respected. They were frequently consulted by their neighbors to ease afflictions like insomnia, cure a rash, or break a hex caused by the evil eye. Many were asked to cast a spell or divine the future. By candlelight or by a glowing hearth, they'd cast their spells and empower them with everyday ingredients found in their cupboard or pantry.

These magicians were also keenly aware of the rhythms of nature. They knew when and where certain herbs would be growing, when to harvest them, and how to use them magically and medicinally. The Wise Ones could "read" the signs of nature and were able to sometimes predict the weather. And, like any herbalist or village Witch, they worked with the appropriate phase of the Moon.

The history of kitchen magic stretches back into antiquity. Recipes for herbal remedies using ingredients such as onions and mint have been found in ancient Egyptian tombs. And the Greek doctor Hippocrates realized the medicinal value of hundreds of herbs, many of which are still used today.

There are no strict rules about kitchen witchery. Since occult practices were strictly forbidden at certain times over the past few centuries, there is little information written down about this practical form of folk magic. Most of the kitchen magic we know and use today was passed down orally through the years. Despite persecution, it has managed to survive in certain rural areas and among some ethnic groups.

A Kitchen Blessing

Although kitchen magic isn't high ceremonial magic, it is still a good idea to purify your kitchen with the simple blessing that follows. This will ensure that your kitchen is transformed into a sacred space that will aid in the success of your spells and charms.

To bless your kitchen and to help increase positive vibrations, tie together three protective herbs, such as basil, parsley, and rosemary. The should be fresh. Drench this herbal bouquet with plain tap water. Hold them in both hands and inhale their scents. Using the herbs as a wand, walk clockwise around your kitchen and gently sprinkle the water all around. Pay special attention to cabinets, countertops, drawers, the refrigerator, and oven—anywhere you plan to perform your magic. Gently crush the herbs in your hands; inhale their scents again. You may hang the herbs to dry, or use them immediately in a recipe. Repeat this ritual as needed.

In addition to the above described ritual, you may also bless appliances by using the sacred oil of the Greek goddess Athena—olive oil. Olive oil promotes peace and protection. For a blessing, simply anoint an appliance by taking a drop of olive oil on your finger and trace a holy symbol, such as a cross or pentagram, on each appliance. As you do so, concentrate on asking the appliance to give you years of service.

Once you've consecrated your kitchen as a place to work magic, you'll be able to create simple, powerful magic suited to your needs. If you're new to the magical arts, you're about to find that the ingredients for many types of magical practices are as close as your cupboard or refrigerator. Best of all, you can begin to perform magic *now*. Here are a few suggestions on how to use some basic kitchen supplies to bring about positive changes into your life. Let's begin!

Salt and Pepper

Found in almost any kitchen, salt and black pepper (used separately or combined) are among the most purifying and protective of all kitchen seasonings.

Salt is the symbol of purity. It's related to feminine energy and the Earth. Pepper is masculine, fiery, and protective. It's sacred to the god Mars.

An old-fashioned magical charm to protect the home is to sprinkle salt at every exterior doorway, then lean a broom across the threshold. To ward off evil influences, you may simply combine equal parts salt and pepper and scatter it about your property.

To repel the evil eye, try this: combine salt and pepper and sprinkle outside your front door in a spiral pattern. The belief is that the evil power will follow the spiral design, become trapped, and its energy will weaken until it becomes harmless. When you feel the salt and pepper have done their work, sweep it away from your home.

Garlic

No kitchen Witch should be without garlic. Since ancient times, garlic has been used to purify, protect, and give courage. Hung in the kitchen, on the front porch, or near livestock, garlic will protect against any hostile energy.

To protect the home, cut a garlic clove into three sections and combine with salt. Sprinkle this mixture on your doorstep. Combine this mixture with pepper and you'll have a magical blend to protect against thieves.

To repel an enemy, crush a garlic clove then spit on it three times. At night, during a waning Moon when you won't

be disturbed, throw the crushed garlic in the direction of your enemy. Their influence on you will begin to fade.

As an offering of thanks, bury a clove of garlic at a quiet crossroads as the ancient Greeks did. This was done to receive the blessing of the goddess Hecate, the Queen of Witchcraft and Magic.

Taken internally, garlic has many healing qualities. It's said to reduce the number of colds a person may contract and to boost the immune system. Odorless garlic tablets, which can help regulate the circulatory system and lower blood pressure, are available at drugstores. As with any drug, you should check with a health professional first before beginning a garlic supplement regimen.

Some magical practitioners even pray over garlic to give them protection and to keep away all envy and jealousy.

Love Magic

The village Wise Ones of long ago were frequently called upon to work love charms. Here is one such charm using some love-attracting herbs. As with any love magic, don't think of any specific person as you cast this spell—that would be a form of manipulation, which has no place in positive magic. This spell is only meant to attract the perfect person to you.

You'll need one teaspoon each of crushed almonds, sugar, and grated orange peel. Blend the ingredients and set aside. Select a taper candle in one of the following colors: pink for friendship; orange for a steady, lasting love; or red for a hot, passionate affair. Also have on hand a square piece of red fabric about the size of a handkerchief.

Select a night just before a Full Moon and light the candle in the color of your choice. Relax and gaze at the flame for a few moments. Begin to sprinkle the sugar mixture around the base of the candle and speak these words:

With orange, the fruit of love
With almonds, ground fine as dust
With sugar, pure and white
Bring to me, my heart's delight.

Gaze intently into the candle's flame; you may catch a glimpse of your future love. Let the candle burn out, then place the sugar mixture in the middle of your red cloth and tie up the corners. Hide your magic bundle. You may repeat this spell in one lunar month if you wish.

To magical practitioners of years ago, orange was the fruit of choice for love spells and love sachets. The peel or seeds are equally potent, and if a marriage is desired, orange blossoms should be added to the spell.

If you wish to cook up some love magic, prepare foods and baked goods with warm spices such as cinnamon, clove, and ginger. Men especially find these flavors and scents alluring. If you have no time to bake, try this bit of kitchen witchery. About ten minutes before your lover walks in the door, spray a baking sheet with nonstick baking spray. Sprinkle the sheet lightly with a dusting of cinnamon and place in the oven; set the oven at its lowest setting. The scent of warm cinnamon will set the mood for romance.

A Prosperity Spell

To begin this spell for prosperity, you will need a plain sheet of white paper and a plain envelope. On the paper, write the amount of money you need—be sure it's a reasonable amount. Over the paper, crumble a pinch each of these three money-attracting ingredients: mint, oatmeal, and wheat germ. Fold the paper like a letter and seal it in the envelope. Keep the envelope in a secret place or carry in your purse. When the spell has done its work, burn the envelope and contents in a heatproof dish or fireplace.

Spells to Break a Curse

Breaking a curse was one of the most important activities of the village Witch. The ingredients needed to break a spell were usually common. Here are some examples.

One interesting method involves toast and herbs. First, toast a slice of bread until it is burnt and crumble it on an old, clean dish rag. Add a bit of dried chamomile tea and a bay leaf to the toast crumbs. Crush this mixture by hand; visualize

the curse being destroyed. Tie up the corners of the rag and bury on your property. Leave it undisturbed.

To protect the home against a curse or the evil eye, cut an onion in half. Rub the cut side of the onion along the blade of the knife. Raise the knife with your power hand. As you do this, see a protective blue-white light streaming from the tip of the blade in your mind's eye. Walk clockwise around your home until your house has been psychically sealed.

Another way to break a curse is to combine herbs and fire. Grind together dried basil, red chili pepper flakes, and cumin powder—just a pinch of each will do. Cast this herbal mixture upon a fire and say: "Curse be turned, fire burn. With these herbs, this spell I bind. Leave only good behind." As the fire dies, so will the curse.

Honey and Apple Cider Vinegar

Growing up on my grandparents' farm, I remember honey and apple cider vinegar being staples in our pantry, and now I know why. They are both superb to use in healing and purifying the body and spirit.

To heal a minor burn, dab on a bit of honey. Adding a spoonful of honey to an herbal decoction and soaking a clean cloth in it will make a healing poultice. To bless a new home, blend a small amount of honey with crushed almonds, then anoint the threshold with it. This will ensure a happy home.

If you need a cleansing bath to rid yourself of negativity or renew your spirit, add a cup of vinegar to the bath water. This is great before a ritual, too. To cleanse your system, begin every morning by mixing a tablespoon each of honey and apple cider vinegar in a glass of warm water. Drink this about a half-hour before breakfast, and it will give you a feeling of general well-being.

Conclusion

Creating magic in the kitchen will give you a feeling of empowerment. Knowing that the ordinary seasonings and foods you probably have on hand can help you create powerful magic every day will open up a new door of magical possibilities. And you are drawing upon the ancient wisdom of our ancestors by doing so.

If you wish to create herbal spells yourself, remember the odd-number rule: The most powerful spells usually contain an odd number of ingredients. Three, five, seven, and nine have been the favorite quantities of ingredients used by magicians over the centuries. To learn more about the magical associations of herbs, ask around to see if any herb clubs or herb farms in your area offer workshops.

For Further Study

Cunningham, Scott. *Cuningham's Encyclopedia of Magical Herbs.* St. Paul, MN: Llewellyn Publications, 2002.

Family as Coven

by Sybil Fogg

Sometimes people seek out others who share their religious preferences and desire to belong to a congregation—or, in the case of the Pagan community, a coven. Some Pagans prefer solitary work, and still others work their magic with their family. But can a family truly be a coven? A coven is a community of like-minded individuals who gather to worship and honor the divine together. A family is composed of people who live in the same household and more than likely share the same religious affiliation. Most Wiccan parents practice the Craft with their children because they want to impart a view of the natural and spiritual world to their offspring. This is one reason to consider forming a coven within the family. Other reasons include feeling more comfortable with family members, convenience of all being in one place when needed, and represention of the different stages or cycles of life.

It would be hard to practice any religion without including your children. Imagine the amount of energy it would take to wait until the young ones went to bed for sabbat celebrations or Full Moon spells. What about daytime gatherings? Would you skip Pagan Pride Days just so your own kin wouldn't know about your faith? And what does this say about your faith if you're ashamed of it? There is a level of hypocrisy if your belief system is embarrassing or seems dangerous to those dearest to you. If you have children and are hiding your religious affiliation from them, perhaps it is time to question and reconsider your faith.

Oftentimes, following a spiritual path feels very personal. Many Pagans tell stories of how at some point they needed to practice alone. Sometimes this meant being physically away from people, at others just practicing in a quiet, private manner. Feeling comfortable casting spells and chanting mantras in public or small groups might never happen for those of us who are shy and/or introverted. The family is where many people feel safe. A supportive, loving familial network can aid our spiritual growth, allowing us to take magic to a higher realm because we are safe from the trappings of awkward public settings. Even when families disagree or have a dispute, it is more likely to be worked out, if for no other reason than that family members must eventually see each other again. Other covens may experience power struggle or disagreements and break apart because sometimes it is much easier to move on and start over than to stay and try to reconcile our differences.

One challenge of the regular coven system is getting everyone together. We have all experienced situations where we needed to schedule a meeting or circle and this person had this obligation and that person had that responsibility. It can be hectic enough to make many people throw their hands up in frustration. Many a coven has succumbed to the stress of scheduling problems.

On the other hand, gathering the family takes little more than calling them all to the kitchen table for supper. Especially when our children are young, we

know where they are, which tends to be somewhere physically near to us. We can hold impromptu meetings as well as rituals and magic. Any moment of the day can become spiritual, experienced by all members. A day at the beach can turn into an educational opportunity about ecology, environmentalism, and the elements water, air, earth, and, with a little ingenuity, fire. As children age, it obviously becomes more difficult to bring them all together, but an advantage of living under the same roof is that filling in for the absent coven member is a relatively easy task.

Which brings up another reason families make good covens: they represent the stages of life. Females travel through maiden, mother, and crone phases. For the men of the family, they move through youth, father, and grandfather phases. The act of birth itself is an initiation. For the infant, it is an initiation into the world and family, as well as into the coven. For the woman, she moves from maiden to mother if it is her first child, and each additional birth is a confirmation of her stage as mother. Birth is a journey that travels near death for both mother and child. Despite the wonderful advances of modern medicine, every pregnant woman has a certain awareness that she is creeping close to the valley of the shadow of death. There is no other initiation ritual that is more spiritual than that of the process of giving birth to another human life.

The very young children of a family coven represent innocence. We have an awesome responsibility to teach them about the planet we live on and the creatures we share it with. What we adults show them will determine the future for everyone. Think of the youngest members as an opportunity to educate even ourselves by viewing the world through their eyes and slowing down. We have a chance to really learn about our religion while we break it down for our children. This also affords us the opportunity to appreciate the natural and metaphysical world around us. A child's imagination is expansive—a necessary tool for all magical workings.

The middle-childhood group members of the family will often question and push, but they are also the most active in their belief. In our household, these children fight for animal rights and bring Pagan projects to school to educate their friends, fellow students, and teachers. They want to know everything there is to know about the Goddess and God, the holidays, the elements, and the Moon cycles. They are gluttons for knowledge, gorging and ever growing. Middle-childhood members bring ideas to the table, organize celebrations, and have input at every stage. Similar to the newest members of a non-family coven, they are the most eager and willing to assist in all aspects of coven work.

The maiden or youth members of the family coven begin to exert their independence. They might leave, either emotionally or physically, to follow their own pursuits or to seek their own answers about the world. From my experience, this is a time when they really begin to practice the Craft, but want to do so either with friends or on their own—they aren't always willing to participate in family events. Similar to when novices leave a coven to strike out on their own, the best reaction is to let them go. Unlike members of a nonfamilial coven, they will return, even if only to eat and celebrate holidays. Eventually, they will have families of their own and will bring their children back into the fold to learn from the elders.

The beauty of raising children in a family coven is that you will likely someday be a grandmother or grandfather. You will enter this last material stage and complete the circle of life within your family. There is a good chance in a family coven that all stages of life will be represented at some point, perhaps even all at once. There is so much we can learn from our mothers, fathers, and grandparents, not just about Earth worship and magic, but also how to care for the other people who walk this Earth with us. That is a journey best taken with your family.

Family Moon Wish Spell

Time: Any Full Moon
Tools: Bonfire or fire pit (or small cauldron)
Scraps of white paper
Silver and blue markers, pens, colored pencils,
    or crayons
Herbs: jasmine, rose, lavender, and rosemary

1. Set out a bowl of the mixed herbs for each member of the family who will be participating.

2. Gather in a circle around the bonfire or cauldron. (If it is too cold to do this spell outside, sit around the kitchen table with a cauldron or bowl in the middle.) Hold hands and meditate for a moment, mentally casting the circle. Have someone call each of the four directions.

3. Pass around the paper and writing instruments. Have everyone write down everything they wish to manifest by the next Full Moon. Do not hold back on this step, even if it seems ridiculous, put it down. The younger members who cannot write yet can draw pictures or have older members help them. Remember to vigilantly watch anyone younger than ten around the fire.

4. Welcome the Moon Goddess by saying:

Tonight we welcome the Moon
Round as the mother's womb
We send our wishes out into the night
To be heard by the Goddess bright
From full to dark and then full again,
Please grant us our wishes by then.

5. Have everyone throw their wishes into the fire, followed by a handful of herbs to seal the spell.

6. Clasp hands again and watch the papers curl and burn. Meditate on the idea of your wishes soon being fulfilled.

7. When you are ready, break the silence and open the circle. Do not forget to thank the Goddess and God.

8. Bring out snacks and drinks and enjoy the fire. Feast and talk. Remember that it is moments like these that confirm the family as coven.

Family covens are groups that have dedicated themselves to incorporating their belief system into their everyday life. This includes how they raise their children and honor their spirituality. They might attend public rituals and gatherings, but they generally are not interested in teaching or including members outside of their family. Sometimes they are very closed off from the rest of the Pagan society and other groups, while other family covens might be very vocal and active in the community. They are the same as other covens in that they worship the same deity and appreciate many of the same aspects of Paganism, and have simply chosen to do so with their closest loved ones.

Alternatives for the Solitary

by Boudica

For many solitary practitioners, working alone is a distinct choice they have made. For others, a working group is simply not available in their area. But the solitary practitioner is not an isolated person in their practice. Rather, many solitaries would like to have the option of occasionally working in a group or celebrating some sabbats or esbats with others. Many solitariy practioners choose an occasional group gathering or working—once you have experienced a group setting, you realize that you are not a lone soul on the edge of a practice, but a member of a small community.

For open practioners who actively choose to be solitary (and those who somehow "end up" being solitary), it sometimes seems that there is nothing you can do. You have your books, you have your practice, and you will plug away at it by yourself until you think you've got it right.

For those who are not "out of the closet" to their friends, family, or neighbors, working in a group could present all sorts of issues. Many solitaries are not on the Internet, nor do they have a computer. So what options are there?

Covens

Covens are the most obvious group setting. However, even if they are available in your area, covens can present issues. The wrong practice, the wrong people, the wrong place; this can make the coven a bad idea or not a viable option. Covens also take time—more time than some people have—by requiring regular attendance. For those of us with busy family lives, game schedules, PTA meetings, and jobs must come first. A coven just won't figure well into many people's busy lives.

Study Groups

But there are other ways! I am sure you have friends; maybe one or two know you practice. They might know your spirituality is not mainstream or they could even be closet practitioners like yourself. Maybe you want to learn, but you don't feel you have the knowledge or the ability to be "teachers." You just want to study and progress on your own chosen paths.

What is wrong with studying together? How about an informal study group? This is nothing new, study groups have been around in various forms for a long time. Put your heads together and work on understanding, practicing, and improving your rituals. This kind of group will prove to be nurturing, and it can be as informal as having a cup at a coffee shop or some shopping time at a bookstore.

I've listened to people say that their local group only offers elements that they do not want to associate with. Yes, there are folks out there with some strange ideas on what we do, and yes, they call themselves Pagan; and no, we don't want to be involved with them. But, not everyone is weird, off the wall, or stupid. There are working groups in our communities that offer the chance to socialize, have rituals, and make connections on a community level. What you need to do is "shop around" for one that's right for you and your practices and not withdraw just because one local group is actually just role playing or full of weirdoes. We are finding now that areas usually have more than one group, and you need to get out and find them. They are not going to walk up to you and drag you out. You need to first be willing to socialize.

As in all things, a level of trust must exist among all the members for the study group to work. I always suggest meeting new people in public locations and not inviting anyone to your study group until you know that person well enough to invite them to your home. Everyone should agree to the addition of a new member.

A study group is not a teaching group; it is an exploring group, a reading group, a group that works toward understanding together. You learn by trial and error. Working together allows you a second or third opinion, an additional eye on the practice, and sometimes just the motivation you need to get into what you are doing. Like a good exercise program, it's always easier to do if you have someone else who is also interested to keep you focused.

Any good study group starts with a plan. Even if there are only two of you, go over what you want to do. Discuss interests, books and authors, practices and beliefs. Here's an easy way to do it: Write down what you discuss and work a plan out from there. Do not limit yourselves to what you know—be willing to explore the unknown. Be flexible, allow for time off, time lost to uncontrollable issues, and allow time to work together when you do meet. Remember, an hour for shopping or lunch is fine, but you really should put aside at least one afternoon each month to work on a practice or spirituality as a group, or one afternoon every two weeks to work individually.

Make sure you have everything you will need to make the most of the time you spend together. Supplies should be thought out in advance, written down, and responsibility for bringing the incense or the "eye of newt" should be decided before you meet. A phone call a few days before can assure that everyone brings their Book of Shadows and supplies.

Supplies can bring up the issue of money, but sharing supplies means that you spend a little and everyone benefits. Mixing a brew or making mojo bags can be a shared expense, and buying in bulk can lessen the fiscal responsibility. Find economic suppliers and make sure you have enough for everyone.

Not only can you share the burdens of practice, but you can also share your successes. Compare notes, discuss flopped kitchen experiments, or just work on elements of your practice. As you discuss problems with your friend or friends, you will find that issues you may not have been able to work out yourself can be worked out easily as a group.

Events

Pagan meet and greets can connect you with local Pagan groups, be it near or far. You can find out about these events from flyers posted at local esoteric shops, Pagan stores, and spiritual stores. Some groups will post to bulletin boards at coffee shops and

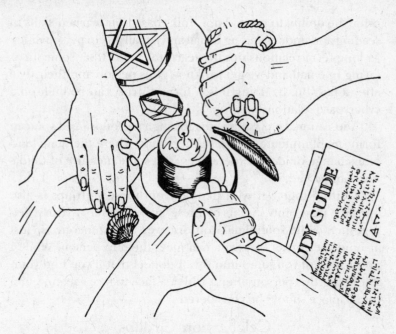

book stores, it all depends on where you are. Again, do not rush into the study group concept with a local group, but do take the time to see if there is anyone you may feel friendly about. Get to know them and see if there is common ground in personality and beliefs.

Local events or statewide events also offer a personal connection. One of those weeklong camping events will give you a chance to meet others. Discussing location with some of the attendees will give you a good idea of who is in your area, and further correspondence is an option. Many of these events offer day-tripper or single-day rates, and attending for just a short time will let you know if this is the kind of thing that would interest you.

Online

If a computer is available and you can access the Internet, another option to augment your solitary practice is an online study group. This is a bit more complicated, because you usually don't know the people you end up with in chat rooms or email groups. However, recent studies suggest that cyberspace does offer the ability to get to know folks based on learned skills in reading and understanding e-mail and e-mail group personalities. In long-term relationships, we learn to "read" what someone is saying in email and we get to "know" this person and their style after a fashion. By doing this, a form of trust can be built on a cyberspace relationship.

You can make cyber-friends through e-groups. And you can form small, intimate online study groups, where the same kind of exchange of ideas, experiences, and some measure of validation can be had.

Getting together with people from these e-groups is also another possibility. Some of these groups offer a yearly get-together, while sometimes you discover that someone is "just around the corner" and you can meet them in person. While I never suggest you jump into this, I do feel that if you find yourself liking this person after a while, a face-to-face meeting in a public place should be considered.

Celebration Groups

Ritual can also be an issue with the solitary practitioner. While working your own holidays gives you a certain freedom, there is nothing like community celebration to add to the season.

Again, the emphasis is not on isolation in our solitary magical practices. You may prefer to work on your own, but you should not be antisocial. There is something to be said for the occasional gathering for celebration, ritual, and sharing good food and conversation.

We go back to your friends and that little study group you have going. What about the occasional Full Moon together? Or celebrating Yule together? Again, this offers an opportunity to explore what you've learned, exercise your skills to write a ritual, or just celebrate in a simple or generic fashion. There can be as few as two of you; you do not need large numbers of people to make a study group or celebration group. And to be honest, ritual is not even necessary. How about the two of you standing in the moonlight, each holding a candle, asking your deity for blessings and thanking them for special favors, and then sharing a meal? That is all that's necessary to make a celebration.

These small groups make it easy to plan road trips. Try sharing a ride to a neighboring town to explore other Pagan stores, or maybe visiting an event that you have always wanted to check out but never would have attended alone. You can travel by bus or train to one of these events together. Go on a day-trip or a short overnight stay. Having a friend with you offers you a measure of safety and security that you may not have when traveling by yourself.

Friendship

Finally, we come to something rarely discussed in the Pagan community. While I do encourage group working for study, ritual, or events, this can be and should be expanded into the more personal area of friendship. There is much to be said for a friend with whom you have some common beliefs or ideas. Discussion does not have to be focused solely on Paganism or spirituality or ritual all the time. How about going shopping with a study partner? Don't you just love it when you can shop for those colorful dresses you love to wear and your Pagan friend doesn't say "That is so Sixties!" How about grocery shopping? Discussing "green" cleaning with a Pagan friend is so much easier than having to explain and/or defend your choices in soap, green paper products, free-range chicken, and cage-free chicken eggs. Expanding your experiences outside the study group can result in good, strong friendships.

There are many group alternatives for the solitary practitioner, as long as you remember that you may need to take the first step. Be careful, but do not isolate yourself. There is a lot to be said for small solitary communities.

The Sacredness of Stones

by Nancy V. Bennett

Older than time they stand, their ancient mysteries kept within. The carefully placed stones of Stonehenge, the moving stones of California, the stone medicine wheels left by the First Nations people in parts of Canada and the United States, and there are even stones that fell from the sky. There are stones that we leave messages on, long hidden in tombs or caves. There are stones we have carved that will stand long after we ourselves have turned to dust, and some that we pass on through generations. Stones are everywhere, all around us, and these are but a few examples of sacred stones to awaken your imagination.

The Lords of Light and the Stone of Destiny

In Ireland, there are more than 50,000 stone circles and many more tombs and standing stones. A friend who recently returned from the British Isles had one in her backyard and noted that, though the locals did not make a fuss over their stones, they would not dream of moving or disturbing them. For that reason, crops are planted around them and roads bend to their stony will.

Other stones can be moved, and some are even stolen—by royalty no less. Such is the case of the Stone of Destiny. According to legend, the Liath Fail, or Stone of Destiny, was brought to Ireland by the children of the Goddess Danu, who were also known as the Lords of Light. They had supernatural powers and so disguised themselves as mortal magicians to travel among the people. One of the gifts left after they had gone was the Stone of Destiny. The stone was used by the kings of old Ireland, who were crowned upon it until about AD 513.

To further complicate matters, the Scottish claim the stone as their own, starting its history around 840. It was used by Scottish kings for their coronation rituals, and then, in 1296, Britain's King Edward the First stole the stone. It entered the realm of the British court, where it sat under the coronation chair until 1996, when it was returned to the Scottish people. But was it ever really out of Scotland?

It was a common-looking enough stone, a block of red sandstone chiseled into an oval. It was believed by some that when the monks of Scone (where it was stored) saw King Edward coming, they hurriedly replaced it with a similar decoy stone. The real stone was hidden in a peat bank, where it remains. Did the Scots outsmart the Brits with a substitution? Speculation continues to this day.

The stone may go even further back than the time of the Lords of Light! More than 3,000 years ago, a royal princess known as Scota, the daughter of Ramses II, left her home in Egypt in search of her own promised land. Scota's journey took her across the waves, and she supposedly settled on the North Coast of Ireland 1,000 years later. Among the things she brought with her from the land of the pharaohs was the Stone of Destiny.

Was the stone of kings and dreams lost to the people in a peat bank, or does it reside in Edinburgh Castle, waiting for the next royal to take an oath upon it? Only the Stone of Destiny knows for sure, and for now, it's keeping mum.

Stones that Move

In Death Valley on a dry lake bed, strange tracks have been found. The tracks aren't the mark of animals, or even the result of tumbling weeds—these tracks are made from moving stones. Some of the tracks are thousands of feet long, with a stone at the ending of the trail. These are not mere pebbles, but fairly large rocks, some weighing as much as one hundred pounds.

The sailing stones, as they are called, remained a mystery for many years, though a number of theories have been brought forth. In 1967, Robert Sharpe, a professor of geology, concluded that a light rainfall must cover the lake beds from time to time, and when it is accompanied by strong gusting winds, the stones are moved by the gusts. Later studies concluded that it was only the wind that moved the stones, and no rainfall is necessary. The mystery continues to play out in our world in the not so silent desert, where once every two to three years, stones dance across the desert as if they were sliding across a pond of ice.

In Alaska and parts of Norway, intricate stone circles, as well as labyrinths and polygon-shaped forms have been found in the plains of some of the most isolated areas. There are no aliens here, nor crop circle fakers. Instead, the freezing and thawing cycles in the ground create the wonderful mosaics in the ground, moving stones to make complicated patterns. Science explains it rationally, but could stones have some will in the movements they make?

According to two French geologists, stones, like us, are living entities. Arnold Rheshar and Pierre Escollet say that not only do stones move, they also breathe, though much slower than humans. An average stone breath can take days to weeks, and a stone heartbeat can take from two to three days. This could help explain the power that can be found in crystals and sacred stone places. Nothing is dead, it seems, on a living planet, where even the stones come alive and move.

Medicine Wheels Lost and Found

In various cultures, stone circles were used to mark a special place, and the people of the First Nations tribes were no exception. From the stone circles along Frenchman River in Saskatchewan, to the medicine wheel at Big Horn, South Dakota, these ancient sites were used not only for yearly gatherings, but also in rituals.

Stone circles are most commonly found in the prairie areas of Alberta, Saskatchewan, the Dakotas, and Wyoming. Among the tribes believed to be responsible for their creation are the Lakota, the Ojibway, and the Blackfoot.

Ancient sites in Frenchman River have revealed a simple circle of stones in the center of a well used area, also including tipi rings and remnants of cooking pits. The medicine wheel at Big Horn, in contrast, is quite large and has rays of rocks extending outward like the spokes on a bicycle wheel. Many of these circles are very old, dating back more than 4,000 years.

Theories abound on what was the true reason behind the creation of these circles. Many people believe that the stone circles were set out to follow cosmic star charts or mark the changing of the seasons. Others believe that the circles were a place of gathering for special rituals and events. With the loss of much of the native culture in the last century, we may also have lost the true reasons behind these circles. But out of our ignorance sometimes comes new beginnings.

In recent years, the interest in medicine wheels has grown. Some modern-day people are creating new stone circles in an attempt to connect with the natural world around them. Rituals of healing and of unification for all people are performed within these new medicine wheels. The Earth's natural cycle of creation, from the brightest stars to the smallest insects, is given homage within these sacred stone circles.

Standing Stones in Britain, Stonehenge Revisited, and Menhirs Masked

The earliest known written record of Stonehenge comes from a fourteenth-century English manuscript. Here we see a picture of the great magician

Merlin receiving the aid of giants to build the sacred structure. Legend says the stones came first from Africa, then to Ireland, before being placed on Salisbury Plain. In reality, the sandstones were probably from Wessex, and the stone circle was made sometime around 2100 BC.

Bone axes and antlers were used to dig the large pits that hold the structure upright. The rocks are aligned for viewing the rising Sun in the Winter and Summer Solstices. Early Druids claimed that it was not Merlin who built Stonehenge but a Celtic Druid queen known as Boudicca. With a resurgent Druid interest in the eighteenth century, Druids started to conduct ceremonies at the site. Many believe Stonehenge was a giant astronomical calendar by which phases of the Moon and the growing seasons could be observed. An ancient calendar attuned to the stars? The work of giants? Or the meeting place of some powerful and magical religion? Only the stones know.

Menhirs are another type of standing stone in Western Europe. For thousands of years, local people would pay homage to these ancient markers. They were often found inside or next to crop circles. It is believed that these stones were able to change negative energy, which might lay inside a crop circle, and could be used to focus positive energy that ran along the ley lines.

When Christianity swept over the land, many of the great stone circles and Menhirs were denounced, and the church wanted them destroyed. But the destruction was not always successful, so the church tried its own form of graffiti. Those "idols of Paganism" that could not be moved were masked by having crosses cut into them.

An article on stones would not be complete without a look at the great stone chambers that dot the British landscape. Wayland's Smithy is such a chamber, which lies in the Oxfordshire area of Britain. It is more than 5,500 years old, and measures more than 50 feet long. The remains of fourteen people were found inside when excavations were conducted in the 1960s.

The name Weyland comes from the Saxon God of metalwork, Wayland, and so does the legend attached to the area. According to ancient local belief, if your horse lost a shoe on the road, you need only to leave a coin and the animal at the stone chamber. When you returned, the coin would be gone and the horse's shoe would be in place. The state of the horse after being shod by a Saxon god was never revealed!

That Which Falls From the Sky

When the sky opened up and spewed forth great rocks upon the ground, these stones were said to be magical. In Scandinavian myth, the egg-shaped bits of iron or stone were thought to have come from the god Thor, who struck down his mighty hammer so hard that pieces flew down to Earth. Among the ancient Greeks, such a stone from the sky was housed in the Temple of Apollo at Delphi. Other nations have similar stories associated with thunder gods and the stones that are sometimes found after violent storms.

In the West African nations, thunderstones became a symbol of power passed on from generation to generation. So strong was the pride in these objects that it is believed many were smuggled to America on slave ships. In Central Africa, these stones were believed to be messages sent from the ancestors, and they were carefully kept in baskets in the village.

Other cultures thought that thunderbolts had landed on Earth in the form of well-polished axes. For Asian people of olden times, lightning and thunder were akin to the teeth of a dragon. But when lightning struck, it was oddly enough the thunder that was blamed for any resulting destruction. Stone axes were thought to have healing properties and to provide protection against the wrath of the storms.

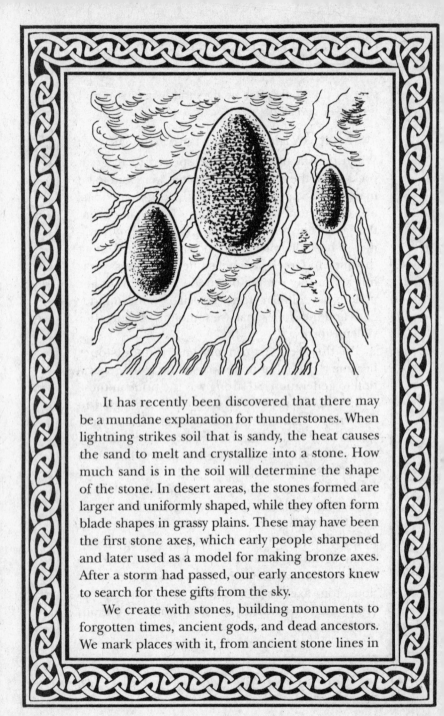

It has recently been discovered that there may be a mundane explanation for thunderstones. When lightning strikes soil that is sandy, the heat causes the sand to melt and crystallize into a stone. How much sand is in the soil will determine the shape of the stone. In desert areas, the stones formed are larger and uniformly shaped, while they often form blade shapes in grassy plains. These may have been the first stone axes, which early people sharpened and later used as a model for making bronze axes. After a storm had passed, our early ancestors knew to search for these gifts from the sky.

We create with stones, building monuments to forgotten times, ancient gods, and dead ancestors. We mark places with it, from ancient stone lines in

Europe to the standing shapes of Inukshuks in the Arctic. Sometimes it falls from the skies to inspire us to create weapons or to remember our ancestors. It is within the stone caves to the north that the old knowledge is found, so I have been taught in my Wiccan training, and this is evoked on my altar at home by a rough bit of copper and gold my husband drew from an old mine.

Strong and ancient these stones stand, waiting for you to find them. Discover and relish their sacredness, for the stones are no longer silent.

Bibliography and For Further Study

Bahn, Paul G., ed. *The Cambridge Illustrated History of Archeology*. New York: Cambridge University Press, 1999.

Dimitrakopoulos, Sandra. "Stonehenge." Discovery Channel. http://exn.ca/mysticplaces/enigma.asp

Fletcher, Lena and Anne Nester. "The Mystery of the Rocks on the Racetrack at Death Valley." http://sophia.smith.edu/~lfletche/deathvalley.html

Forces of Nature. "Stones That Move." Oracle Education Foundation ThinkQuest. http://library.thinkquest.org/C003603/english/phenomena/stonesthatmove.shtml

Komsomolskaya Pravda, translated by Guerman Grachev. "Stones are living creatures that breathe and move." Pravda. http://english.pravda.ru/science/earth/12-07-2006/83225-stones-0

Krystek, Lee. "The Impossible Rocks that Fell from

the Sky." The Museum of Unnatural Mystery. http://unmuseum.mus.pa.us/rocksky.htm

Kumf, Tom Quinn. *Ireland Standing Stones to Stormont.* Boulder, CO: Devenish Press, 2004.

Leylines and Dowsing. "Megalithic monuments." http://www.leylijnen.com/megalithic_monuments.htm

Rouge Foundation, The. "Medicine Wheel." http://www.rivernen.ca/med_1.htm

Royal Saskatchewan Museum. "Stone Circles along the Frenchman River." http://www.royalsaskmuseum.ca/research/what/stone.shtml

Stephens, Tim. "Scientists explain formation of stone circles, other strange patterns in northern regions." UC Santa Cruz currents online. http://www.ucsc.edu/currents/02-03/01-20/patterns.html

Thunderbird, Shannon. "Medicine Wheel Teachings." http://www.shannonthunderbird.com/medicine_wheel_teachings.htm

Undiscovered Scotland. "Stones of Scone." http://www.undiscoveredscotland.co.uk/usfeatures/stoneofscone/index.html

Whicombe, Christopher L. C. E. "Stones and the Sacred." Sacred Places. http://witcombe.sbc.edu/sacredplaces/stones.html

Wikipedia contributors. "Thunderstone (folklore)." Wikipedia, The Free Encyclopedia.http://en.wikipedia.org/w/index.php?title=Thunderstone_%28folklore%29&oldid=153741537

Charming Household Items

by Elizabeth Hazel

People use many items and tools in the daily course of life. Athames and chalices are regularly consecrated and dedicated for ritual use. But why limit it to that? Everyday things can be made special and sacred with charms. In ancient times, people personalized the few possessions they owned, either by carving or painting a rune on it or by identifying it with a special mark. It wasn't unusual to see a pastor blessing a new barn, house, or plow.

Now, it is so easy to get new things that old items can be discarded without thought. Tools are easily replaced and aren't always well made when new. Applying charms to household and everyday items is a good reminder to value the service these items perform. Charms give an item a special, personal magical charge.

Any of the spells and charms given here can and should be applied to new items, but it's never too late to charm familiar tools that have served well. Older items should be cleaned before they are consecrated or charmed. Who knows? New results may come once they've been spruced up with a little magic.

Kitchen Items

The central item in any kitchen is the kitchen table. So much happens around this table: family discussions, study, and the ingestion of daily nourishment. Charming a kitchen table can ensure that the people who gather around it do so in peace and mutual respect, and that it is a source of learning and wellness for all who sit there.

At the Full Moon, wash the tabletop and the four legs using water with a pinch of consecrated cleansing salts. Smudge it with sage. Create a magical talisman for the table by drawing on a piece of parchment symbols of what is desired at this table: a peace sign, a protection rune, or a protective bind-rune; a crescent Moon symbol for emotional contentment and nourishment; a circle that contains the names of all family members; a square within a circle to show the integration of all four elements, etc. Use symbols that express your hopes and wishes for what will happen (or what will not happen) at the kitchen table.

Fix a light-blue candle with consecration oil, light it, and set it at the center of the table. You may create a magical circle around the table with consecrated sand before casting the charm, or you might sprinkle a little sand at the four corners. When the circle is finished, chant:

Kitchen table, circle and square –
All the family is centered there;
Seasons come and seasons go,
All are fed here through the flow.
Knives, forks, and spoons are placed around,
Plates and drinking glasses are found;
By this charm, you are now bound:
Peace be at this table, day by day,
Wisdom be at this table, day by day,
All who are fed here are filled,
All who talk here gain wisdom,
All who rest here are revitalized.
As I will and charge, so mote it be.

Place the talisman in a small envelope and sprinkle some consecrated sand or salt or some blessing herbs into the envelope before sealing it. Tape the envelope under the center of the table surface. Allow the candle to burn all the way down. This charm can be renewed (and the talisman remade) before any feast or special gathering in the kitchen.

Turn a favorite wooden spoon into a "Moon Spoon" by charming it on the night of a Full Moon. After it is washed and smudged, put the spoon on your altar or magical working space. After the circle of protection has been evoked, place the spoon on a tray of consecrated sand or salt, or on a paten with a pentagram. Say this charm:

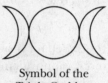

Symbol of the
Triple Goddess

> *Now I bless this wooden spoon,*
> *Underneath the glowing Moon,*
> *Stirring pots in Brigid's name,*
> *Bless the tree from which you came,*
> *All you make, be stirred with love,*
> *In honor of the sacred grove. Blessed be.*
> [ring bell]

Use a permanent ink marker to inscribe the symbol of the Triple Goddess onto the handle of the spoon. Each time you use the spoon, you'll see the symbol and remember that everything you stir is made with love.

And even those small, unassuming objects in your kitchen can be charmed for a magical boost: car keys, measuring cups and spoons, electric can openers, food mixers and processors, and any other frequently used cooking equipment, such as pots, bowls, and pans.

Cooking bowls should be rinsed thoroughly with cleansing salts. Swirl the salt water around the bowl with your Moon Spoon while you chant:

> *Bowl of cooking, bowl of mine,*
> *Blessed for making both sweet and brine;*
> *In thee all ingredients marry,*
> *From thy depths my wishes carry.*
> *So mote it be.*

When you use the bowl, whatever you're thinking about or feeling will be transferred into the food. (Be sure to read or watch *Like Water for Chocolate* before you get carried away while making food for others!)

Since cooking pans are used with heat, they should be consecrated with flame. Rinse and smudge the pan, then dry it carefully. Light a red candle and hold the pan over it while chanting:

Cooking pan, do my will,
Food from you can bring no ill.
Absorb the fire, own the flame,
Food be never burned again.

After the pan has been charmed, use nail polish to paint your
wizard mark or initials on the handle.

Beauty Items

Tools used for beautification and grooming are intensely personal,
and it is unhygienic to share combs, brushes, and toothbrushes—
even more reason to consecrate them with a personal charm.

Beauty is the province of Venus. Charms may be worked when
the Moon is waxing or full in either Venus-ruled signs—Libra
and Taurus—or when Venus is transiting through Taurus, Leo,
Libra, or Pisces. Choose the zodiac sign that complements your
Sun sign. Grooming tools should be dedicated to Venus, who fully
appreciates the effort of a beauty regimen.

When the right time has been determined, clean the grooming tools (comb and brush, for example) with salt water and a
sage smudge. Place them on your altar in a bowl of dried rose
petals or lavender, or burn rose or lavender incense to evoke the
goddess. When this has been prepared, chant:

Aphrodite, goddess of love and loveliness:
Bless these tools to my hand!
May my beauty ever grow when I use them.
Infuse this comb and brush with your powers
So that my natural beauty is enhanced with your aid.
By beauty refined, this thing be mine.

Using nail polish or a permanent marker, mark these tools with
your personal initials, symbol, or a Venus glyph. Tie a pink ribbon
around the handle of a brush. This charm can be adapted for
other beauty tools such as curling irons, blow dryers, and other
makeup equipment. Hand mirrors are especially beloved by the
goddess Venus.

Mass-market perfumes should also be blessed and consecrated for personal use. Unlike handmade magical oils, mass-market perfumes have not been consecrated in any form. Before using any bottle of commercial perfume, place it on your altar, sprinkle rose petals over it, and say a little charm, such as:

> *The scent of beauty comes from thee,*
> *By flower petals, herb, and tree.*
> *When I use this essence sweet,*
> *I follow the path of Ishtar's feet.*

Cleaning Supplies

Never let it be said that a Witch didn't have a consecrated broom. But a consecrated vacuum? Sure! Housekeeping can be turned into a sacred task with magical benefits. It helps if the tools for doing the job have a magical mandate. Vacuums, buckets, dusters, and even squeegees can be consecrated.

Vacuuming is not a favorite task for most people. The noise bothers human and pet ears and lots of things can go wrong. Have you ever sucked up a toy or other small item in a vacuum? Consecrating a vacuum will help you avoid these little problems. Wipe the vacuum clean and put a new bag in it. If it's a bagless model, make sure the dirt cup is clean. For models that use bags, write a magical protection symbol on the bag, and put a tablespoon of lavender inside of it. Have another handful of lavender ready when you say this charm:

> *On the floor and all around,*
> *Be silent your obnoxious sound,*
> *Avoid all dangers on the ground!*
> *Charmed you are and charmed you be,*
> *As you suck up dirt, three times three,*
> *This vacuum be charmed, so mote it be!*

Toss the lavender on the floor, plug in the vacuum and run it over the dried lavender. The vacuum will smell terrific every time it's used.

Making a magical bucket is just plain easy. Wash the bucket out with consecrated salts and wipe it dry. Use a permanent ink marker to draw a magical symbol on the bottom of the bucket. That's it! Accompany your magical bucket with a magical mop.

Mops should be carefully cleaned and wiped off before charming them. Stretch the mop across two chairs, and pass a sage smudge back and forth across the length of it, while chanting:

Back and forth, I push and pull;
Mop, be good and never spill.
Every floor will gleam with light;
Mop, be good and make it bright.

Tie a red ribbon with three knots to the top of the mop to bind good luck to it.

Fill your magic bucket with water and add some regular floor detergent and either a pinch of cleansing salts or a few drops of an oil to attract prosperity. Agitate the contents of the bucket with your magical mop, squeeze out the excess water, and start mopping the floor. As you mop the floor, tell the house the things you want to be drawn into it. Make wishes for things you want, or for things you want to happen. Play your favorite music while you're mopping and put your heart into the wishes and prayers you've said. When finished, throw the water out the back door and yell, "Evil, be gone!"

Another magical mopping ritual is to put silver coins into the bucket before mopping. As you mop the floor, chant:

As I mop this dirty floor,
Good luck comes straight to my door.
As my floor gets good and clean,
Prosperity flows in gold and green.

Repeat this chant while you do the task. Wash off the front door stoop with this water. When you are finished washing the front stoop, throw the dirty water out of the back door (along with the coins) and say loudly:

Poverty is banished,
Cast from my door.
Poverty is banished,
Return here no more!

Frankly, magical cleaning rituals make cleaning tasks rather fun, and it's amazing how well these humble rituals work.

Items of Contention

There are certain items in every house that are prone to causing quarrels, such as television remotes. Holding a remote is like holding a kingly orb: all the power is invested in one pair of hands! Try zapping your TV remote control with a peace charm. On your altar, make a circle with consecrated sand around the TV remote. Holding your hands above the item, visualize peace and harmony as a cocoon of pink and white light around it. Chant:

> *Remote control, you'll always be*
> *Surrounded with peace and harmony;*
> *White light cleanses, pink light warms,*
> *Power for good, never for harm.*

Develop a charm for any item that causes arguments between family members. Or take a more magical approach to arguments between children. Designate a special binding box, where you place any toy or item that has caused a quarrel, saying "Trouble, trouble, you will stay / Until the quarrel is put away." Put a skull and crossbones on the front of the box. Let children know that once a cursed, quarrel-causing item is in the binding box, it won't come out until the quarrel has been resolved and you lift the bane spell from it. "Peace is here, good will abounds / Toys are shared with love all around; Blessed Be!"

Charming household items will help you have a more merry and magical home!

Magical Inks

by Elizabeth Barrette

Writing has always been considered a somewhat mysterious and magical process. The invention of ink—and papyrus, parchment, and paper—made it possible to write quickly and easily on portable surfaces. The improvements over older methods, such as clay or stone, helped to spread both reading and writing to more people, places, and purposes.

Most of the early inks were herbal, although some were based on mineral or animal products. Among the most famous of inks is oak gall ink. It combines tannic acid with ferrous sulfate to create a fairly durable ink that starts out a deep blue-black and slowly fades to brown. Oak gall ink dates back to about AD 400. The main drawbacks to this ink are its tedious, complex preparation and its high acidity. Because the acidic ink damages the paper or parchment it's written on, old texts are very fragile.

Magical inks are related to ordinary inks. They use some of the same ingredients, but also include more exotic elements. They must function well as ink for writing, yet also be able to hold magical energies. Herbs can provide fragrance, color, and enchantment to magical inks. These inks can then be used for writing in a Book of Shadows, scribing runes on rune staves, writing out incantations on paper that will later be burned as part of a spell, and so forth. Different magical inks have different properties. Note that most magical inks come in bottles and are intended for use with quills or dip pens.

Ingredients

Ink can be made of many different ingredients. Most basically, it needs a **carrier** and a **colorant**. The carrier allows the ink to flow over the page and dry. The colorant makes the lettering show up, and it can be any color at all. Inks may also have binders to help them stick to the page, fragrances for scent, preservatives to extend their life, and other ingredients. Here are some common ingredients and their purposes.

Alcohol serves both as a carrier and a preservative. It creates a strong, fast-drying ink. Alcohol is also good for dissolving resins and other materials that are difficult to dissolve in water. Denatured alcohol is pure and clear, an excellent solvent for making ink. However, you can also use such things as brandy or vodka. Red wine helps make a bright red or purple ink; brandy is good for yellow to brown inks.

Dragon's blood is a deep red-brown resin derived from the dragon tree (*Dracaena draco*). This ingredient adds

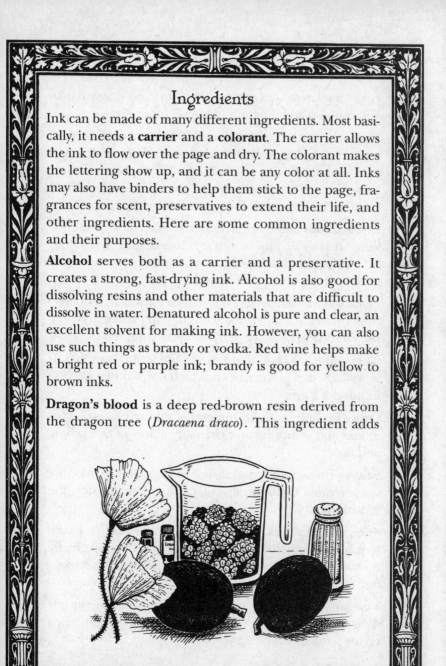

color, thickness, and staying power to most magical inks. You can also add dragon's blood oil for fragrance.

Egg makes an excellent carrier for ink that will be used immediately. Egg white (albumen) is relatively clear and does not affect color. Egg yolk is yellow and works beautifully with red, orange, yellow, or green colorants. Both plant and mineral colorants work well with egg carriers.

Essential oils add fragrance to inks that use a strong solvent, such as alcohol or vinegar. Cinnamon, clove, dragon's blood, lavender, mint, rose, and rosemary are some of the common scents used in inks.

Floral waters such as lavender water, rose water, or orange-flower water add a delicate scent to water-based inks. Floral waters don't survive well in solvent-based inks.

Gum arabic is a resin that acts as a binder in many inks. It is available as a powder or chunks, but works best for inks in powder form.

Ochre is a soft, crumbly mineral often used as a colorant in inks and paints. It comes in many shades of red, yellow, and brown.

Salt is a preservative used mainly in berry or egg inks that are intended for fairly short-term use. It helps slow the growth of mold.

Soot, or lampblack, is carbon dust that makes an excellent black pigment in ink. Some recipes depend chiefly on soot for their color, but you can also use it to darken and thicken any deep-colored ink.

Vinegar acts as a preservative and a solvent. White vinegar does not affect the color of ink. Red wine vinegar helps create a red or purple ink.

Recipes for Magical Inks

There are many different ways to make magical inks. Some are simple; others are quite complex, relying on sophisticated chemical reactions that take a long time to complete. Some inks, like those based on oak galls, are highly acidic. Others are not very colorfast; while not ideal for long-term uses such as writing in a Book of Shadows, these inks still work fine for short-term uses, such as writing spells on scrolls to be burned or buried.

The simplest way to make magical ink is to enchant ordinary ink. India ink (black) and calligraphy ink (various colors) make suitable bases to which you can add magical components. To add the energy of a fragrant herb to ordinary ink, mix in 3 to 5 drops of essential oil into a 1-ounce bottle of ink; rose- and lavender-scented inks are especially popular. Less fragrant herbs may be added in the form of finely ground powder, 1 or 2 pinches of herb per ounce of ink. However, this creates sediment; you can either strain it out after some time, or dip your pen carefully to avoid stirring it up. Traditional magical inks include Bat's Blood, Dove's Blood, and Dragon's Blood.

Bat's Blood Ink

    12 oz. denatured alcohol
    2 oz. dragon's blood resin powder
    ½ oz. myrrh resin powder
    2 drops cinnamon oil
    5 drops lavender oil
    ½ oz. gum arabic

This ink is best made at night. Place the alcohol in a clean, dark glass bottle. Add the dragon's blood and myrrh. After they have dissolved, add the cinnamon and lavender oils and the gum arabic. Shake the bottle to

blend the ingredients. Store this ink tightly sealed in a dark, cool place.

Bat's Blood Ink originally consisted of or included the blood of an actual bat; modern recipes use other ingredients instead of real blood. This ink is used in binding and banishing and spells for discord, tension, or hexing. All the "blood" inks can be red, but this one is often colored blue or black.

Dove's Blood Ink

    10 oz. denatured alcohol
    1 oz. dragon's blood resin powder
    2 drops bay oil
    2 drops clove oil
    5 drops rose oil
    1 oz. gum arabic

This ink is best made during daylight. Place the alcohol in a clean, dark glass bottle. Add the dragon's blood. After it has dissolved, add the bay, clove, and rose oils and the gum arabic. Shake to blend. Store tightly sealed in a dark, cool place.

Dove's Blood Ink originally had bird blood in it and now does not. This ink is used for love, peace, gratitude, and other positive applications. It is usually red, occasionally pink or purple.

Dragon's Blood Ink

15 oz. denatured alcohol
1 oz. dragon's blood resin powder
1 oz. gum arabic

This ink is best made at noon. Place the alcohol in a clean, dark glass bottle. Add the dragon's blood. After it has dissolved, add the gum arabic. (You may also add several drops of dragon's blood oil if you wish.) Shake to blend. Wait at least one week, then strain before using. Store tightly sealed in a dark, cool place.

Dragon's Blood Ink never had draconic blood in it, but rather is named after its key ingredient, the resinous herb dragon's blood, which gives it a dark-reddish color. This ink is used for adding power or fire energy to spells.

Note that modern recipes for Bat's Blood and Dove's Blood contain dragon's blood resin for coloring and binding; if you want to keep them more distinctive, you can substitute red ochre (color) and gum arabic (binder).

Celestial Ink

15 oz. white wine
½ oz. frankincense resin powder
½ oz. myrrh resin powder
1 pinch saffron
1 oz. gum arabic

This ink is best made in the morning. Place the wine in a clean, clear glass bottle. Add the resin powders. After they have dissolved, add the saffron. The more saffron you use, the darker the ink will get. When you're satisfied with the color, add the gum arabic. Shake to blend. Strain before using, and store tightly sealed in a dark, cool place.

This is a yellow to orange ink, probably inspired by the use of saffron-colored inks in India for certain spiritual purposes. It is variously called Angel Ink, Seraph Ink, or Celestial Ink. This ink has a very high, bright vibration that is useful in celestial magic or spiritual writing. If you can't afford saffron, turmeric gives a similar color though somewhat less energy.

Herb Inks

There are many inks made from herbs, usually with flowers, berries, or tree bark. These contain the energy of the original plants. They can be further enhanced by adding essential oils, floral waters, or other ingredients.

You can make magical ink from almost any herb that possesses a strong color and/or fragrance. Use the recipes here as inspiration, look up other traditional ones, or invent your own from scratch. Color correspondences suggest which colors of ink best suit various types of magical workings—e.g., red for love spells or brown for grounding spells. Look up herbs to find which ones have the powers you want to capture in your ink. Finally, remember to keep records of your attempts, so that if you discover something terrific, you'll be able to repeat it!

Berry Ink
1 c. ripe berries (blackberries, blueberries,
    mulberries, strawberries, etc.)
1 tsp. red wine vinegar
1 tsp. salt

Crush the berries in a strainer, catching the juice in a bowl. (Blackberries and blueberries yield shades of blue and purple. Mulberries and strawberries yield shades of purple to reddish pink.) Add the vinegar and salt to the juice. Test for consistency. If the ink is too thick, add a little more vinegar. Strain through cheesecloth before using. Seal the ink tightly in a glass jar and store in a cool, dark place.

This ink is easy to make but it doesn't keep very long, so only make as much as you'll need in the near future. It's good for spells relating to plant magic, cooking, and hearthcraft, among others.

Poppy Ink

1 c. field poppy (*Papaver rhoeas*) petals
1 ½ c. boiling water
¼ c. denatured alcohol

Place the poppy petals in a heatproof container. Pour over them enough boiling water to cover the petals. Allow to steep overnight. Add the denatured alcohol. Strain and bottle the ink. Store in a cool, dark place.

This reddish or orange ink is good for magic relating to love, sleep, flowers, or faeries.

Walnut Ink

12 black walnuts with hulls
water
denatured alcohol

Gather black walnuts when their hulls are turning brown. Place the walnuts in a pot and add enough water to cover them. If you use a glass or aluminum pot, you'll get golden to medium-brown ink. If you use a cast-iron pot, or throw in a handful of rusty nails, you'll get ink so dark a brown that it looks black. Simmer the walnuts until the husks come off. Remove the nuts, leaving the husks behind. Boil until the mixture is dark brown and begins to thicken. Strain first through a colander and then through cheesecloth to remove all the hulls. Gradually add denatured alcohol to thin the ink until the desired consistency is reached. Bottle and store in a cool, dark place.

This ink is good for earth magic or spells relating to security, strength, and success.

For Further Study

Bennett, Jim. "Calligraphy for Everyone." Studio Arts Net. http://www.studioarts.net/calligraphy/

Bremness, Lesley. *Complete Book of Herbs: A Practical Guide to Growing & Using Herbs.* New York, Viking Studio, 1988.
> *Covers cultivation, cooking, crafts, etc. See "Making Ink" on pages 202 and 203.*

Cunningham, Scott. *Cunningham's Encyclopedia of Magical Herbs.* St. Paul, MN: Llewellyn Publications, 1991.
> *Magical uses of herbs and spices, with correspondences.*

Forest, Crystal. "Magickal Inks." http://crystalforest1 .homestead.com/CRAFTinks.html

Grebenstein, Maryanne. *Calligraphy: A Course in Hand Lettering.* New York: Watson-Guptill, 2006.
> *Introduces tools and supplies, lettering techniques, and projects for novices.*

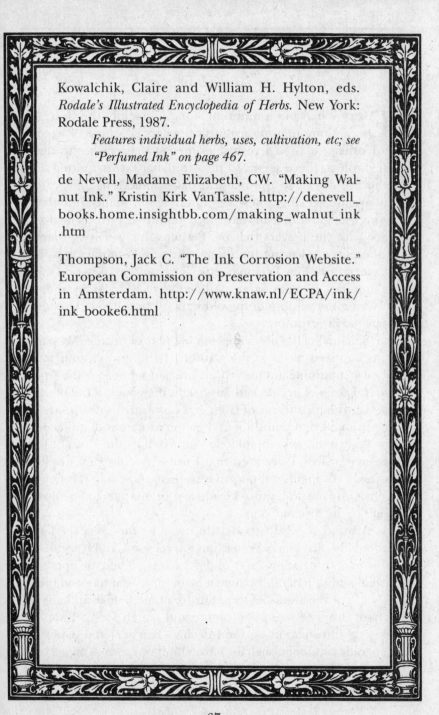

Kowalchik, Claire and William H. Hylton, eds. *Rodale's Illustrated Encyclopedia of Herbs.* New York: Rodale Press, 1987.

> *Features individual herbs, uses, cultivation, etc; see "Perfumed Ink" on page 467.*

de Nevell, Madame Elizabeth, CW. "Making Walnut Ink." Kristin Kirk VanTassle. http://denevell_books.home.insightbb.com/making_walnut_ink.htm

Thompson, Jack C. "The Ink Corrosion Website." European Commission on Preservation and Access in Amsterdam. http://www.knaw.nl/ECPA/ink/ink_booke6.html

Life as a Teen Witch

by Abel R. Gomez

Every Witch has a different story. For some, the Craft is something that miraculously appears in a time of need. For others, it is an irresistible interest that refuses to die. Regardless, there seems to be a unifying factor uniting all who are drawn to the magical path, something that calls us. We are seeking a new definition of spirituality, one that brings magic into everyday life, a path that puts us face to face with the powers that be. Perhaps this is why so many adherents are leaving traditional faiths and embracing Neopagan spirituality. Personal experience and exploration are taking the place of dogma, and people of all walks are rediscovering the wisdom of the old ways for transformation and spiritual progression.

Spirituality has always been a big part of my life. My parents baptized me into the Catholic faith, and church was always important. I attended a Christian school for the first several years of my life and was taught the basics of the Bible, the Christian concepts of God, and how Christ's death saved me from eternal punishment. I gathered statues of saints on my nightstand and completely lost myself in the church. By the age of five, I declared that I would become a Catholic priest, a distinguished person who speaks to God on other's behalf. My mission was to be a healer of our age, to lead lost souls to the love of God.

Around the fifth grade, during my years at a secular school, the first Harry Potter film was released, and it seemed as if my entire school was under its spell. The concepts of magic and Witchcraft became a main topic of interest in our school conversations. During our free time before and after school, students would go online and search for spells and magical information on the Internet. Teachers and parents generally condoned such an activity, as it was seen as an act of our creative expression and a game for our imaginations.

I can still remember my first spell. Through our occasional book catalogue, I had ordered a book called *A Wizard's Handbook*, a somewhat fantastical guide to magic aimed at grammar school children with colorful images of Witches from movies. For me, it was an invitation to explore my magical side and do magic just like Harry Potter or Gandalf from the world of J. R. R. Tolkien. The day the book came in the mail, I spent all my free time reading it, savoring each word as if it were the word of God Himself.

When I got home, I decided I would cast my first spell, a spell to bring rain. I created an amateur circle as the book suggested, drew a picture of my intention, and chanted a nonsense utterance involving rain. After my spell was complete, my heart raced as I hurried to the window to see if my spell had worked. Just as I hoped, rain poured down for hours. It had not mattered that the skies were cloudy all day or that I had no idea what I was doing. I had cast a spell that worked and, for the moment, that was all that mattered.

I continued reading books on magic, specifically those geared toward children interested in Harry Potter. The information was not completely incorrect, but it did have a flare for the fantastical. Though I was able to learn some basic concepts, I was still blissfully unaware of the inherent spirituality of magical practice. Still, it excited and terrified me that I was entering a world of real magic, so much so that I decided it was not the path for me. Instead, I decided to explore "lighter" metaphysical practices, such as tarot, dream work, and yoga.

Touching the Great Mystery

My magical practice had all but completely stopped until two years later. A book I was reading mentioned Witchcraft as an alternative spiritual path, and I thought it would be interesting to look into it again. At the time, I had been working on a paper about the gods of Hinduism, and the parallels between Hinduism and the Craft piqued my interest. I began reading about these mystical traditions and realized that there were alternatives to what I was taught. "What other paths are out there?" I wondered. If the Hindu practices were indeed valid, genuine paths to spirituality, what of the other world religions? Are they equally valid?

During my studies I came upon *The Inner Temple of Witchcraft* by Christopher Penczak and decided to dedicate myself to study it for a year and a day. After my homework, I would do the meditation exercises suggested and explore magical theory. I also read a number of other books, and I learned basics of witchcraft and magical practice; I was taken on an incredible journey of growth and transformation. The Earth was alive and I was immersed in a world of beauty, mystery, and endless exploration. I became aware of my personal power and how to manifest magic in everyday life. Life's purpose became clear, and with each book and magical experience came a deeper passion for spiritual understanding and reverence toward Mother Earth and all living things.

It seems like the feeling of "coming home" is common among practitioners of modern Paganism. It was certainly present when I first got involved in the Craft. The concepts of the Goddess, the four sacred elements, and reverence toward

nature all seemed to fit. What struck me as particularly appealing was the level of tolerance and pluralism within the Pagan community. Not only do Pagans accept diversity, they encourage it! Witches teach "there is no part of us that is not of the gods" and that to truly grow in magic, we must accept ourselves, even the parts of us society tells us are dirty or profane. What's more, Pagan practice embraces creativity, rejects dogma, and upholds the idea that we must create our own spiritual paths and identities.

But there was trouble in paradise. My parents were unaware of my practice and made it quite clear that they did not want their son to be engaged in Witchcraft. My rituals and study were done completely in secret, and I worried constantly about how my parents would react once they discovered that I was a Witch. It hurt me that I could not share with them the practice that filled me with so much purpose and joy. Most teen practioners feel the same way, I think, especially if they're brought up in a Christian or fundamentalist religion. The "broom closet" can be a scary place, and the realities of Witchcraft are usually regarded with fear and skepticism.

Though the fear of rejection or disapproval forces some to stay in the "broom closet" for their entire lives, I knew I had to be honest with my parents and the people that I love. I decided I would write my parents a letter and leave them with some books before spending the night at my grandmother's house. I thought it was important to give them time and space to think about my decisions and prove to them not only that the Craft was a religion rooted in compassion and beauty, but that I was dedicated to learning and applying the teachings of Witchcraft into my daily life to grow into an ethical and mature human being.

Many of the teen Witches I have met are troubled that their parents have not accepted the Craft as a valid spiritual practice. Perhaps what many of these young Witches fail to understand is that the concern and fear of magic and the Pagan religions is not a punishment but a display of love and thoughtfulness. In my own life, I came to understand that my mom's intentions for restricting my involvement with the Craft came from a place of love and compassion. Fortunately, she came to understand that I needed to find my own answers and has since allowed me to practice my Craft freely.

Weaving the Web

When I first began practicing the Craft, I wasn't acquainted with anyone who knew even the slightest about Paganism, much less practiced it. Though it felt like I was alone in my magical pursuits, I believed the loose ends would somehow come together when the time was right. It has been said that when the student is ready, the teacher will appear, and while I now accept this as true, it was hardly plausible to me as a young Witch. I wanted to find magical friends instantly and decided to write a cord spell to draw such people my way. To my amazement, I discovered several days later that a teacher at my school was a Witch. I hadn't even cast the spell!

Around that same time, I discovered the *Copper-Moon* e-zine, an online magazine for teen Witches created by author Gwinevere Rain. At the time it was called *Teen Witch News*, and I began submitting articles about deities, sabbats, and my ideas on contemporary Witchcraft. I felt a great sense of community among other teen Witches, and it was great to know that I was not the only person my age interested in occultism. Still, I did not know any of these teen Witches outside of online forums and, although they brought me some sense of community, I still felt very alone.

It wasn't until several years later that I was able to find any concrete sense of community. I had formed a friendship with Neopagan Priest and author Raven Digitalis through e-mail and phone conversations over several years. When his friend Megan (who was also a teen Witch) was in my area, we decided to meet, along with her friend Tobias, at a public Reclaiming ritual. We visited the Haight in San Francisco and Starhawk's collective house before participating in the Imbolc ritual that night.

Later that same month, I was also able to attend Panthea-Con, the largest Pagan gathering in my area. Though I'd never

attended such an event, I anticipated a festive and educational experience about what the Pagan community looks like. To my delight, I was able to see a diverse range of Pagan practitioners and how they interacted with one another. Additionally, I was finally able meet my friend Raven Digitalis in person, as well as two of my favorite authors, Christopher Penczak and T. Thorn Coyle. It was an eye-opening experience for my mother as well; she was able to see that the community I was stepping into wasn't as scary or dangerous as she initially expected.

I continued to attend Reclaiming rituals in San Francisco and was introduced to an array of wise and progressive Witches dedicated to their Craft and to creating a more compassionate world. Ritual planners and attendees treated me with respect and honesty, and one priestess even offered to give me her cell phone number in case I ever wanted to learn more. There was a real sense of community within the Reclaiming group, and their innovative rituals and avant-garde politics really struck a chord with me. What's more, I was able to meet more like-minded individuals who were interested in the Craft.

It was the attitude of political activism that really intrigued me about the Reclaiming community. Reclaiming is the activist branch of the Feri Witchcraft tradition. It fuses spellcasting and ritual technique to create beneficial energies for political demonstrations. These Witches teach that we must never be complacent about the injustices around us, and in order to effectively create change, we must be willing to devote our time and energy to the preservation of Mother Nature and the sanctity of all life. Inspired by these concepts, I engaged in my first political action with members of Reclaiming during a peace march on the fourth anniversary of the Iraqi war.

Living Magic

From my first spell five years ago, I knew my life would be forever changed. As I continued studying Witchcraft, I realized that even the most simple acts are extraordinary. Magic is not just for ritual spellcasting for me; it is every breath, every step, every moment. Our thoughts have the power to move mountains and create change in the world around us. I gained a sense of power-from-within and an alternative set of values and ideas that has grounded and guided me through the difficult periods of teenage life.

Through my studies and experiences with magic and ritual, I have come to learn that the true heart of Witchcraft is healing. When we cast our circle and connect with the gods and the elements of life, we return to wholeness, reconnecting to all that is. Our ritual protocol is rooted in the concept of divinity within all things, and we are invited to radiate our own divinity into the world as well.

Though we may be approached with fear or skepticism, to be a teen Witch is truly to align oneself with the divine and the further progression and liberation of all beings. Our age need not restrict us from questioning and exploring the vastness of our magical universe and experiencing the sublime every moment. As teen Witches, we herald the dawn of a new generation, one that honors Mother Nature and all creatures in an effort to bring healing and reconnection back to a deeply damaged world.

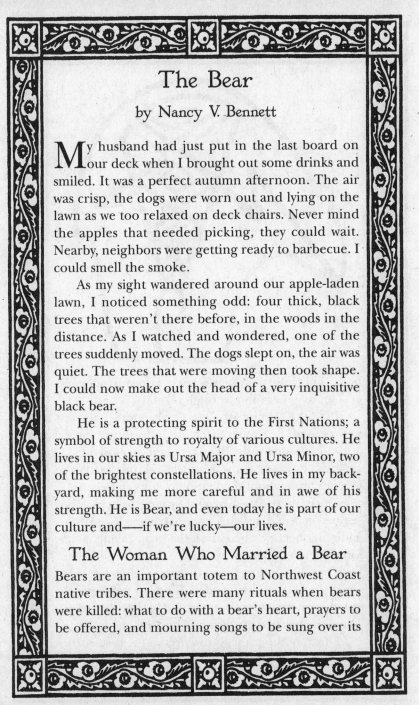

The Bear

by Nancy V. Bennett

My husband had just put in the last board on our deck when I brought out some drinks and smiled. It was a perfect autumn afternoon. The air was crisp, the dogs were worn out and lying on the lawn as we too relaxed on deck chairs. Never mind the apples that needed picking, they could wait. Nearby, neighbors were getting ready to barbecue. I could smell the smoke.

As my sight wandered around our apple-laden lawn, I noticed something odd: four thick, black trees that weren't there before, in the woods in the distance. As I watched and wondered, one of the trees suddenly moved. The dogs slept on, the air was quiet. The trees that were moving then took shape. I could now make out the head of a very inquisitive black bear.

He is a protecting spirit to the First Nations; a symbol of strength to royalty of various cultures. He lives in our skies as Ursa Major and Ursa Minor, two of the brightest constellations. He lives in my back-yard, making me more careful and in awe of his strength. He is Bear, and even today he is part of our culture and——if we're lucky—our lives.

The Woman Who Married a Bear

Bears are an important totem to Northwest Coast native tribes. There were many rituals when bears were killed: what to do with a bear's heart, prayers to be offered, and mourning songs to be sung over its

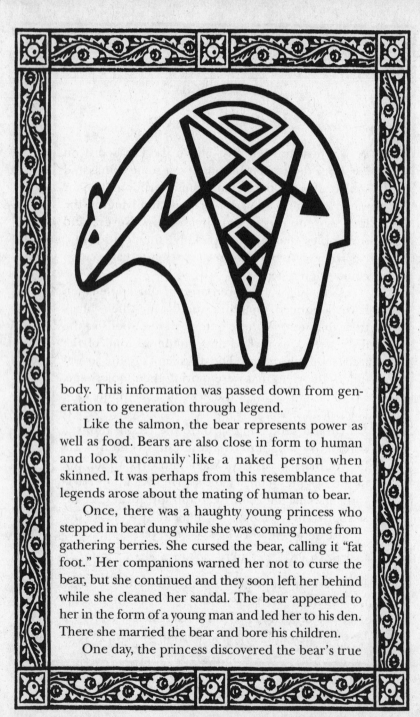

body. This information was passed down from generation to generation through legend.

Like the salmon, the bear represents power as well as food. Bears are also close in form to human and look uncannily like a naked person when skinned. It was perhaps from this resemblance that legends arose about the mating of human to bear.

Once, there was a haughty young princess who stepped in bear dung while she was coming home from gathering berries. She cursed the bear, calling it "fat foot." Her companions warned her not to curse the bear, but she continued and they soon left her behind while she cleaned her sandal. The bear appeared to her in the form of a young man and led her to his den. There she married the bear and bore his children.

One day, the princess discovered the bear's true

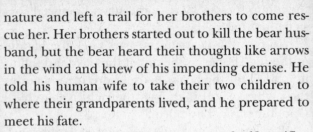

nature and left a trail for her brothers to come rescue her. Her brothers started out to kill the bear husband, but the bear heard their thoughts like arrows in the wind and knew of his impending demise. He told his human wife to take their two children to where their grandparents lived, and he prepared to meet his fate.

Was the bear performing an act of self-sacrifice for the salvation of mankind? In other versions of the story, after the father has been killed, the two children come home with their mother instead of being taken to their father's parents but are treated badly by their human relations. Eventually, all three change to bear form and kill the mother's brothers. Is there perhaps a bit of bear in every mother?

The Bear Who Lives in the Stars

For generations, the Big Dipper has been a guiding star in the Northern Hemisphere. Ursa Major is the name of the constellation containing the Big Dipper, which is Latin for "Greater She Bear." The legend of how the bear constellations came into being casts blame on the Greek god Zeus and his wandering ways.

Zeus fell in love with a maiden of Artemis called Callisto, and she bore him a son. Hera, wife of Zeus, became jealous and turned Callisto into a bear but left the child as a human. One day, the bear mother came upon her son and rose on her hind legs to greet him with a hug. The child did not recognize his mother and drew his bow to slay her. Zeus was watching from above and, seeing the dilemma, grabbed the bear mother and her son and threw them into the sky. Here they remain immortal constellations to this day.

To find the bears in the stars, seek the handle of the Big Dipper as the tail of the bear and follow it forward for the bear's body. Above Ursa Major in the night sky and slightly to the right is her child, Ursa Minor, or "Little Bear."

Because this star group is closer to the horizon in autumn, it was believed by some of the First Nations people that the stars in this cluster, like the bear, were looking for a place to hibernate for the winter. For the Iroquois people, however, the stars depicted a bear hunt. The stars in the handle represented the hunters who were chasing the bear, including one carrying the cooking pot! As autumn approached, some of the hunters left the chase and, as their stars began to fade, the bear continued to escape into the night.

The Bear Who Stole the Chinook
A Blackfoot Legend

Those on the prairies welcomed the warm winds that came before winter, known as the chinook, so they could gather game and prepare. But one year, it did not come. Instead, the cold winds brought in the snow and the people were very hungry. In the tribe was one young orphan boy whose only friends were the animals. One day, he gathered his animal friends together in his teepee to decide what to do.

The magpie, who knew everything and was a bit of a gossip, said that his relatives had told him that the reason why the chinook had not come was that a bear had stolen it. He was a large bear who lived

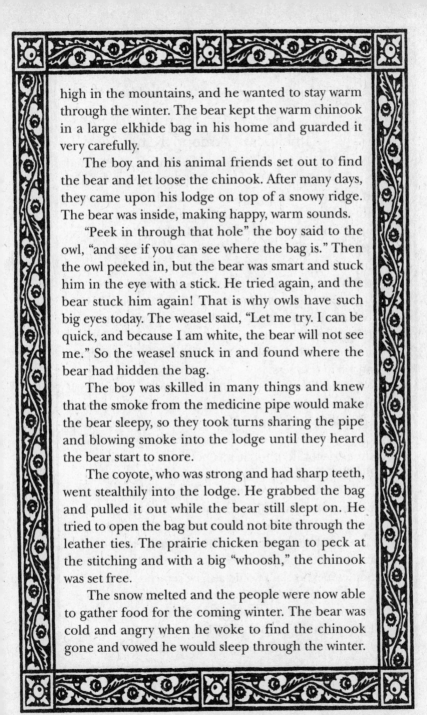

high in the mountains, and he wanted to stay warm through the winter. The bear kept the warm chinook in a large elkhide bag in his home and guarded it very carefully.

The boy and his animal friends set out to find the bear and let loose the chinook. After many days, they came upon his lodge on top of a snowy ridge. The bear was inside, making happy, warm sounds.

"Peek in through that hole" the boy said to the owl, "and see if you can see where the bag is." Then the owl peeked in, but the bear was smart and stuck him in the eye with a stick. He tried again, and the bear stuck him again! That is why owls have such big eyes today. The weasel said, "Let me try. I can be quick, and because I am white, the bear will not see me." So the weasel snuck in and found where the bear had hidden the bag.

The boy was skilled in many things and knew that the smoke from the medicine pipe would make the bear sleepy, so they took turns sharing the pipe and blowing smoke into the lodge until they heard the bear start to snore.

The coyote, who was strong and had sharp teeth, went stealthily into the lodge. He grabbed the bag and pulled it out while the bear still slept on. He tried to open the bag but could not bite through the leather ties. The prairie chicken began to peck at the stitching and with a big "whoosh," the chinook was set free.

The snow melted and the people were now able to gather food for the coming winter. The bear was cold and angry when he woke to find the chinook gone and vowed he would sleep through the winter.

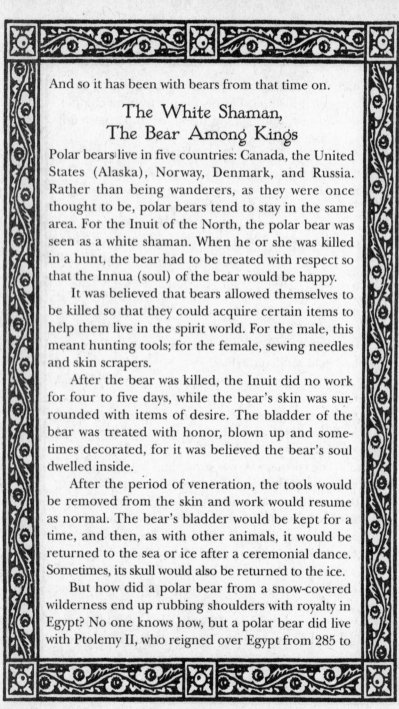

And so it has been with bears from that time on.

The White Shaman, The Bear Among Kings

Polar bears live in five countries: Canada, the United States (Alaska), Norway, Denmark, and Russia. Rather than being wanderers, as they were once thought to be, polar bears tend to stay in the same area. For the Inuit of the North, the polar bear was seen as a white shaman. When he or she was killed in a hunt, the bear had to be treated with respect so that the Innua (soul) of the bear would be happy.

It was believed that bears allowed themselves to be killed so that they could acquire certain items to help them live in the spirit world. For the male, this meant hunting tools; for the female, sewing needles and skin scrapers.

After the bear was killed, the Inuit did no work for four to five days, while the bear's skin was surrounded with items of desire. The bladder of the bear was treated with honor, blown up and sometimes decorated, for it was believed the bear's soul dwelled inside.

After the period of veneration, the tools would be removed from the skin and work would resume as normal. The bear's bladder would be kept for a time, and then, as with other animals, it would be returned to the sea or ice after a ceremonial dance. Sometimes, its skull would also be returned to the ice.

But how did a polar bear from a snow-covered wilderness end up rubbing shoulders with royalty in Egypt? No one knows how, but a polar bear did live with Ptolemy II, who reigned over Egypt from 285 to

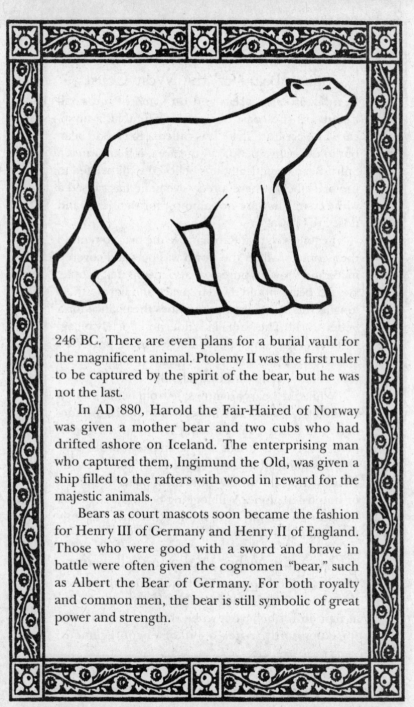

246 BC. There are even plans for a burial vault for the magnificent animal. Ptolemy II was the first ruler to be captured by the spirit of the bear, but he was not the last.

In AD 880, Harold the Fair-Haired of Norway was given a mother bear and two cubs who had drifted ashore on Iceland. The enterprising man who captured them, Ingimund the Old, was given a ship filled to the rafters with wood in reward for the majestic animals.

Bears as court mascots soon became the fashion for Henry III of Germany and Henry II of England. Those who were good with a sword and brave in battle were often given the cognomen "bear," such as Albert the Bear of Germany. For both royalty and common men, the bear is still symbolic of great power and strength.

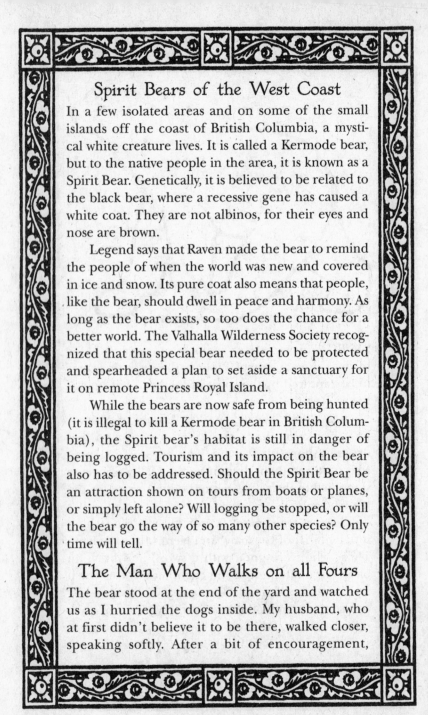

Spirit Bears of the West Coast

In a few isolated areas and on some of the small islands off the coast of British Columbia, a mystical white creature lives. It is called a Kermode bear, but to the native people in the area, it is known as a Spirit Bear. Genetically, it is believed to be related to the black bear, where a recessive gene has caused a white coat. They are not albinos, for their eyes and nose are brown.

Legend says that Raven made the bear to remind the people of when the world was new and covered in ice and snow. Its pure coat also means that people, like the bear, should dwell in peace and harmony. As long as the bear exists, so too does the chance for a better world. The Valhalla Wilderness Society recognized that this special bear needed to be protected and spearheaded a plan to set aside a sanctuary for it on remote Princess Royal Island.

While the bears are now safe from being hunted (it is illegal to kill a Kermode bear in British Columbia), the Spirit bear's habitat is still in danger of being logged. Tourism and its impact on the bear also has to be addressed. Should the Spirit Bear be an attraction shown on tours from boats or planes, or simply left alone? Will logging be stopped, or will the bear go the way of so many other species? Only time will tell.

The Man Who Walks on all Fours

The bear stood at the end of the yard and watched us as I hurried the dogs inside. My husband, who at first didn't believe it to be there, walked closer, speaking softly. After a bit of encouragement, the bear moved on in the forest at a slow, almost methodical pace.

For this bear to appear at the time it did, a time when my husband was facing questions and frustrations about his work, meant only one thing to me: that we were being offered strength. As we worked toward changing our life plan, the bear hung around. We saw his tracks and heard him crashing in the woods. When we walked the dogs, the rocks and stumps showed themselves to be bears, watching us from a distance, silently protecting.

We were not afraid, for Bear is our totem. He has chosen us.

For Further Study

B.Wise Productions. "The Great Bear Constellation." http://www.souledout.org/nightsky/ursamajorandminor.html

BC Lions Society. "Spirit Bears in the City." http://www.lionsbc.ca/events/spirit_bears.shtml

Davids, Richard C. *Lords of the Arctic: A Journey Among Polar Bears.* New York, Macmillan, 1982.

Fraser, Frances. *The Bear who Stole the Chinook: Tales from the Blackfoot.* Seattle, WA: University of Washington Press, 1991.

Loveless, Evan. "About Spirit Bears." Klemtu Tourism Ltd. http://www.klemtutourism.com/html/about_spirit_bears.htm

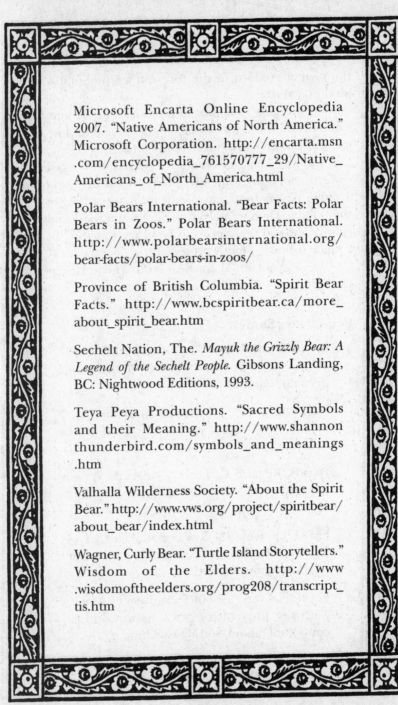
Microsoft Encarta Online Encyclopedia 2007. "Native Americans of North America." Microsoft Corporation. http://encarta.msn .com/encyclopedia_761570777_29/Native_ Americans_of_North_America.html

Polar Bears International. "Bear Facts: Polar Bears in Zoos." Polar Bears International. http://www.polarbearsinternational.org/ bear-facts/polar-bears-in-zoos/

Province of British Columbia. "Spirit Bear Facts." http://www.bcspiritbear.ca/more_ about_spirit_bear.htm

Sechelt Nation, The. *Mayuk the Grizzly Bear: A Legend of the Sechelt People.* Gibsons Landing, BC: Nightwood Editions, 1993.

Teya Peya Productions. "Sacred Symbols and their Meaning." http://www.shannon thunderbird.com/symbols_and_meanings .htm

Valhalla Wilderness Society. "About the Spirit Bear." http://www.vws.org/project/spiritbear/ about_bear/index.html

Wagner, Curly Bear. "Turtle Island Storytellers." Wisdom of the Elders. http://www .wisdomoftheelders.org/prog208/transcript_ tis.htm

Air Magic

Bells: Sacred and Mundane

by Lily Gardner

Men's death I tell by doleful knell;
Lightning and thunder I break asunder;
On Sabbath all to church I call;
The sleepy head I rouse from bed;
The tempest's rage I do assuage;
When cometh harm, I sound alarm.

Of all the tools in the Witch's closet, the bell is the least understood and written about in Pagan literature; yet, the bell continues to play an important role as a sacred tool and as a cultural symbol in modern life. The history of the bell dates back to the Copper Age, with the earliest bells discovered in China as far back as 3900 BC. Many cultures believed a bell's ring to be the echo of the primordial vibration. Its hollow, cupped shape symbolized the divine feminine, and the relationship between clapper and bell suggested Earth and the heavens.

Religions of every stripe have rung bells during ritual to focus and delineate between the sacred and the mundane. Buddhist temples hung small bells from the rafters to hear their heavenly voices. The bell, with its clear ring and fading vibration, suggested to the Buddhists the law of impermanence, a reminder to be fully present in the here and now. Just as we ring the bell three times upon casting our circle and calling in the quarters, so the Catholics ring bells to call attention to the moment their offerings of bread and wine become the body and blood of Christ. The Siberian shamans wore bells for incantations and prophecies. The bells sewn in the hems of the shaman's robes summoned the gods who spoke through

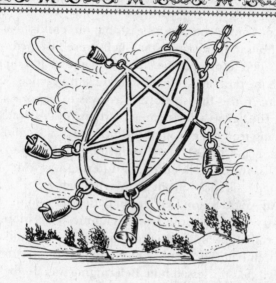

them. Perhaps the practice of reading tea leaves came from the bell's power of prophecy, for what are bells but inverted cups?

For many centuries, bells were used as fertility amulets. In Great Britain, Morris dancers, wearing leggings to which many small bells were attached, danced over newly plowed fields to ensure good crops. Fertility bells from Europe to China were dressed to resemble a sown field or decorated with rows of nipples. In times of drought, an old rain charm was to fill a bell with water and sprinkle it on the fields. In Egypt, the feast day of Osirus, the fertility god, opened with bell ringing. Ringing bells over the fields at harvest time ensured a bumper crop.

Bells have also been used across cultures for protection. The bell created a magic circle and held at bay such threats as outlaws, wild beasts, and the terrors of evil spirits. Cattle, goats, sheep, and camels wore bells as a way to locate strays, but their primary function was as a protective amulet against the demons of sickness and danger.

Bells not only protect our beasts but our children as well. For thousands of years, small bells were fastened over a baby's bed to protect the child from ghosts and demons. The baby rattle is a relic of that ancient practice. An old custom in the British Royal Navy was to baptize a baby using the bell as a christening bowl. In West Africa, mothers hang iron bells around the ankle of a sick child. Folk wisdom said that demons could not abide the tinkling of bells. An old folk cure for stuttering was to have the afflicted child drink from an inverted bell.

An Anglo Saxon bell charm dating back to the tenth century cured people from demonic possession. The spell called for an infusion of thirteen herbs drunk from a church bell. The liquid caused the person to vomit out the evil that possessed him. Bell ringing was also believed to lift a curse. The German *schrecklauten*, or "fright bells," were rung to frighten away trolls and goblins.

In times of pestilence, bells were rung to clear the air of corruption. An old Korean belief told that a ringing bell would ease a person's pain. Bells hung on the corner eaves of pagodas drove away negativity, and bells were also hung over the doors of homes and businesses to protect the inhabitants from evil influences. The shop bell is a present-day survivor of this ancient custom. The origin of wedding bells was to protect the newlyweds from spirits envious of their happiness.

Bells were also thought to drive away tempests. Church bells were rung vigorously during violent thunderstorms. Farmers rang bells over their fields and said: *Fulgara frango dissipo ventos,* or "Lightning and thunder, I break asunder." For those people living on the coastlines, the practice was to fill a bell with seawater and fling the water out into the storm to diffuse its destructive powers and spare the property.

The "passing bell" is rung slowly at the time of someone's death, a ring for each year the person lived. The ringing bell was a prayer for a happy death and a protection for the mourners against any envious ghosts. The Chinese rang bells to communicate with their dead. From eighteenth-century France, we have instructions for a bell through which one was able to speak to the dead. This bell was cast from a combination of gold, silver, mercury, tin, iron, and lead. Once the bell was cast, it was wrapped in a square of green taffeta and buried in a graveyard for seven days to pick up the vibrations from the grave. After the seven days, the bell was able to summon the spirit of the dead person.

If a bell rang of its own accord in a villager's house, it was said to presage a death in the family. In sixteenth-century Russia, a bell was heard to ring by itself when Dmitri, son and heir to Ivan the Terrible, had been assassinated. The bell was given 100 lashes and its handle cut off so it could no longer be hung. The bell was then imprisoned in a windowless room in a nearby monastery.

Often, bells were named and took on a personality. They were said to refuse to ring if insulted or to sweat blood if terrified. In medieval France, people believed that their church bells traveled to Rome on Good Friday. The villagers stayed indoors so as not to disturb the bells' flight. If the bell was unable to make its Good Friday pilgrimage, the village would suffer bad luck for the year.

Bells marked the hours as the town's timekeeper, giving people a sense of order that stayed off the forces of darkness and anarchy. The word *clock* comes from the Latin *cloca*, meaning "bell." The practice of ringing bells on the hour is called clocking in Great Britain. Bell towers were heard over long distances, providing country folk, too poor to be able to afford a clock, a sense of time.

The *taozhong*, a primitive Chinese bell, rang when it was time for the villagers to leave work and enjoy themselves. In Western Europe, bells are rung beginning at Yule and extending through Christmas Eve to announce the end of work and the beginning of revelry. A folk belief in England was that the devil died on the night that Christ was born. They called the Christmas bells "The Devil's Knell." Then, there's the age-old practice of ringing out the old year and ringing in the new. The logic was perhaps twofold: both to keep time and to drive away ghosts and demons so they didn't seize the opportunity to slip into the world of the living, and bring their dead bad luck with them.

Bells were used to warn citizens of invaders and storms. At sea, bells protected boats from running into each other during periods of low visibility. The bell held an important place in the life of the ship and the seaman. The ship's bell was named and consecrated, only retiring when the ship was also retired. The ship's cook was responsible for the bell's upkeep.

Originally only the provinces of the aristocracy, bells were later used by the government and the clergy. In China, the emperor hung bells on the four sides of his palace, the prince was permitted bells on three sides of his house, the minister on two sides, and the government official on one side. In 1799 republican France, a scandal erupted when a group of schoolgirls broke into the bell tower and rang the bell to mark the feast of Saint Catherine. It was against the law to ring the bell for religious purposes, but the villagers backed the girls' right to ring the bells in celebration of their beloved saint.

When invaders conquered a new province, they often destroyed bells they found as a symbol that the newly conquered people no longer had any power. Bells were

held as patriotic symbols or as war trophies. America's Liberty Bell, as an example, rang to announce the United States' independence from England on July 8, 1776. Both the Greeks and the Goths fastened bells to their shields to summon the gods as they went into battle and a great ringing of bells occurred when they were victorious. Chinese soldiers, until recently, went into war with a loud peal of bells. William I, the eleventh-century Norman conqueror, used the curfew bell to warn his Saxon subjects to be indoors with their lights extinguished in order to prevent discontented citizens from plotting his overthrow. Since that time, the curfew bell has been used to suppress targeted groups of people or to maintain public order or health.

Bringing Bells into Your Magic

How can we incorporate all these bell traditions in our rituals? Begin by cleansing and blessing the bell as a sacred tool. Using a modified version of an old Christian bell baptism, cleanse the bell with holy water (pure water set out in the light of a Full Moon) and salt. Dry the bell with a white cloth. Dress the bell with fresh flowers and call upon the powers of air and say, "May this bell be made sacred and consecrated in the name of the Lady and the Lord. Blessed Be!"

Using a small censor, burn myrrh incense so that the smoke fills the cavity of the bell. Say:

May the powers of air,
Winds and breath,
The dawn of each day,
The spring of the year,
Clouds, sunshine, moonshine, and starshine;
The winged creatures,

Movement, flight, intellect, and song,
Commit this bell to your use,
Infuse this bell with your power.

Use your sacred bell to cast your magic circle. Incorporate it into any spells that call upon the powers of air or spells for protection. Hanging a bell from your child's door-knob and over your front door provides a protective field around you and your family. Wear a small bell as an amulet and ring a bell when you begin meditating to reflect on the impermanence of life.

With a deeper understanding of bell traditions, we have the opportunity to forge a richer relationship with this sacred tool.

Flying Ointment in Fact and Fancy

by Magenta Griffith

Witches flying through the skies . . . it's one popular image of Witchcraft. From ancient times, Witches were thought to possess secret ointments (also called unguents) that enabled them to fly, turn themselves into cats and other animals, and perform other feats of magic. Could Witches really fly, or was it just imaginary? What exactly was in those potions, and would they work today?

An ointment is any medicinal preparation based on an oily or fatty substance, such as olive oil or lanolin, with herbs or other additives. Many different recipes can be found for flying ointments. Most flying ointments are made by heating or boiling various herbs in lard or some other animal fat. The heat extracts the active ingredients, all of them toxic to some degree; the ointment is meant to be applied to the skin, not taken internally. Typical ingredients in these recipes include hemlock, belladonna, aconite, and henbane. This was often called "the green ointment" or "green oil" because the herbs made the mixture green in color.

Witches were supposedly able to fly to Sabbath on a broom by using the ointment. Riding brooms probably originates from the phallic nature of the broomstick. Old folk customs include people riding around fields on brooms and leaping high to show the grain how high to grow. These people weren't necessarily trying to fly on their broomsticks, but the image stuck. In the early days, flying was associated with turning oneself into an animal, usually a bird, owl, or bat.

The Golden Ass (also known as *The Metamorphoses of Lucius Apuleius*), was written by Lucius Apuleius in AD 160. The book was written in the first person, so the author is assumed to be the protagonist. The story takes place in Thessaly, an area of Greece associated with Witches. Lucius spies on a Witch named Pamphile. She takes her clothes off, rubs herself all over with an ointment, recites a charm, then turns into an owl and flies away. Lucius is having an affair with the Witch's maid and asks her

to get him the ointment the Witch used. Lucius applies it, but without the correct incantation, he turns into an ass. He can't fly, and, because he is an animal, he can't talk—he can't recite a charm to change back. He spends the rest of the book trying to turn back into a man, finally succeeding at the end of the story.

Flying ointments were first specifically described by Johannes Hartlieb in 1456. They were also mentioned by the Spanish theologian Alfonso Tostado in *Super Genesis Commentaria* (1507), which supported the idea that Witches traveled to Sabbath by flying. While numerous references to flying ointments may be found in Inquisition literature (and, less frequently, in medieval and early modern magical literature) there is no consensus among scholars. Some dismiss the phenomenon entirely as part of the Inquisition campaign against Witches, who were accused of many ridiculous acts.

In *The Book of the Sacred Magic of Abramelin The Mage*, which may date back to 1458, the author mentions a flying ointment given to him by a Witch: "She then gave unto me an unguent, with which I rubbed the principal pulses of my feet and hands; the which she did also; and at first it appeared to me that I was flying in the air in the place which I wished, and which I had in no way mentioned to her." Later the narrator says, "I felt as if I were just awakening from a profound sleep, and I had great pain in my head and deep melancholy. I turned round and saw that she was seated at my side. She began to recount to me what she had seen, but that which I had seen was entirely different." This implies that what happened to the narrator was probably a dream or hallucination.

De Miraculis Rerum Naturalium, published in 1558, discusses the "Lamiarum Unguenta" (the Witches' Ointment) and gives one list of ingredients as: celery, aconite, poplar leaves, and soot. Another flying ointment recipe combines sium, acorus, cinquefoil, the blood of a bat, nightshade, and oil. The book goes on to say, "Then they smear all the parts of the body, first rubbing them to make them ruddy and warm and to rarify whatever had been condensed because of cold . . . And so they think that they are borne through the air on a moonlit night to banquets, music, dances and the embrace of handsome young men of their choice."

Modern science suggests that most of the flying ointments contained hallucinogens that gave people the illusion of flying. Another possibility is that they contained chemicals that produced vertigo, dizziness, and disorientation. Some of the combinations suggest that both the sensation of flying and visions of the Witch's sabbat resulted from the ointment's use. Herbs that are hallucinogenic include many plants of the nightshade family, such as belladonna or Deadly Nightshade (*Atropa belladonna*), which often appeared in recipes for these ointments.

Other plants that may have been used in flying ointments include mandrake (*Atropa mandragora*) henbane (*Hyoscyamus niger*), thornapple (*Datura stramonium*) hemlock (*Conium maculatum*), and monkshood or wolfbane (*Aconitum napellus*). All of these plants are toxic and can cause death in sufficient quantities. These plants contain a variety of alkaloids that produce such symptoms as dizziness, vertigo, delirium, and hallucinations. Under their influence, you might think you were flying and might see things that would later seem to have been a gathering or ritual, especially if you were primed with stories about the Witches' sabbat.

Belladonna is so dangerous that the genus, *Atropa*, is named after the Greek Fate, Atropos, who cut the thread of life. It was thought that when a mandrake root was pulled from the ground, it would emit a shriek that would madden, deafen, or even kill an unprotected human. Occult literature contains complex directions for harvesting a mandrake root in relative safety. A dog would first be tied to the upper part of the root. The dog was then called from a distance and would pull up the root when responding. The dog would then die instead of the person harvesting the plant. In medieval times, the thornapple was considered an aid to the incantations of Witches. During the time of the Witch and wizard mania in England, it was unlucky for anyone to grow it in his garden. Henbane was used to produce a deep sleep; some thought it was so powerful that washing the feet in a decoction of henbane or just smelling the flowers would cause sleep.

Yet another flying ointment recipe combined belladonna or mandrake, poplar leaves, and soot in a base of clove oil. Poplar would give the mixture a pleasant scent, and clove oil would make the areas it was rubbed on slightly numb, as well as giving a mild "high." (Clove oil's numbing effect is still used to relieve toothaches.) A few recipes called for nutmeg, which is also hallucinogenic in large quantities. Acorus refers to a group of plants, including sweet flag and yellow flag. It was used medicinally, as a tonic, and for stomach problems. There is evidence it may be hallucinogenic in large enough doses.

Other plants were less toxic. Sium, mentioned earlier, is a root vegetable related to carrots and parsnips. Cinquefoil is a common grass that was often used in magical preparations in the Middle Ages. It was useful as an astringent and to cure fevers, but seems to have no psychoactive properties.

The exact names of the plants contained in some flying ointments are a bit of a mystery. While some recipes call for plants by names that we can identify (like monkshood, a form of aconite), others were identified by various secret names for the plants, sometimes based on appearance or some other attribute. It has been speculated that the Witches' chant at the beginning of Shakespeare's *Macbeth* that begins, "Double, Double, Toil and

Trouble," is actually a list of plants for flying ointment or some other magical preparation. For example, "tongue of dog" might refer to hound's tongue, *Cynoglossum officiale*, a plant with known medicinal properties.

The precise recipe of a true flying ointment is still open to speculation. Some have suggested a mixture of nightshades and poppies. While it is true that the effects of the nightshades would be balanced by the opiates, this is improbable for several reasons. One is that the ointment is described as being applied to the skin. The active ingredients in poppies—opiates—would have little or no effect when used this way. Also, the balance between the two sets of alkaloids would have to be very precise, more so than could be pulled off in the average Witch's cauldron. Even though they can be used as antidotes to each other, just a little too much of either one could result in death. More important, none of the recipes that have come down to us include poppy by any of the usual names.

Flying ointment would be rubbed on the forehead, hands, wrists, and feet. The ointment may have also been applied to the genitals and arm pits. Applied this way, it would increase the absorption of an effective dose through the skin and possibly the genital area. However, henbane and several herbs mentioned would blister mucous membranes, so it is doubtful that it was regularly applied to anything that came into contact with the genitals. Atropine and other active ingredients in the herbs commonly listed in flying ointments are absorbed through the

skin, and so the ointment would still be effective when it was applied externally.

Gerald Gardner, the founder of modern Witchcraft, was initiated into a coven in 1939 in the south of England. He learned the members of the coven made an ointment from bear's fat, not for the purpose of flying but to keep themselves warm in the forest at night while performing their rituals skyclad—that is, naked.

Modern Witches do not know for certain of a recipe that is safe to use. Instructions for compounding a flying ointment are available, but they almost always involve herbs that are safe and nontoxic. You'll need fat or an oil to keep the ingredients together. Fat goes rancid, so this concoction was prepared immediately before use, or else a preservative was added. Below is one example of a modern flying ointment recipe. A copy of this recipe can be found at the Web site "Inner space, outer space, and hyper space."

Flying Ointment Recipe

¼ tsp. dried cinquefoil
¼ tsp. dried mugwort
¼ tsp. dried thistle
¼ dried vervain
¼ c. lard or solid vegetable shortening
½ tsp. clove oil
1 tsp. ashes from a ritual fire
½ tsp. benzoin tincture

Using a mortar and pestle, crush the dried herbs until almost powdered. In a small cauldron or saucepan, heat the shortening over a low flame until it is melted completely. Add the herbs, the clove oil, and ashes to the melted fat and mix well. Add the benzoin (a natural preservative). Stir together clockwise 13 times, and then simmer for 10 to 15 minutes. Strain it through cheesecloth into a small heat-resistant container and allow to cool. Store the ointment in a cool, dark place until it is ready to be used. On a night of the Full Moon, cast a circle for protection. Rub a small amount of the flying ointment on your temples and third eye (the middle of the forehead). Be careful to avoid touching your eyes when applying the ointment. For external use only.

Personally, I think these ointments all sound much too messy, and the authentic ones were probably quite dangerous. I'd prefer to do my flying on a 747!

For Further Study

"Flying Ointments: Their Ingredients and Their Use." http://www.angelfire.com/electronic/awakening101/flying_ointments.html

Hansen, Harold A. *The Witch's Garden*. Santa Cruz: Unity Press, 1978.

Harner, Michael J. "The Role of Hallucinogenic Plants in European Witchcraft." *Hallucinogens and Shamanism*, edited by Michael J. Harner. New York: Oxford University Press, 1973.

"Inner space, outer space, and hyper space." http://www.geocities.com/lavenderwater37/flying_ointment.htm.

Wikipedia contributors, "Flying ointment," *Wikipedia, The Free Encyclopedia*, http://en.wikipedia.org/w/index.php?title=Flying_ointment&oldid=145664872

Pet or Familiar?

by Sybil Fogg

Odin liked the bird. He sat by its cage constantly and I'd be surprised if that bird didn't like Odin right back. The tabby cat would press his head against the bars of the cage and the little yellow bird groomed him by fluffing Odin's fur with his beak, plucking out parasites and debris. Odin and the parakeet belonged to a friend of mine who had many animals, everything from lizards to pug dogs, with many cats in between. One of those cats was her favorite and she considered him her familiar. When I asked her how she knew, she said it was obvious: "He found me, I wasn't looking for him." I thought about that and wondered what other telltale signs there were to determine whether you had a pet or a familiar.

Most Witches I have spoken with insist that they did not seek out their familiar, the animal found them. In my friend's case, her kids brought the cat home, and though she tried to ignore him, he wouldn't go away. In fact, he followed her from room to room, out to the car, through the neighborhood—essentially anywhere she went—and was quite dedicated. She expected he'd play with her children, but he didn't. The cat slept with her at night, lounged behind her head on the sofa, and was most intrigued whenever she cut herbs, baked sabbat bread, or did other regular Witchcraft tasks.

Common Pagan knowledge has it that at one time the prevalent belief among non-Pagans was that familiars were given to Witches by the devil or bought or inherited from other Witches. It was also believed (and is still so in many Pagan sectors) that a Witch can call for a familiar through psychic meditation, ritual, or Moon magic. Of course, today it is ridiculous to entertain the thought that the devil is handing out black cats, especially as the general public has become more aware of Witchcraft, Wicca, and Paganism and more people know that there is no link between Satan and the Witch. It is still possible to inherit a familiar from another practicing Witch, whether it be a parent, friend, or mentor, in the same way one might be given a Book of Shadows, athame, or other magical tool. Many modern Witches have sent out a call to attract a suitable familiar to them.

On the other hand, it is a widely held belief that pets should be acquired through careful thought and consideration. People who want to add an animal to their household will often adopt from the local shelter, talk to a friend who has a litter, go to the pet store, or pore over the want ads in their quest to find the perfect pet. This seems contradictory to letting a familiar find you. Is it possible for a familiar to find its match through careful pet adoption?

It is a common story: someone will go to the local animal refuge thinking they want a specific pet, such as a cat, and end up leaving with a dog *because the dog chose them*. When I was twelve years old, I acquired what I consider to be my first familiar, the brazen money cat, Cleopatra. My friend's cat had just given birth to an unexpected litter and my mother and stepfather allowed me to pick a kitten out. I went with the intention of getting a male cat, hopefully a solid black one. There were no black kittens in the litter and every one of them was sleeping except for this little orange, brown, and red spitfire who was climbing up one of the posts of a four-poster bed. She immediately ran up my pant leg and I knew she had to come home with me.

As the years have passed, I have never had to go to a shelter or a pet store to get a cat. Most of them have come from my friend with the many animals. That is how I ended up with Odin, sans the bird (not that I didn't try). Whenever I was at her place, Odin would work his charms on me, following me around, rubbing against my legs, and sitting on the couch next to me. He had also picked up the unhealthy (unhealthy in the sense that it was rapidly wearing out his welcome in that home) habit of picking on my friend's familiar. As the older cat aged, he became more and more testy about Odin's playful attacks. Eventually, my friend asked me to take Odin away, and I did.

But Odin is no ordinary pet cat. He is not particularly affectionate. He won't sit on my lap or request love. In fact, he doesn't like to be scratched anywhere but his head. Sometimes, he'll sit on the opposite end of the couch and purr. He doesn't sleep on my bed at night and prefers to be outside. During the day, he sleeps on the altar. Many times, I have caught him drinking out of the chalice as though it were left just for him.

Odin is also an excellent judge of character. There have been a few people in my life who have either dragged me down or have had a negative effect on my psychological state, and Odin has always known beforehand who was going to be unhealthy. He snubs those who are offensive and loves those who he knows have benevolent and compassionate qualities.

When I do magical work, Odin is always there, whether it's kitchen magic or a high ritual. When I sit at my dining table to cut and dry herbs, craft dream pillows, bake bread, or make sachets, Odin will appear and climb onto the table. Although he knows this isn't usually allowed, he understands there is a time and place when it is okay. Usually he will sit across from me, watching intently, but not interfering.

On holidays, Odin is always present for the ritual gathering with the family. He can sense a circle is about to be cast. Even if he's been exploring the neighborhood for the past three days, he will suddenly appear and make himself part of the festivities. Summer and autumn pit fires are one of his favorites activities. When he stretches out in front of one, there is no doubt in my mind that this old tomcat is filled with magical potency.

Full Moon magic is Odin's favorite type. He will plunk himself in the middle of the altar. It is obvious by the charge he lets off that magic within his presence is much more effective than before he came to live with me. Odin and I share a psychic link that assists all magic endeavors. That, combined with the fact that I wasn't looking for a pet when he moved in, his personality, and his inherent magical qualities, leads me to believe he is not simply a pet—he is a familiar.

It has been said that familiars are more serious, intelligent, and aware than the average pet. This is because they are not simply pets. They possess all the qualities of the animal shape they are in, but they are also psychically in tune with their Witch. They can sense negative energies, either unseen or emanating from people that dabble in the dark arts or have an evil intent. This intuition is one of many reasons Witches will seek out a familiar.

Thanks to the entertainment industry, cats are generally the most common animal associated with witchcraft. We've all seen the Halloween depiction of the Witch's black cat, but any animal can be a familiar. Other than the cat, the most common throughout history have been dogs, toads, lizards, birds, and snakes, though any animal a Witch feels an affinity with has the potential to be a familiar.

According to the literature, familiars also aren't always animal-shaped. Sometimes they are in human form, and occasionally they are of astral essence. Whatever they look like, they are said to be mentally linked up to their Witch because she or he called the familiar forth, whether with intent or unconsciously. The part they play is that of magical assistant.

Back to the debate: can a pet be a familiar? Or should the question be: can a familiar be a pet? How does one know if they have a familiar or a pet? And is it possible to have both in one animal? In my experience—yes!

Things to consider when determining whether or not your pet is your familiar are:

- How did the animal find you?
- What is the animal's personality?
- What type of relationship do the two of you share?
- What kind of role does the animal play in your magical endeavors?

And what if you don't have any animal—pet or familiar—and decide that you want one? The best way to obtain either animal is via adoption at a shelter. Although wild animals are mesmerizing and definitely mystical, they do not make suitable familiars for the same reasons that they should not be kept as pets. If a wild animal wanders to your home consistently and eventually shows up for magical workings, then it is more than likely a familiar. For your health, and that of the animal, it is not wise to venture into the forest to acquire an animal.

Before you head to the animal shelter, it's auspicious to do a call for a familiar. This is best done on a Monday during a New Moon in Cancer. Take a white candle that has been consecrated with water and salt, and on it carve a New Moon symbol and images or hieroglyphs of the animal traits you hope to seek. Don't perform the call seeking a specific kind of animal; instead, focus on the qualities of your desired familiar. Remember: although you are carefully preparing to add an animal to your home, you must still allow your familiar to choose you. Anoint the candle with sweet clover, amber, and lavender oils. This is best done a couple of days before you do the call so that you aren't fumbling while the Moon is growing fat and round.

Sit with your candle outside, if possible, or near a window where you have a view of the Moon. Take three deep breaths to cleanse your mind. Take another three to clear it of any thoughts. Light the candle and meditate on its flame, thinking of the animal traits you would like to have come to you.

Continue this until the candle has burnt itself out. Thank the Goddess and God because you are ready to go to the shelter. It is wise to do this within a couple of days of doing the call.

When you arrive at the shelter, explore all the animals, keeping your mind clear of any type. Try to seek your familiar with your mind. You will know as you approach your familiar. This animal might be friendlier than others, might be aloof, but you will know that this creature is meant for you.

Something to remember about all animals is that they need attention. Although familiars tend to be more self-sufficient than the average pet, they will still need your care. Make sure your animal gets adequate affection. You will need to handle it, play with it, exercise it. All animals need regular food and water, and you should expect veterinarian visits and bills. Odin doesn't require much; he likes food in his bowl and access to water and the outside world, but he does need to stay up to date on his vaccines and last year he burst a blood vessel in his ear that required surgery and a hefty veterinary bill. His head is now a bit lopsided, but that just adds to his mystical appearance and quality as a magical familiar.

Connecting with Kabbalah

by Winter Wren

The Kabbalah, with its origins in ancient Hebrew mysticism, is a multifaceted magical tool. Kabbalah is derived from the Hebrew QBLH, which means, "to receive." It has come to be viewed in a variety of ways, to the point where even spellings of the word vary. Many overlook the value of this system due to misconceptions of its usability. The Kabbalah does not have to be out of reach; in fact, through some basic visualization and meditation, the Kabbalah can provide magical practitioners with another foundation for their workings.

The core of all magical working comes from within. A practitioner of magic who is not connected with their inner self cannot hope for successful practice. The knowledge of the self is a continual journey. The Kabbalah can be a deeply useful tool in both the practice of magic and in coming to know the inner self. However, many magical practitioners avoid the use of this powerful tool for lack of understanding how to connect with it.

Connections to the foundations of the Kabbalah can be made through the Tree of Life. It seems pertinent to point out that the Tree of Life is not exclusive to the Kabbalistic traditions. It is a foundation in many ancient belief systems. The Tree of Life is the Yggdrasil of the northern European traditions; it is the Bodhi Tree of the Buddha; it is the World Tree of the Mayans and the Aztecs. The Tree of Life is a pictorial diagram of the elements of the Kabbalah. The diagram consists of ten circles (the ten sephiroth) arranged in one standard and two inverted triangles along three vertical pillars and the twenty-two pathways linking the ten circles. It has been said that this diagram explains the beginning of creation and is the map to both the universe in which we live and to our own selves.

The core Tree of Life diagram is pictured here.

The ten circles, the sephiroth, are considered the facets of the divine being. You will note that the numbers of the sephiroth read right to left as do ancient Hebrew writings, rather than left to right.

The highest triangle of spheres is the highest abstract energies of the divine. This is the triangle of love. The crowning sphere of these three is the Kether (1), standing above the center pillar, the divine glory of the light of the Sun. It corresponds to the element of air, the color of white, the crown chakra, and the ace cards in tarot. To the right is the active pillar, and at its top is Chokmah (2), the sphere of the Father, corresponding to the element of fire, the color of gray, the third eye chakra, and the kings and twos in tarot. To the left is the passive pillar, and at its top is Binah (3), the sphere of the Mother, corresponding to the element of water, the color of black, the third eye chakra, and the queens and threes in tarot. Together, these three spheres are the root of all life and the soul of the divine creative spark that creates all life forms in the universe.

The second triangle is inverted. This is known as the ethical triangle and is a reflection of the higher triangle. To the right is Chesed (4), the sphere of Love and Mercy, corresponding to the element of water, the color of blue, the throat chakra and the fours of tarot. Its opposite on the left pillar is Geburah (5), the sphere of Limitations and Mortality, corresponding to the element of fire, the color of scarlet, the throat chakra, and the fives of tarot. Centered below these two on the main pillar is

Tipareth (6), the sphere of Beauty, reflecting the energy of the godhead at the crown of the pillar. Tipareth corresponds with the element of air, the color yellow, the heart chakra, and the knights (princes) and sixes of tarot.

The third triangle is also inverted. This is the magical triangle, the place of Earth. To the right is the sphere of Netzach (7), the realm of Attraction and Cohesion, which corresponds to the element of fire, the color of emerald, the solar plexus chakra, and the sevens of tarot. Balancing Netzach on the left pillar is Hod (8). Hod is the realm of the Mind and of Reason, corresponding to the element of water, the color orange, the solar plexus chakra, and the eights in tarot. At the lower point of this inverted triangle is the sphere of Yesod (9), the place of Balance and the ordered paths of Time. It corresponds with the element of air, the color violet, the root (genitalia) chakra, and the nines of tarot.

At the lowest point of the center pillar, standing alone, is the sphere of Malkuth (10). Malkuth is the sphere of the Kingdom. The sphere corresponds to the element of earth, the color of citrine, the feet chakra, and the pages (princesses) and tens of tarot. Though it corresponds to earth, since the Tree emanates from the heavens, this sphere is actually the top of the tree rather than the root.

In observing the preceding diagram, one will note there is an unnumbered sphere located along the center pillar between the spheres of Kether and Tipareth. This sphere does not actually exist on the numbered Tree of Life diagram. This unnumbered sphere is the nonsphere of Daath, or Knowledge; it is a conjunction of Chokmah and Binah. It is the void that separates the finite from the infinite. It is believed that to reach the sphere of Daath is to gain union and wholeness with the divine, the ultimate goal of practitioners of higher magic.

Many magical practitioners work with the Kabbalah astrally, creating temples to each of the ten realms in their minds through meditation. One of the most established meditation exercises of the Tree of Life is known as the Center or Middle Pillar meditation. As with most things of this nature, there are many forms of this ritual meditation. It can be found in a complex and detailed form in *The Middle Pillar* by Israel Regardie from Llewellyn. What follows is a more simplistic form that I use as I prepare for my work as a reader each day.

Center Pillar Meditation

Settle yourself in a comfortable position that will allow you to sit with your back straight for twenty minutes to half an hour. There is no "absolute" position for good meditation. Respect the limitations of your own body. It is very difficult to focus on any meditation if you have placed yourself in an uncomfortable position.

Once you are settled, begin relaxing the body. Become aware of your breathing and allow your breath to become deep and regular. Do not begin the visualizations themselves until you are truly settled into a calm and relaxed meditative state. The more you work with meditation, the easier it will be to attain this calm state.

Now, picture a sphere of bright, glowing white light about the size of a good grapefruit just above your head. See this sphere as a shining source of illumination that brings light to a dark space. This is the sphere known as Kether. While focusing on this shining force, invoke the divine name of the sephora three times: EH HE YEH. Let the sound resonate with your being. Kether is the concept of the universal consciousness existing "beyond" and throughout everything. Concentrate on making the sphere glow more brightly with each exhalation. Feel it warming and illuminating your being.

Next, envision a blue sphere in the area of your throat. This is the non-sphere of Daath, of Knowledge. This is the place of connection, where the source of light above makes connection with the self below. It is also the source of sharing wisdom. That which is learned and seen is shared through the voice, which emanates from the throat. While focusing on the glowing blue sphere, invoke the divine name of this non-sephora three times: YE HOH VOH E LOH HEEM. Concentrate on making the blue sphere glow more brightly with each exhalation of breath. Feel the sphere and light freeing your voice to speak the truth as you embrace the day ahead.

The next sephora is Tipareth, the realm of beauty. Centered at your heart, the center of your physical being, this sphere is filled with glowing golden-yellow light. Visualize the sphere in this place as the light of the Sun pouring out energy. See the sphere of yellow light pouring out its own healing energy, drawn down from the spheres above through the shaft of the center pillar that joins each of these spheres. This is the center of you, the point of balance. As you focus on the warming energy of this sphere engulfing your heart, invoke the divine name of the sephora three times: YE HOH VOH EL OAG YE DA ATH. Once more, concentrate on making the sphere glow brighter with each out breath.

The next sephora is Yesod, the foundation of the being. Visualize a purple sphere of light in the groin area. This is the root of instinct, emotion, and perception. Again, feel the flow of energy coming down from Kether through each of the spheres, down the center pillar to this point. Feel the root of your being connecting to the astral plane. Feel the awakening of the aware- ness deep within you. As you focus on the pulsating violet of this sphere, invoke the divine name of the sephora three times: SHAH DAI EL CHAI. Concentrate on making the sphere glow brighter again as you expel each of your breaths. Visualize all this energy flowing down through your being.

The sephora of Malkuth lies at your feet: Malkuth, known as "the kingdom" is the sphere of the Earth and matter, the source of your physical body as a whole being. The sphere in this place is one of glowing citrine, a rich russet hue of warmth. Maintain the feel of the energy flowing down the planes from Kether all the way to Malkuth, flowing from the universal source to the connection of your human being, your physical form. As you focus on the radiating glow of this sphere, invoke the divine name of the sephora three times: AH DOH NAI HA AH RETZ. Concentrate on making the sphere glow brighter as each breath departs your being.

Now, see this energy flowing through you and broadening itself out into a spherical cocoon of yellow-orange light centered at the heart chakra and surrounding your entire being. It extends outside the bounds of your physical body. It is elastic and moves with you. It expands to hold you within should you reach out. Relax, continue breathing deeply and evenly. Let all the spheres of the system integrate and all of your self to feel energized from these forces. Let yourself feel the wholeness you are creating.

As with all forms of meditation, it is a good idea to end in a structured way. Take the time to make sure that you ground yourself properly through gradually returning to the awareness of your physical body. It is never a good idea to simply pop out of a meditative state and right into some form of activity. Take the time to focus the energy you have created toward the work of the magic you set forth to do or the work of your day. If you are not working in a magical setting, focusing yourself though this mediation can bring awareness of the self to even mundane daily work.

The Tarot Connection

As I am an artistic being, I am a very visual person. I comprehend things better if I can see them before me. I also find my meditations are stronger with visual keys. In coming to deepen my understanding of and connection to the Kabbalah, I chose to turn to the magical tool with which I have the greatest knowledge and comfort: tarot.

The link between Kabbalah and tarot has been documented since the writings of Eliphas Levi. By the end of the nineteenth century, A. E. Waite and S. L. Mathers of the Hermetic Order of the Golden Dawn determined the Kabbalistic connection with tarot applied not only to the twenty-two major arcana, but also to the full seventy-eight card tarot deck. With these connections firmly established, I feel tarot is a viable tool for connecting with Kabbalah on a deeper level.

I noted in the correspondences of the sephiroth which tarot minor arcana cards associate to the spheres. When I am seeking to connect more strongly with a particular sephora, I lay out the cards corresponding to it and study them for a time. Once I am comfortable with the images, I settle in for meditation in my usual manner and then visualize the cards in my mind's eye. When I have the images clearly focused, I create a dialogue with the residents of the cards, inquiring of them what they can share to help me form a stronger connection to the energies of that particular sephora. Sometimes, I consult with them individually; sometimes, I create the concept of a panel discussion. Always, at the end of each meditation, I thank these worthies for their energy and wisdom.

The major arcana of tarot are associated with the paths between the sephiroth rather than the spheres themselves. Meditating on the arcana card linked to the pathway allows one to gain a better understanding of the flow of energy between the spheres, in the world and within the self. Regardless of whether I am working with the minor or the major arcana, I am always asking these dignitaries for wisdom and guidance. What further information can they help me see to add to my knowledge base?

In seeking out tarot diagrams for the Tree of Life, one will find that many such diagrams exist and can differ greatly. For the purpose of this article, the diagram on the opposite page is my foundation.

The Kabbalah and its associated Tree of Life are a useful foundation of knowledge for each practitioner to work with and connect with over time. As you begin this journey, understand that it is the work of a lifetime. At times, it may give you just as many questions as answers, if not more. But questions are the foundation of growth, and growth is the foundation of magic. It is the journey of a lifetime. Journey well.

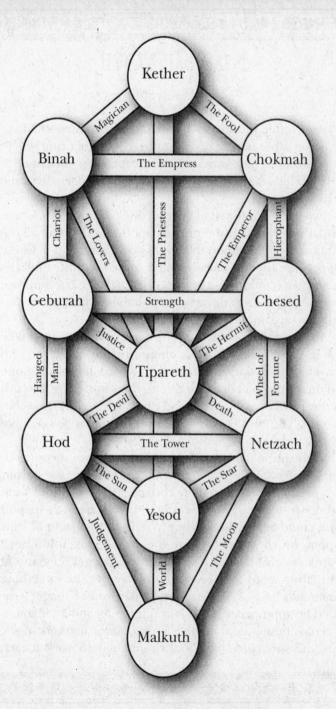

Magical YOU!

by Paniteowl

People often think of spellworking as something you do to affect other people or situations. For a practicing Witch, the basic awareness is that the first thing a spell changes is YOU. So let's talk about a relatively simple spell where the focus is on YOU!

Everyone has heard of voodoo dolls and poppets, where sympathetic magic is the primary motivation. Forget all the negative mumbo jumbo that Hollywood has created, where poppets are used to harm or bind someone. Instead, focus on how you could use a poppet on YOURSELF, to improve your life and change those negative habits or tendencies that you know are not helpful to you!

You may have heard about some practices that take "the measure of the Witch" when initiating someone into a coven. This is simply using a strong cord and placing one end under the heel of the dedicant, then stretching the cord up the back, over the head, and down again until it touches the toes. The cord is cut at that point and may be used as a belt for ritual robes.

To begin making a poppet, take your own measure by wrapping a cord around your head (or from the base of your neck in back) then stretch the cord over the top of your head and down to the area below your chin. For men, the cut-off point could be the Adam's apple. This is the height of your poppet, which will determine the overall size. You'll need approximately half a yard of fabric. You can get remnants at most fabric shops for a really good price. Or, use something you already have. A T-shirt, shirt, or skirt you no longer wear would be appropriate, especially if it has meaning for you.

Fold the material in half. Using magic markers, place your "measure cord" on the fabric and make a mark at each end. One mark will be the tip of the head, and the other mark will be the tip of the toes of your poppet. Now draw an outline of your shape between those two marks. Think of those old-fashioned, cloth-bodied dolls, or think of poppets you may have seen, and don't worry if your drawing skills are not museum quality! Keep it simple, and picture yourself as you draw the doll. This is your basic pattern. Cut the fabric along your drawing lines. You should have two pieces of fabric in the shape of your poppet. If your fabric has a pattern or texture on one side, place the right sides together. Stitch along the edges to join the two pieces together, leaving the head area open, to be closed after you stuff the poppet. Now turn the poppet inside out so the seam edges are on the inside. The purists recommend stitching by hand, but we're modern Witches, so a sewing machine is fine!

The next thing to consider is what you will use to stuff the poppet. What kind of person are you? Some people may want to use the standard stuffing material you can get at any craft store. That's fine—as long as it is biodegradable. However, some people choose to use items that are more personal. Scraps of fabric you have lying around the house, old stockings and socks, even cotton balls can be used. Also, straw, raffia, and soft packing materials come in handy in a pinch. You're putting together a representation of YOU. Think about what would be appropriate to your personality. Another thing to consider when stuffing the poppet is what you want to focus on to change your life. I've known people to place a candy heart in the poppet, based on their own need to be more loved and loving. I've put a piece of chocolate candy in my poppet because I'm a diabetic, and one of the things that is important to me is to constantly be aware of what I'm eating to maintain my health. (Just for your information, I'm also a chocoholic! When I incorporated my craving for chocolate into my poppet, the craving did indeed lessen.)

Other items to consider placing inside the poppet are notes to yourself about things you need to deal with or pictures of people and things you feel have been a negative influence on your life. Remember, the poppet is about YOU, and how YOU deal with issues in your life. It's not about changing anyone else!

OK, now that you've decided what needs to go inside of the poppet, it's time to look at the outside. What is going on in your life that needs to change? What things seem to constantly drag you down? One of the simplest ways to work on the external things in your life is to use buttons. Most of us have a stash of buttons someplace in our homes—lost buttons, one of a kind extra buttons, and even some buttons we've picked up as souvenirs in our travels. Take a look at them and decide what each will represent. A large red button may represent a short temper or anger-management issues. A green button could represent having a problem with your finances. A yellow button could remind you of being envious or jealous of someone. As you select the buttons, simply sew them onto the poppet, reminding yourself that these are things that you need to be more aware of, and that you truly want to change.

Some people have used superglue instead of sewing the buttons. That's fine! This is YOUR poppet, and there's

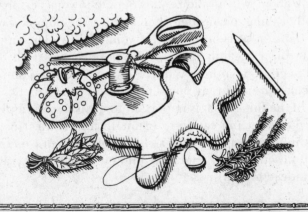

no "right" way to define yourself. Others have used specific things instead of buttons. I know one woman who attached a cigarette to the poppet with craft wire. She was trying to quit smoking! Another person glued coins to his poppet because he consistently got into financial problems. I remember one poppet that had a couple of small bottles of vodka tied to both arms, like those served on airplanes. Can you guess what that person's issue was?

I hope you're beginning to get the picture of what the poppet represents. There are personality traits we've all developed over the years that can be improved upon. There are hopes and fears and phobias that lie deep within our personalities that can hinder our enjoyment of life. As we confront our deep-seated internal issues and name them, we use sympathetic magic to imbue our poppets with those traits by calling them to our conscious attention.

Then there are those things that we pick up as practices, habits, and behaviors that have more to do with our environmental experiences. We smoke, drink, or overeat because our families and friends do so in our social situations. We get hooked on things because that's the way our immediate circle of friends and relatives behave. You might paste a page out of the *TV Guide* onto your poppet if you're "hooked" on soap operas! How about attaching the receipt from the payment of your latest traffic ticket? Maybe combining a big red button with the traffic ticket would be a significant way of describing road rage? This poppet is all about YOU! It's YOURS! Once the poppet has been stuffed, the opening stitched closed, and all of your "issues" attached to it, now you have to live with it for a while.

Our Trad usually does this work around the Summer Solstice. It's a turning point on the Wheel of the Year, and it can also be a turning point for you to take control of your life. Change doesn't happen overnight, but the beginning for change can happen in the blink of an eye.

Choosing to change is much more satisfying than being forced to do so!

As many times as I've shown people this working, I am always surprised at the way the poppets turn out! Some will have faces, either drawn on with magic markers, or hand stitched like a piece of artwork. I've seen people draw a face on the poppet using their own makeup kits, even giving a blush to the cheeks. I've seen some with wigs and some with yarn hair. I've seen some "dressed" and some simply left plain. There is no "right" way. When you are working on yourself, it is entirely up to you as to how the poppet is put together, decorated or not.

However, when you look at the differences in the poppets, you will also notice that the people making them do put their own concerns into the doll! Just doing the project helps tell what kind of person you are. Did you use a plain piece of scrap material? Did you decide to get a colorful, patterned piece of cloth? Does that fit with your personality? Someone whose appearance is very important to them will tend to pay more attention to the "beauty" of the poppet, while someone who is less concerned with fashion would probably be more comfortable making their poppet out of old scrap fabric.

The lesson in this working is to bring out who YOU truly are. What is important to YOU is the focus. Again, there is no "right" or "wrong" way.

Once your poppet is finished to your satisfaction, decide what you want to do with it. You can put it in a prominent place in your home where you see it every day and think about those things that need changing. You can carry it with you in a purse or place it on the console of your car. You can take it to work and use it as a paperweight! Just remember that it must be within your sight and reach every day. It's a work in progress. It's a reminder of how you feel about things, and what you want to see changed.

My poppet helped remind me to change my eating habits after being diagnosed with diabetes. My poppet sat on top of my refrigerator, and every day I had to make food choices based on the looming poppet. I also took her with me when I went out to eat. Yes, sometimes I got strange looks when I sat her on the table at a restaurant, but if anyone asked, it was a good conversation starter! In fact, one of those conversations was with a woman in a popular weight-loss program. After I explained what I was doing and the significance of the poppet, she asked if she could do the same thing to help her lose the weight. I gave her my phone number and helped her put her poppet together. Some time later, she called me and told me that she had a get together with other friends who were on the program and they all made their poppets and focused on sticking with it—it worked!

The external focus of the poppet is beneficial, but I think the internal working of self-improvement is even more worthwhile. To reprogram oneself takes a lot of energy and commitment. The poppet allows you to get a better perspective by externalizing your hidden feelings and emotions.

The poppet is a magical tool. Use it as you will. I've known people to take exceptionally good care of their poppet and not let anything happen to it. I've known others who will throw it across the room or stick pins in it when issues crop up in life. Whatever method you need to use to get you where you want to be is OK!

If you start at Summer Solstice, plan to complete the spellwork by Samhain. Oh yes, there is a time limit on this. You have approximately three months to work on YOU! Look at your poppet every day. Reinforce the things you want to change. Take courses in self-improvement, anger management, finances, human relations . . . whatever areas you have identified as needing improvement. It doesn't mean you have to complete all those courses within the three months, but it does mean that you should be exploring and finding out what is available to you so that you can accomplish your changes.

And now we come to the Samhain celebrations. You've lived with your poppet, you've considered your opportunities, and you've seen some progress. It's a beginning for change. Now it's time to take your poppet to the Samhain fires. Yes, you're going to burn that poppet and send the intent for change and improvement into the fire so that it changes to smoke and ash. It's now time for you to let go of those negatives in your life that were hindering your personal progress. As the poppet burns, feel the release of old baggage in your life. You are now ready to take the next steps toward permanent healing and self-improvement. In order to do this, you need to truly look at yourself. The self-analysis that went into creating your poppet is very important. The self-awareness as you live with your poppet is very important. The release of those emotions, habits, and behaviors is extremely important. Now it's time to move forward.

Can you create another poppet for yourself? Of course you can. After all, none of us are static. Life evolves, changes, and moves forward. I would recommend waiting at least three months before redoing this spellwork. At that point, you will re-examine those things you need to work on. Some may be the same old, same old stuff you've been carrying around for years. Sometimes you find a whole new list of projects to work on. And sometimes, if we're very lucky, we find that it's not necessary to create a poppet at all, and we continue to grow, evolve, change, and find joy and satisfaction in our lives because of our own efforts and perspectives.

After all, I think what we all seek is a better way to live within our own niches. We all want to be happy and satisfied with ourselves and our lives. It's up to us to make the

best of what we have. And isn't that what our studies of the ancients teach us? We are the descendents of those who went before and created the world we know today. Not just the scientists, and the inventors, but the wise ones, the cunning ones, those who listened to the nature within and the nature without. We are the survivors!

Blessed Be!

P.S.: This is a teaching method for 1st Degree Initiates of our Trad. We don't usually tell our students that the poppet will be burned at Samhain. Finally, the way the poppet is treated, by each individual, becomes part of the teaching as to how "attached" we become . . . and how difficult it is to truly let go of behaviors and habits that may be harmful to us. I guess the cat is out of the bag now!

Dance of the Merry Muses

by Laurel Reufner

Sing to me of the man, Muses, the man of twists and turns
Driven time and again off course, once he had plundered
The hallowed heights of Troy
                    —Homer, Book I, *The Odyssey*

He is happy whom the muses love . . .

                                        —Hesiod

We all seek inspiration at one time or another. Many an artist has gone looking for their own personal muse. In ancient Greece, to be remembered by the muses meant fame, fortune, and good luck. (The muses were also referred to as the *Meneiae*, or Remembrances.) It can be the same way for artists today, for to be truly moved by the muses inspires one to create something outstanding that stands the tests of time.

While today a personal muse can be almost anyone or anything that inspires you to create, we have the ancient Greeks to thank for the original concept of the muse. By learning the history and background of these marvelous ladies, you'll be in a better position to either welcome them into your life and work or to create a muse of your very own.

Since the muses spoke directly through the poets of the time, any poet with a brain would remember to thank the source of his inspiration. This mention often came at the beginning of their work, with the poet representing himself as the person who had merely written down what the muses told him.

In the beginning, in a time before memory, there was only one muse. While her name has been long forgotten even by the classical Greeks, her inspiration lived on; in fact, it grew. And while it may be ironic that the original muse's name has been forgotten by history, we have the muses to thank for the inspiration of the great ancient Greek writers.

At times, there were groups of three or four muses with cults at various locations. Delphi once worshiped three muses whose names represented the three strings on a lyre (Nete, Mese, and Hypate) and at other times people worshiped four muses (Thelxinose, Aoede, Arche, and Melete). Mount Helicon, in Boeotia, Greece, had three Muses: Melete (Meditation), Mneme (Memory), and Aoede (Song). It is widely believed that their worship was established by the Aloeidae, Otus, and Ephialtes.

Athens had a whopping eight muses to worship. The island of Lesbos had a cult of seven muses. There are also references to a so-called tenth muse, a group Sappho of Lesbos fell into, thanks to Plato.

Although the muses at Mount Helicon were said to be founded by the Aloeidae, they were certainly not considered the parents of the muses. While several pairings have been named, the most generally accepted parental couple is Zeus and Mnemosyne, a titaness personifying memory.

Apollo was considered leader of the muses because of his musical inclinations and gift of prophecy. He could often be found in their company near various sacred springs. Muses also could be found in the company of the Charities, the Horae, Eros, and Dionysus, among others. They could also be found at banquets upon Mount Olympus, singing and dancing for the gathered crowd.

In addition to performing on Mount Olympus, the muses also were charged with conferring the poetic gift upon those they found worthy. Invocations to the muses were always sincere, even in an ever-increasingly cynical Greek society. Artists and writers always remained grateful for the divine inspiration and patronage of the muses. The muses held sway over all areas of thought: oratory, rhetoric, knowledge, history, mathematics, and astronomy (astrology). They trained Aristaeus, deity of agriculture, in the art of healing and taught Orpheus how to play the lyre.

Some memorable muse performances include singing at the marriage of Harmonia and Cadmus and at that of Thetis and Peleus. The muses sang lamentations at the funeral of Patroclus, best friend of Achilles. The oldest song ever sung is said to be the victory song performed by the muses

after the Olympians defeated the Titans.

The muses were also asked to be judges on occasion, such as the musical contest between Apollo and Marsyas. Of course, Marsyas couldn't hope to best a musical god such as Apollo. Apollo flayed Marsyas alive, nailing his skin to a tree near Lake Aulocrene, all for the crime of hubris against the gods. The muses weren't above handing out punishments as well. Thamyris boasted he could out-sing the divine performers, an insult for which the muses took both his sight and his ability to sing. In another contest, the sirens claimed they could out-sing the muses and lost their wings as a result. The muses did not take challenges lightly.

While no one is sure how nine came to be the official number, in the end that's the number of generally recognized muses. Perhaps it was felt that the spheres each muse represented were the more important categories of academia and fine art. Let us take a look at these divine nine and learn a little about them as individuals.

Calliope, she of the Beautiful Voice, was considered the eldest and wisest of the muses, as well as the most assertive. She was the muse who inspired Homer in his creation of both *The Iliad* and *The Odyssey*. She apparently bore two sons with Apollo: Orpheus, one of the ancient world's foremost musicians and poets, and Linus, the first creator of melody and rhythm. When Aphrodite and Persephone fought over the youth Adonis, it was Calliope whom Zeus sent to mediate between the two goddesses. As a result of her wisdom, each goddess was allowed the young man's company one-third of the year. This allowed Adonis some much-needed time to himself, as well. Finally, she taught Achilles to sing at banquets, something for which the hero became well known. Calliope is usually pictured holding a writing tablet and stylus. She might also be shown holding a book or scroll and possibly wearing a golden crown.

Clio, the Proclaimer, made men famous by proclaiming, or recounting, their deeds of renown. She is most associated with heroic poetry and historical feats. She was the mother of Hyacinth, fathered by Pierus, King of Macedonia. Yes, the same Hyacinth accidentally killed by Apollo, who then turned him into a flower. She may have also been the mother of Hymenaios, Greek god of marriage ceremonies. Finally, she is the one to have introduced the Phoenician alphabet to the Greeks. Clio is usually represented with a scroll or a set of tablets, or perhaps an open chest of books.

Erato, the Lovely, represented lyric poetry and hymns, especially of the erotic or romantic variety. She was also gifted with mimicry. With Arcas, she bore a son named Azan, and had a daughter, Cleophema, with Malus. Little is known of her children and their fathers. Be that as it may, those who followed her became men who were desired and loved. Erato is often shown with a lyre, appropriate for her role in lyric poetry.

Euterpe, the Giver of Pleasure, was the muse of flute-playing, as well as music in general. Later on, her role was narrowed to that of representing classical lyric poetry. She bore a son, Rhesus, with the River Strymon. Rhesus is noted for leading a band of Thracians during the Trojan War. He was killed by Diomedes. Euterpe is often pictured, appropriately enough, with either a flute or a double-flute.

Melpomene, the Songstress, was associated with tragedy, although she's known as being joyous-sounding. She may have been the mother of the sirens, although it's not very likely. Melpomene is usually shown with the mask of tragedy, wearing a cathurnus, which were boots worn by tragic actors. Sometimes, she holds a knife or club in one hand. The club may represent that of Hercules. A crown of cypress is often on her head.

Polyhymnia, the muse of Many Songs, personified both the sacred hymn and eloquence. While Melpomene was known to be joyful, Polyhymnia was meditative and pensive, often appearing lost in thought. She was sometimes considered the muse of geometry, mime, meditation, and agriculture on top of her other attributions. Polyhymnia (sometimes spelled Polymnia) was usually shown holding a finger to her mouth, as if in thought, wearing a long cloak and veil, with her elbow resting on a pillar.

Terpsichore, Delight or Dance, was the muse of lyric poetry and dance. She is another candidate for mother of the sirens, mated with the largest river in Greece, the Achelous. She is usually portrayed sitting and holding a lyre.

Thalia was the muse of comedy and pastoral poetry. With Apollo, she mothered the Corybantes, dancers honoring Cybele. Thalia also shared a name with one of the graces. She was often shown with a comedic mask and a shepherd's crook or wearing a wreath of ivy.

Urania, the Heavenly, was the muse of astronomy and universal love. She inspired those interested in philosophy and astronomy. Also, it was believed that she could foretell the future using astronomy. She may have been the mother of Hymen, god of marriage celebrations (sometimes known as Hymenaious), and Linus, god of rhythm and melody, with Apollo. (Yes, Calliope is also credited with giving birth to those two gods.) Urania is often represented with a celestial globe and staff.

The Muses In Your Life

How do you go about welcoming these inspiring ladies into your life? It can be as simple as setting up a special altar or shrine to the muse of your choice using either images or symbols. Many images can be easily found on the Internet.

Invoke the muses into your workspace in much the same manner as you would the ancients. Remember to dedicate part of your work to them or leave them offerings after you've felt particularly inspired.

Can't decide on a muse to inspire you? Try doing what countless others have done before and create one of your own. You can be as specific as you want, since it's your muse. Create a shrine, altar space, or artwork that represents your muse. Think in terms of color, images, and symbols to give your muse some personality. Most of the Greek muses were playful, but that doesn't necessarily need to be the case for your personal muse. Remember to honor her as is her due. A cranky muse should be avoided!

If you just want to bring the beauty and joy of the muses into your personal space, trying adding a small fountain to your altar. The muses were often fond of hanging out at various sacred springs. If you don't have room on your altar, or that doesn't seem to be the most appropriate place for a small fountain, find somewhere else to put one. There is nothing wrong with honoring divinity in unexpected places—we often find inspiration in the most unexpected of places. If you have the energy, finances, and space, try putting in an outdoor water garden, complete with fountain.

Speaking of unexpected places, get outside! Take a walk in the park or even just down the street. In spite of all the partying and the seriousness of their roles, the muses were nature gals. Get some fresh air, clear the cobwebs from your mind, and find inspiration in the landscape around you. Notice the beauty in that tree's leaves and those flowers' petals. Hear the music in the air around you and know that the muses haven't left us. They've just been waiting for us to rediscover them.

If you'd like more information, check out Wikipedia [http://www.wikipedia.org] and the MythMan [http://www.thanasis.com/homewk01.html] websites online. For more on Greek mythology, I recommend *Women of Classical Mythology*, by Robert E. Bell, as well as *Classical Mythology* by Mark P. O. Morford and Robert J. Lenardon.

Welcome the muses into your life and see what they can inspire within you!

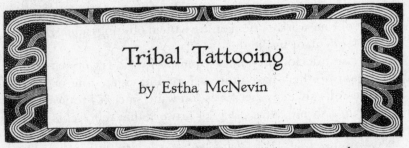

Tribal Tattooing
by Estha McNevin

The history of artistic body modification runs to the very roots of our collective human record. Anthropologists have unearthed well-preserved burial sites around the world that offer amazing evidence of our ancient proclivity toward lastingly embellishing the natural body. Indigenous cultures revered body modification as a rite of passage and a means of infusing or obtaining energy. Designs were often self-chosen for talismanic purposes, and they displayed power, agility, or rank within tribal hierarchies. While the types and styles of modification vary, tattooing is the most common ritualistic practice among all indigenous cultures. Of those civilizations, we have the most documented evidence of Polynesian practices and are able to trace their influence far beyond the expanses of the Pacific Ocean. Tattoo is the persistently significant rite of passage that we know to have been practiced by nearly every indigenous tribe on the planet.

The modern word and tribal practice of tattooing finds its heritage in Protopolynesian Tongan. Within this indigenous Tahitian culture, *tatau* (later *tattow*) was a sacred and ritualistic rite of passage. The term itself was onomatopoetic, a linguistic imitation of the sound made by the double striking technique of the ancient art form. Protopolynesian culture played a large role in the island nations of the South Pacific. During the Paleolithic period (or Old Stone Age, roughly 2.5 million to 10,000 BC) they were the largest ethnic group in the region. The vast clusters of the Pacific archipelago evolved into vigorous trading networks. From a context of mutual benefit, the Islands shared metaphysics, celestial navigation, art, and tools, as well as harvested and cultivated goods.

The lush culture that emerged stretched from Taiwan to New Zealand to the Pacific Northwest and is often referred to as the Polynesian triangle or Lapita. Polynesian culture is believed to be largely responsible for the popularity and survival of tattoos. Through this culture, the art and tools of tattoo were shared with many other tribes on both sides of the Pacific, eventually spreading to Central and Pacific Native American tribes as well as westward through Central and West Asia into Europe.

Even to this day, body modification holds an ancient and sacred energy within Polynesian tribal cultures, and it is believed to be truly rejuvenating for the mind, body, and spirit. The ritualistic significance of tattooing involved sacred ceremonies that enhanced qualities or dispelled weaknesses, often acting as rites of passage. These observances punctuated stages of personal development and were aligned to the acquisition of skill, characteristic, or intensity.

Tā Moko

The Māori Tribe of Aotearoa/New Zealand is one of the last indigenous tribes to continue to use tattoo in its traditional and sacred forms. Permanent patterns were added to the flesh as an act of transformation and courage. The face, upper arms, thighs, and buttocks were marked with chosen or earned designs that often marked tribal status. Tā Moko practices did not involve needles originally, but used *uhi* (delicately sharpened Albatross bone) to chisel intricate line and spiral patterns into the epidermal flesh. These immutable grooves were then packed with natural dyes stored in vessels (*okos*).

Oko ink was considered a sacred element for the power that Tā Moko could invoke. The black coloration was achieved by using burnt timber inks of varying shades. Minerals provided early rosy hues. The dyes to mimic flesh tone were a bit more of an obscure harvest. Grassland caterpillars, Awiteto, infected with a fungus were ground down and used for this particluar dye. The dyes were so sacred that Tohunga Moko, moko specialists, would bury their inks when not in use. Stored with the utmost devotion in lavishly painted earthenware pots, many inks were passed down through the generations of Tohunga Moko. The meticulous Tohunga Moko training was undertaken mostly by men. Women began to practice and pass down moko traditions during the twentieth century, and they have upheld the tradition to the present day.

Colonial exploration and the East India Trading Company greatly changed the face of the South Pacific. With them, Westerners brought Christianity and unknown exotic luxuries. When they left, Western sailors carried with them strong impressions of the Polynesian lifestyle and forever linked the roughish bravery of nautical travel with tattoo art. Pressures from colonial authorities and Christian conversion initiatives led most men to stop practicing moko in the 1860s. Surviving Tohunga Moko were quick to learn modern tattoo techniques, most of which were a crossover from the English engraving and metalwork trades; the first modern tattoo gun was of English design and little more than a refitted electric engraver.

Today, Tohunga Moko have taken to combining the traditional moko with more modern tattoo practices to improve sanitary standards and lessen the occurrence of infection. Among the younger generations of Māori, modern tattoos of traditional patterns and designs offer a new and welcome evolution in moko. There is a genuine resurgence of Māori language and culture in Aotearoa/New Zealand, and modern Māori tattoos have rekindled a local and global interest in the sacred traditions of moko. Among the tribal patterns of the world, the Māori alone are the most commonly recognized. Inspired by the dramatic paradise of the South Pacific, the self-creative and transfiguring ceremonies of Māori culture remain one the most enduring links we have to traditional tribal culture.

Irezumi

A more modern Pacific tattoo tradition, the Japanese Irezumi has evolved to a sacred and secretive art form. The indigenous people of Japan, the Ainu, were an ethnically darker Polynesian tribe.

The Ainu used and revered tattoos for decorative and ceremonial purposes. Chinese colonization forced many of the early tribes of Japan northward and brought with it extreme ideas of ethnic prejudice. From AD 300 to 600, tattoos were used to mark convicted criminals and social outcasts. Many of these early tattoos were character groupings or mottos that conveyed the transgression publicly as an extension of punishment. The result, as one might imagine, is a strong Japanese association linking tattoos and rebellious factions of society.

There is much speculation in Japan, though there seems little evidence, that ancient Irezumi techniques emerged in an effort to cover or conceal these criminal markings. These theories bank on the secrecy of modern Irezumi Masters and purport that larger, more ornate designs were indicative of a multitude of offenses. As a result, tattoos in Japan were often related to exiled criminal sects, few of whom favored Chinese Imperial colonization.

During the Edo period, around 1600, the influence of a Chinese printed book titled *The Water Margin* (also known as *The Outlaws of the Marsh*) led to a boom in the tattoo trade. The story was loosely based on a Chinese borderland outlaw named Song Jiang, including detailed woodblock prints showing the outlaw and his companions defending their familial territory and redeeming their ancestral property from corrupt imperial officials. Decorated with ornate tattoos of dragons, mythical beasts, flowers, tigers, and religious images, the outlaws appeared as rural heroes struggling to maintain familial and clan identities while being engulfed by the imperial Chinese territory. The stories of the outlaws struck a chord within occupied Japan. The demand for tattoos caused a resurgence in traditional technique. Tools from woodblock printing were borrowed and used in conjunction with traditional bamboo and steel needle implements.

Many woodblock artists found fame and fortune in the medium of the flesh. They employed chisels and gouges along with Nara ink, known for its distinctive blue-green hue. By the 1800s, Irezumi had manifested its own cultural customs and distinctive secrecy. During the Meiji Period, Irezumi was outlawed as imperial Japan attempted to modernize and stamp out overt tribal influences. However, tattoo art has long been honored in some of Japan's most sacred traditions, like those of the Samari and Geisha.

Irezumi evolved to invoke the power and symbolism of natural and mythic figures. The Irezumi Masters used rigorous training to encourage focus and skill, teaching disciplined students the art of bringing mythic archetypes to life through their work. To this day, each person who receives an Irezumi does not select the details, color, or subject of their own design. This information is channeled by the artist to ensure that the final images blend together in destined symbolism, not ego-based desires. It is largely believed that Irezumi is an outward representation of the plot of the soul and will only be imbued with life and the power to animate life if the image and the soul are an exact match.

In 1945, tattooing was legalized with the U.S.-led occupation of Japan. Though legal, tattoos generally remain an exception rather than a rule within Japanese culture. Public bathhouses and many traditional public hot spring pools forbid anyone with tattoos to appear publicly nude, and many outright ban participation. In such subtle ways, Irezumi has never lost its link with taboo. The modern Japanese mafia, the Yakuza, are renowned for their belief in the protective and summoning energies of Irezumi. The stereotype is so prevalent that many gangsters now refrain from tattoos to maintain anonymity and avoid unwanted suspicion.

While the Irezumi tradition has been created and upheld by men, and though women are not allowed to be trained, many female family members of master artists receive Irezumi invocations in honor of their blood connection to what is now considered a sacred and enigmatic Japanese tradition. They are among a limited population of women allowed to witness and receive Irezumi and are sternly dissuaded from pursuing any personal interests in the male-dominated tradition.

Modern designs follow an established ideal of Irezumi secrecy by leaving the center of the body, neck, forearms, and ankles bare so as not to reveal or hint at the extensive tattoos beneath modern business clothing. The practice today is best experienced by introduction and word of mouth. It's not enough to merely seek Irezumi; one must truly be willing to endure long, painstaking sessions once a week for up to five years. Traditional Irezumi designs cost upwards of $50,000—any truly impassioned canvas will spare no expense to coyly bear the living masterpieces of Japan's Irezumi Masters.

Tattoo Magic

Many of the tribal tattoo tools and practices remained unchanged until the 1900s. These early tattoos used methods more akin to scarification than to modern tattoo. Minerals, coal, charred timber, and botanicals provided the first color palettes. Each tribal culture developed its own ink recipes, which were revered and passed down through generations of highly skilled artists.

As in times past, tattoos serve to revitalize and renew our outlook on life. They often function as marks of status or rank, and as symbols of religious or spiritual devotion. In all tribal cultures, they have long acted as enduring amulets or talismans that encrypt human flesh with desired qualities, protect us from our fears, and offer us feelings of hope and empowerment in the face of difficult changes.

Tattoos operate energetically on the same frequency as blood magic. Though these practices can lead to unhealthy obsessions, when observed with objective balance and genuine spiritual need, tattoos offer a truly ancient manifestation of self-transfiguration. Symbols activate our link to the collective consciousness of life. When we bind intended or meaningful symbols to our bodies through blood, we awaken the energy of that symbol within us. The binding nature of blood magic entwines the intent of the symbols simultaneously with our past, present, and future, and our whole body energy shifts. The tattoo thereby results in unmistakable empowerment.

While modern tattoos are little more than a stiff repetitive scratch, traditional methods involved a much greater loss of blood and rather a bit more pain, emphasizing such rites of passage as acts of devout endurance and courage. Infection and unwanted scarring were not uncommon in early tribal tattoos, and disfiguration was always a very realistic threat. Facing those fears and purging the weight of the negative self through such alteration rituals allows the ego to separate from past mistakes and encourages bringing the self into a state of balance. Oftentimes, infections were seen as a sign of rejecting change or resisting a natural empowerment or destiny. Seemingly wallowing in infectious weakness or stagnation was unlucky business within tribal communities.

Presently, Anglo-European culture is obsessed with the revival of its tribal roots. Celtic, Germanic, and Scandinavian designs are among the most common modern tattoos patterns. The Western world as a whole seems to be seeking deeper associations of cultural heritage. As religious customs merge together within modern borders, we all search for meaning to the toil and necessity of life's cycle. As monotheism loses favor and environmental issues draw growing numbers of people back to nature worship, body modification—particularly tattoos—have become more broadly accepted in mainstream culture.

The time in which we live is one of amazing information, and there seems to be a true resurgence of tribal ideology. This revival is fueled by growing concerns over global sustainability and alternative natural resources. Many find that shamanic philosophy and integrated religious practices—such as Wicca and the occult—provide non-dogmatic structures that one is free to adapt to personal beliefs. The political freedom to believe as we choose is a new development within human culture; it has yet to take sway the world over. Tattoos can provide modern Pagans and magicians with a link to their past and offer an effective platform for spellwork and transformative magic. Through tracing our own bloodlines and reviving the symbols of our heritage within our lives, we open ourselves to the innate energy of our collective human history and awaken the dormant tribal spirit within us. So mote it be.

Ganesha's Birthday

by Elizabeth Hazel

On September 21, 1995, a man in New Delhi, India, woke up before dawn when Ganesha told him, in a dream, that he was thirsty. The man went to the nearest temple, where the statue of Ganesha consumed the milk offered to it. Word spread, and soon people all over India were offering milk to Ganesha statues. Miraculously, the milk was being consumed! Scientists couldn't explain it. Statues of Shiva, Parvati, Nandi, and Naga also consumed milk. News of this miracle spread like wildfire, and people offered milk to Ganesha statues on every inhabited continent on the globe. The "Milk Miracle" is considered the most important event of the century for Hindus. It is known that statues of the deities accept offerings once about every 100 years and will continue to consume liquids for eight or nine days after the miracle begins.

Ganesha (Ganeśa and Ganapati are alternate names) is the happy, elephant-headed god of India. How can anyone not like this jolly, helpful deity who is Lord of Order and Remover of Obstacles? While some gods are august and remote, Ganesha is an immediate, accessible god who operates close to the material plane. This deity should be treated like a friend. So, when it's time for his birthday, throw Ganesha a party and he'll bestow his blessings on you through the coming year.

Birthday Preparations

Ganesha's birthday, the *Ganesh Chaturthi*, is celebrated in August or September. Hindus follow a lunar calendar for festivals, so it is a moveable feast that occurs four days after the New Moon in Virgo, during the Hindu lunar month of *Avani*. The 2009 Ganesh Chaturthi begins on August 23.

Doing this ceremony at home requires some preparation. The full *puja* or ritual of worship for Ganesha may be too elaborate for some, but this is a god who loves to be acknowledged and is satisfied with whatever offerings are shared. The celebration can last from two to ten days, depending on preference.

A special altar should be prepared for Ganesha. The altar should be decorated to look like a forest and decorated with banana leaves, mangos, coconuts, bananas, other fruits, and red and white flowers. Substitute leaves and fruits that are locally available. Offer shredded coconut in a small bowl. A small tray with a selection of tandoori spices is a favored gift.

Ganesha has a sweet tooth, and his favorite cookie is the modaka ball. Modaka balls are made the same way as steamed Chinese dumplings (Dim Sum), except the filling is a blend of brown sugar, coconut, and butter (ghee). In shape, these sweets greatly resemble garlic bulbs, and Ganesha is often portrayed holding a modaka ball in his trunk. Ganesha, however, is quite fond of any sort of cookie, candy, or chocolate.

A Ganesha Murti

Several days before Ganesh Chaturthi, obtain some modeling clay. Make a small statue, or *murti*, of Ganesha. This is a favorite task for children. Do not fire the clay, simply allow it to air-dry. After the statue has dried, paint the statue in bright colors with acrylic paint. Ganesha is usually depicted with four arms. With three hands, he holds the goad, the noose, and a modaka ball. The fourth hand makes a blessing gesture, called a *mudra*. Sometimes seeds are used for eyes. This statue should be formed with great love and a longing to see the god face to face.

Make a clay pedestal fitted for the base of the statue decorated with eight lotus petals on the edges. When this is dry, paint it, too. Uncooked rice and leaves are to be placed on the flat surface of the pedestal, and the statue sits on top. The altar and statue should be placed on a south wall facing north, or on a west wall facing east.

Prepare pieces of different-colored cloth to wrap around the statue. Place goddess statues on either side of Ganesha. He is closely associated with Lakshmi, the goddess of wealth and plenty. In one tradition, his two wives are Buddhi and Siddhi, wisdom and success—he seems to enjoy the company.

The Party Starts

On the fourth day after the New Moon in Virgo, the birthday party begins. Start at a time you can repeat every day. Have the cookies, fruit, and other offerings ready to bring to the altar, and bathe before beginning the ritual. Enter the altar area with the gifts on a tray, and bow or prostrate in front of the statue. Walk clockwise three times around the sanctum and meditate on the Ganesha form. Pick up the statue of Ganesha and breathe to invoke life into it. This is called *pranapratishtha*. It is believed that the god inhabits the space slightly above his image.

Breathe deeply before starting the ritual. Begin with the mantra of concord, "Aum Ganesha Tat Sat Aum." Ganesha is evoked by the word *aum*. In the human body, Ganesha lives in the *muladhara* chakra (the house of the sleeping serpent) at the base of the spine. Saying *aum* spins the chakra clockwise and makes the individual feel uplifted. From this location, he helps to block the negative influences from the lower chakras at the knees and feet and helps remove obstacles in the upper chakras so the kundalini energy fire can awaken.

Address the god with an invocation, something like: "Great Ganesha, I am honored to have you as my guest in my home, and offer you these fruits, flowers, and gifts to make you feel welcome here."

A greeting mantra is "Aum Shri Ganeshaya Namaha" (Praise to the Lord Ganesha). This mantra invokes blessings for auspicious beginnings. The most famous root mantra is "Aum Gam Ganapataye Namaha." The *bija* or seed word *gam* amplifies the qualities of Ganesha, and this mantra brings knowledge, peace, and spiritual assistance.

For each day of the birthday celebration, Ganesha is treated like a friend or a baby. Wake up the statue with an invocation, bathe and feed the statue, and wrap it in a fresh cloth. Offer fresh gifts. Every night, gently put the statue to bed. This level of dedication, called *bhakti*, is noticed and appreciated.

Mantras are strictly regulated in order to get results. At the same time each day, the mantra is repeated 108 times. Keep count with mala beads, a rope of 108 prayer beads.

Invocation - Supplication - Adoration

After the invocation, the god is in close proximity. This is the time to address specific prayers or wishes to Ganesha. Prayers to Ganesha should be made with loving devotion and complete surrender. In other words, one can't offer Ganesha worries and then go worry over them some more. Once troubles have been given to Ganesha, they are out of one's hands. Trust Ganesha to remove obstacles and take care of the problem.

A special mantra to offer to Ganesha if things are going really wrong is "Aum vakra tundaya hum." The word *hum* is like a hurry-up request. The mantra means that when the world is curved and negative, Ganesha will straighten the way.

Finish the ceremony with devotions and adorations. Indicate thankfulness by offering the statue some sweets, like cookies or honey. You may say a thankful prayer of your own devising to close the morning ritual.

When the statue is put to bed at night, circle the sanctum three times, breathe deeply, and sit in front of the altar. Mantras and prayers can be repeated and additional gifts offered. At the end of this short ritual, unwrap the cloth from the statue and put the statue to bed. Place the statue in a cloth-lined basket and cover with a blanket. Remove the food, fruit, flowers, and gifts. Food has been blessed by the god and may be consumed as a "return gift."

The next morning, prepare a fresh tray of food and gifts before starting the ritual. Repeat all of the steps exactly. The ritual can be repeated for two, five, or ten days. Any number is acceptable.

Ganesha Visarjana

This is the end of the party, when the hosts say good-bye to Ganesha. The departure is a special ceremony in itself, because it is a fond farewell to a beloved god. In India, parades of thousands of people make their way to the banks of rivers. The procession follows Ganesha, who is carried in a decorated palanquin accompanied by music, dancing, and noise. Rivers and streams are often the boundaries of a district, so symbolizing that the god is returning to his own realm. The first public *Visarjana* (release) was held in the United States in 1988 in San Francisco and continues to be celebrated in the Bay Area.

Prepare to convey the god to the water in a home-made palanquin. A small child's wagon could be decorated to serve this purpose. Fill the wagon with flowers and fruit, so the guest will leave with gifts. Take bells, tambourines, or other musical noisemakers. The statue is taken to a beach, riverbank, or some other source of moving water. Place the Ganesha statue in the water and allow the statue to float away, saying "Ganapati bappa morva, purchya varshi laukariya" (O father Ganesha, come again early next year). If performing the release ceremony at a flowing body of water is impossible, the simplest substitute is to dissolve the Ganesha statue in a tub of water at home. Another option is to place it outdoors in the rain and allow the elements to dissolve the statue.

Ganesha Every Day

Ganesha is the god of auspicious beginnings and should be invoked at the beginning of any new enterprise. As the Lord of Order, he has control over time, matter, and memory and is considered the Pope of Hinduism. Ganesha helps keep people on their dharmic paths to fulfill their life tasks. He is a loving guide for the spiritual paths of all seekers.

The Blessings of the Sidhe: Celtic Fairy Faith and Fairy Etiquette

by Sharynne MacLeod NicMhacha

Mention the word *fairy* to any Witch or Pagan and you'll conjure up a variety of images, from slender, mysterious, long-eared beings to dangerous or mischievous sprites to demure pixies in teacups. Indeed, when people talk about "the fairies" these days, they may be referring to quite a different type of thing than the next person—anything from garden devas and household spirits to personal spirit allies from a wide and eclectic cornucopia of spiritual or cultural traditions. Many people, however, do seem to perceive some connection between the idea of fairies and the misty landscapes and ancient legends of the Celtic spiritual traditions. As we will see, in Celtic tradition there are very specific beliefs about what the fairies are (and aren't), as well as how to honor and respect them.

So, What to Call Them?

The earliest name for what we might call "fairies" is found in early Irish manuscripts, where they are referred to as the *Aes Síde* (The People of the Fairy Mounds). These síd or "fairy" mounds are actually Neolithic burial mounds created hundreds or even thousands of years before Celtic people came to live in Britain and Ireland. When they arrived, they recognized these as sacred sites and incorporated some of them into local legends and the fabric of their mythological tradition. Later, the Aes Síde were more commonly called the *Tuatha Dé Danann,* (The People of the Goddess Danu). This term refers to the old gods and goddesses of Ireland, a polytheistic pantheon of powerful male and female deities associated with the landscape as well as elements of culture such as healing, wisdom, skill, and so forth.

The Tuatha Dé Danann figure prominently in the myths and legends of Ireland, and were believed to primarily

142

inhabit a variety of síd locations, most frequently fairy mounds but also bodies of water (rivers, lakes, oceans, etc.). In general, they are beneficent, but could be quite formidable if disrespected.

What is most interesting is that many centuries later, when the names of only a few deities like Lug and Bríg (in the form of Saint Brigid) were remembered, these "People of the Síd Mounds" became folkloric figures renowned for their potential blessings or mischievous activities. They were known in Ireland by the Irish term *Síoga* and in Scotland by the Scottish Gaelic word *Sítheachain*. These spiritual entities still lived in the same places as the Aes Síde—fairy mounds and bodies of water—still had the same dual nature, and were still known by similar names in both languages. These similarities held true in Wales as well, although here they were called *Plant Annwn* (The Children of Annwn) or the *Tylwyth Teg* (The Fair Family).

The English word *fairy*, which we commonly use instead of these indigenous terms, is a much later word, and a foreign import at that. It comes from the French word *fée*, brought into English originally as *fay-erie*, a word that referred to a supernatural power of enchantment belonging to the Fay rather than referring to the beings themselves. Many people involved in the Celtic tradition therefore prefer to refer to these entities as the *Sidhe* (pronounced "shee"), a word popularized in the poetry of William Butler Yeats.

In Scottish Lowland tradition (a blend of English and Gaelic tradition, to some degree) there is evidence that these spiritual entities didn't like to be called by the word *fairy* at all. Some folklore sources state they disliked that word (and were especially opposed to the term *elf*) but did seem to approve of the Scots term *seelie wight*. This means "Blessed Being" in Scots, an older dialect of English. In Ireland, they were sometimes referred to as "The Good People," "The Good Neighbors," "The Little Folk," or "The Hill People," as well as just "They." It was believed and hoped that what you called them, they would be; it could be dangerous to call the beings by their proper name without calling or invoking them.

Fairy Realms and Habits

Where do the Sidhe live? In early traditions, they lived in fairy mounds or bodies of water, as well as on otherworld islands located across the water. Their world, however, was not directly located at these physical locations, but existed in another parallel plane of existence; these physical locales served as portals to that world. It was believed that people could most easily access these realms and their inhabitants on the four Celtic Feast days (Imbolg, Bealtaine, Lughnasadh, and Samhain). In later folk tradition, it was believed that they could be seen most frequently at the four turning points of the day (dawn, noon, dusk, and midnight).

The Celtic otherworld was in some ways like our own, but in other ways much more beautiful, with certain aspects reminiscent of dreamtime. Sickness and death were unknown or very rare, and the otherworld was considered to be the source of wisdom, healing, and other such gifts and powers. In

Ireland, the otherworld was known by many names, including *Tír na nÓg* (The Land of Youth) and *Mag Mell* (The Plain of Honey). In Wales, it was called *Annwfn* (pronounced "ah-NOO-vin"), later shortened to *Annwn* (AH-noon). This literally means "un-world" or "not-world," i.e., the world that is not our own.

Originally, the Sidhe were fully human-sized (or even bigger). They were not described as being small in stature (one to three feet tall) until the last few centuries. Perhaps as their stature in religion declined, they were perceived as smaller in physical size. In the folklore records, the Sidhe were of many types with many different appearances. One of the most common descriptions is of a green coat with a red cap, although many other human-type appearances are also seen. In Celtic tradition, the fairies do not have wings, although they sometimes are able to fly or levitate. To do so, they would make use of a magic password in order to fly on transformed grasses, twigs, or the stem of ragwort—much like the legend of the Witch's broomstick!

The Sidhe are said to love music, dancing, hunting, processions, and games and are very skilled at spinning, weaving, baking, metalwork, and crafts. They are traditionally said to value beauty, order, love, fertility, generosity, loyalty, and truth and are generally fair and helpful, showing gratitude for kindness shown to them. It is said that even bad fairies do not lie, they only equivocate. Overall, their code of morality is a little different than ours, which can lead to misunderstandings. It is much like visiting a foreign country and a foreign culture: it's important to find out who lives there, what they consider important, what is polite or impolite, how their society works, and how to show respect and fit in.

Interactions With Humans

Overall, the Sidhe appear to mainly keep to themselves. However, there are certain instances in which they have sought out interactions with humans. These occasions include borrowing, help with babies, and assistance with conflicts. Most fairy borrowings consist of asking for a loan of grain, and they will often return more than they borrowed. Barley meal seems to be their natural grain (seconded by oats), and special cakes were sometimes baked by them for "fairy favorites." They may also ask for the loan of tools or implements, as well as fire. In early stories, human beings were sometimes summoned to the otherworld to assist in certain conflicts or difficult situations, which was in some cases a sort of spiritual or moral test.

There are also numerous fairy tales in which mortal midwives were called to help in the otherworld, usually with nursing fairy babies. It seems that some interbreeding among their own kind was considered to be necessary or beneficial. In fact, certain families in the Celtic countries are known for their fairy blood. In Wales, the Physicians of Myddfai were descended from the three sons of a mortal father and a fairy mother. The fairy mother taught the physicians the skills of herb-lore and healing before she had to return to her home in the otherworld.

My own Scottish clan, Clan MacLeod, is also said to be the result of a fairy-mortal union (mortal king and fairy wife). In this case, the descendants were gifted with *Am Bratach Síth*, "The Fairy Flag," a magical banner that would help the clan in times of trouble. The banner has been used

successfully several times and is on display in Dunvegan Castle, where the clan chiefs still proudly assert the fairy associations of their lineage.

The fairies could also be harmful or mischievous, either due to their personal nature or (more often) human disrespect or misdeeds. A certain amount of homage was paid to the fairies, and this was considered to be almost a necessary protection payment in Ireland. The church frowned on people who had dealing with the fairies, but the country folk were more lenient. Certain folk seers and folk healers even said that they worked through the fairies and obtained cures and information from them.

There were certain dangers inherent in interacting with the Sidhe, however. One could actually be carried away to the otherworld, and it could be very difficult to return, especially if one had tasted fairy food or drink. Those most in danger of being carried off were beautiful children or babies, and good-looking young men or women.

Fairy magic can take many forms, including shape-shifting, flight, and other activities. The English word *glamour* was used to refer to the power of illusion that fairies could cast over human beings in order to prevent the humans from seeing the fairy's true form or location (rather than a power that human beings try to use over the Sidhe, as has sometimes been asserted). In the Irish language, this was known as *pishogue.*

Another misunderstood term has been translated in English as a "co-walker." In Celtic tradition, this is not a fairy helper but a human double visible only to those with second sight. The double's appearance could signify an upcoming visit or spouse, but more often it portended an illness or death. These dangers were balanced out, to some degree anyway, by the possibility of receiving one of the fairy blessings, including fertility, abundance, assistance, music, and other types of special skill. These blessings were usually bestowed upon those who respected the Sidhe, their homes, and their traditions.

What About Fairy Etiquette?

How can we honor the fairies and show respect for their ways? The Sidhe like open and loving people, those who are gentle, polite, and cheerful (but not braggers or boasters). They love music, dancing, good fellowship, and true love. They do not like rudeness, selfishness, gloominess, scolding, wife beating, bad tempers, bad manners, or undue curiosity. Some do not like to be verbally thanked; one may bow or curtsy, though. The Sidhe will expect all questions they ask to be politely answered.

Hospitality is important! The Sidhe must be made welcome in the houses they visit. They are pleased by neatness and order, a freshly swept hearth, a clear fire, clean water, and offerings of milk, bread, or cheese. Honor their privacy, and be able to keep any fairy secrets imparted to you. They are fond of solitude and contemplation and want to preserve their traditional way of life. They may punish those who infringe upon their privacy, steal from them, spy on fairy revels, or boast of fairy favors. Be open, generous, ready to share with those in need, speak the truth about your plans and quests, and be congenial with them.

What about seeing or contacting the fairies? In general, the best rule to observe is that contact is their prerogative! The Sidhe generally present themselves to humans only if they wish to do so. It is sometimes said that they can be seen unaware by using fairy ointment or a four-leafed clover, and that they may be seen more often on the Moon's quarter days. Tradition has it that they may also be seen at the turning points of the day, as well as with the assistance of a naturally holed stone. Those with the Second Sight (in Gaelic, *An Dá Shealladh*, literally "The Two Sights") can occasionally see them—although this is sometimes considered a blessing and sometimes not.

There are some recorded ceremonies and spells to call or see fairies, but these are considered both dangerous and unwise. It is also understood to be an extremely bad idea to try to capture or control a member of the Aes Síde, to take fairy items or treasure, or to try to learn their name. If fairy protection becomes necessary, the most commonly used items were rowan wood, iron, salt, St. John's wort, vervain, or by crossing running water. Physical contact with a powerful Celtic seer was said to enable one to see the fairies on a temporary basis. Overall, however, the best rule of thumb is to learn how to honor and respect the fairies according to their own rules of society and etiquette.

How, then, to honor these wonderous magical beings? We can show our respect to the Sidhe by making fairy altars, leaving offerings, and following the guidelines explained above. Fairies should be honored simply because they are Blessed Beings, with no expectation of gifts in return—these are not guaranteed, other than perhaps purely spiritual benefits! We can also keep the house tidy and make a clean, special area for them with a fire, or perhaps a safe candle or flame. Set out water and food offerings, particularly barley cakes, and remember that they also love dancing and music! Outdoors, people placed flowers on "fairy stones," and in Scotland milk was poured into cup-and-ring marked stones or other stones with natural indentations. Above all, be honest, truthful, positive and respectful, and honor the ways of the blessed inhabitants of the otherworld!

Your Enchanted Magical Chariot

by Mickie Mueller

"The Clean Machine." That's the lyrical name my 19-year-old daughter and I came up with for our brand-new car while singing along to "Penny Lane" by the Beatles on that warm summer day. It's the first brand-new car our family has owned, so it was quite a big deal! We've owned a lot of cars, old cars, because we couldn't afford a new one. Every one of them was kept running—long past the time when they should have bitten the dust—with lots of love and a bit of magic!

One of my coven mates and I joke that between the two of us, we must have the two most "magic-ed" cars in the greater St. Louis area! No matter what car I was driving at the time, it was my magical chariot. Heck, I spent a lot of time in those vehicles, driving to work, shopping, art shows, Pagan festivals, tae kwon do class, even driving my hubby to college. The average American actually spends more than 400 hours per year in their car. So why not turn your car into your magical chariot, with enchantments to shield it from damage and keep it running smoothly, spells for safe travel, and charms to help your vehicle leave the smallest possible footprint on our Mother Earth? It's time to magically connect with that powerful machine that gets you where you need to be!

Workin' Magic at the Car Wash

The first place to start is to clean out that metal beast. Have you been lugging around suitcases, bags of laundry, bricks, a ritual sword, that one-pound crystal ball? Get it all out of there! Your car's engine is working harder to haul that weight; an extra 100 pounds will reduce your fuel efficiency by 1 to 2 percent. If you have any racks on your car, those are costing you up to 5 percent in mpg and making your poor engine work so hard. Removing

150

those racks and storing them until you need them will reduce your aerodynamic drag quite a bit, and your magical car will thank you with better gas mileage.

Once you get your vehicle's interior all cleaned up, sprinkle a mixture of sea salt, rosemary, and basil over the carpet and seats (if they are fabric). If you have been playing "what's that smell," add a thin sprinkling of carpet deodorizer to the floorboards. Allow this mixture to sit overnight, absorbing negative vibes that may be lingering from road rage, angst over running late, or that heated discussion while waiting at the drive-through. The next day, vacuum it out. You can repeat a charm like this several times as you work:

> *Drawing out the dark and unseen,*
> *Leave my chariot bright and clean*

Here is a simple yet powerful way to cleanse, bless, and shield your car without casting a big circle of candles in your driveway and attracting a curious neighborhood audience. Drive to your nearest carwash and, right before you go through it, light a cone of your favorite incense in the ashtray. As the water begins to rain over your car, focus your intent on the water washing away any negativity along with the dirt. You can chant something along the lines of:

> *Element of water,*
> *Dissolve away,*
> *Grime and negativity,*
> *Gone now, gone to stay.*

Next comes the wax cycle. As magical practitioners, we work with wax all the time in the form of candles. Most car wax contains carnuba wax and beeswax. Beeswax has the magical properties of healing and protection and has been used for magic since ancient times. Carnuba wax comes from a palm found in Brazil and is known as the "queen of waxes." It is the hardest natural wax in existence. It also corresponds with protection because it forms the protective coating on the leaves of the carnuba palm; through sympathetic magic, it becomes a powerful magical shield for your car if you enchant it while it is applied. Simply do this with intention by using a chant such as this during the wax cycle:

Hot wax coating, do your thing,
Shield from all damage, rocks, and dings.
Vandal and thief shall stay away,
My protection shield is here to stay.

After you exit the carwash, extinguish your incense in the ashtray. I bet your chariot's feeling more magical already! With everything clean, chi (positive energy) can flow more easily through your car, leaving you more relaxed and at peace behind the wheel, too. If you wish, you can use the same method for hand washing your car at home; simply use the chants silently or under your breath if you want a bit of privacy.

Charming Traveling Magic

What are we looking for out of travel? We want to be safe, protected, and arrive happy and on time to our destination. Not too much to ask, right? Let's bump up the work we've already done by adding the enchantment of some magical amulets to our magical chariot.

It is very important to remember that no magic in the world is a substitute for safe driving habits and common sense. The following ideas for talismans are merely to *enhance* safe driving and maintenance and are not meant in any way to be your sole method for being safe on the road.

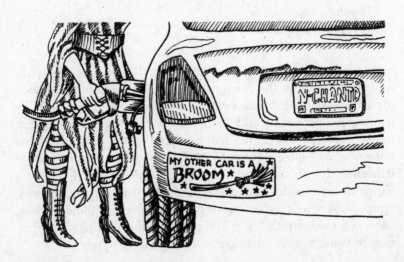

Safe Travel Charm Bag

If you can sew, you can make a small bag out of the fabric and tie it with the ribbon. Below is the no-sewing version, if you choose to avoid that sewing machine. You will need:

- One 6 × 6-inch piece of purple or orange fabric
- 12 inches of purple or orange ribbon

Include any or all of the following:

- Small tumbled moonstone
- An oak leaf or acorn
- A pinch of feverfew, mint, comfrey, flax, Irish moss, or cinnamon
- A found cat's whisker (CAUTION: if you snip or pull one off an animal, not only will the spell not work, but it may have the opposite effect!)

Place the ingredients in the center of the fabric and gather it up into a bundle. Tie it closed with the ribbon, making three knots. As you make each knot say the following:

Safely carry me over the road,
No obstacles will I find,
To my destination then safely home,
My every journey, sublime.

Keep this charm bag in your car. Anytime you wish, hold the bag for a minute in your hands while visualizing yourself arriving safely at your destination. While you're thinking about safe travels, remember that keeping closer to the speed limit helps keep you safe and improves fuel efficiency.

Crystal Car Charm

Here's how to make a lovely and magical amulet to hang from your rear-view mirror to help protect your car and its passengers, and also to keep the car running as smoothly as possible. Once again, this is meant to complement your safe driving habits and regular maintenance, not replace them! To make the crystal car charm, you will need:

- A pinch of dried mint and a few flaxseeds
- Sculpting clay
- Quartz crystal about 1 inch long
- Your favorite Pagan pendant

- 1 inch of wire
- Dark-brown acrylic paint and brush
- Ribbon of your choice

Knead the pinch of mint and flax seeds into the clay. Cover the top quarter of the quartz crystal with clay; the clay should be about ¼ inch thick around the crystal and about ½ inch at the top. Now you can press your pendant into the clay, so that it leaves the impression of the design in the clay. Repeat the design around the circumference of the clay. You can decorate it as simply or intricately as you wish. Take a small piece of clay and roll it into a thin coil the size of a spaghetti noodle. Wrap this coil once around the rough edge of the clay where it meets the crystal to make a nice neat edge; you can end it with a little spiral if you like. Bend the wire to make a loop and push the ends into the top of the clay. This will be the hanger. Bake your charm according to the directions on the clay packaging and allow to cool.

Mix a small amount of water with the brown paint. Paint the clay, coating it well. Using a paper towel, lightly rub the paint off the raised surfaces, leaving the paint in the crevices. Hang the charm with the ribbon from your rear-view mirror. Now watch the sunlight sparkling on the crystal, visualize the energy waking and filling the vehicle. Repeat three times:

Crystal bright, catch the light,
Keep my sweet ride running smooth.
Crystal bright, stone of might,
Protect all riding these wheels, too.

You can re-enchant this charm anytime you feel the crystal needs a little boost.

Riding Out the Storm

When driving in a storm, you may feel as though you are battling the elements to get where you are going safely. Instead of struggling against them, ask the elements for assistance. They are manifest all around you in the forms of rain, snow, wind, lightning (fire), and the road you are trying to travel (earth). If you can't avoid driving in a storm, ground and center, slow down, then try this quick appeal to the elements:

Spirits of air won't blow me from the road,
Spirits of fire keep me brave as I go.
Spirits of water won't let me slide,
Spirits of earth hold me safe as I drive.

Magical Maintenance

With a combination of practical maintenance and crafty magic, you can keep your car running longer and more efficiently. In order to keep your magical chariot running smoothly and in tune with the cycles of Earth, why not plan your tune-ups and oil changes to coincide with the solstices and equinoxes? This planning makes maintenance magical and easier to remember. If you are doing your own oil change, make sure you recycle the oil at your auto parts store. Hold each bottle of fresh oil, visualizing golden light flowing into the oil. If you are having your oil change done at a shop, simply visualize golden light flowing into the oil as it goes into your car. Here is a maintenance chant that you can say aloud or in your mind whenever you change the oil in your vehicle:

Clean and fresh, smooth and bright
Motor oil, stuff of life,
Keep my baby running fine,
All its parts will harmonize.

While you're at it, check your tire pressure, as doing this helps make your travels safer, keeps the air elementals on your side, and—yep, you guessed it—helps your gas mileage by causing less drag. Here's a tip: look in your owner's manual for the proper air pressure, as it will differ for each vehicle because they all have different weights and design. Don't just read the tire, look in the book for the right air pressure. While you are filling your tires, ask the air elementals to bless your tires with long wear as you fill them.

Air elementals, fill my tires,
and bless my travels all the while.

When you're checking the tire pressure, also check the tread wear. The old trick is to put a penny (head down) in the tread; if the tread doesn't at least touch the top of ole Abe's head, you'd better start shopping for tires. Why tempt the fates by driving around on bad tires? All of these little maintenance tips and spells can keep you and your enchanted car on the road longer and safer.

Your magical chariot can become so much more than simply a machine. Like anything else in life, you will get out of it what you put into it. You can grit your teeth and merely bear your commute, or you can put on a peaceful CD, sip some mint tea from your travel mug, and take your enchanted vehicle on a magical ride every time you leave the driveway. When you recognize that a living thing is merely a biological machine—and vice versa—it is really easy to see how a little care and magical energy can keep this metal machine, your personal chariot, a positively magical place to be!

Almanac Section

Calendar

Time Changes

Lunar Phases

Moon Signs

Full Moons

Sabbats

World Holidays

Incense of the Day

Color of the Day

Almanac Listings

In these listings you will find the date, day, lunar phase, Moon sign, color and incense for the day, and festivals from around the world.

The Date

The date is used in numerological calculations that govern magical rites.

The Day

Each day is ruled by a planet that possesses specific magical influences:

MONDAY (MOON): Peace, sleep, healing, compassion, friends, psychic awareness, purification, and fertility.

TUESDAY (MARS): Passion, sex, courage, aggression, and protection.

WEDNESDAY (MERCURY): The conscious mind, study, travel, divination, and wisdom.

THURSDAY (JUPITER): Expansion, money, prosperity, and generosity.

FRIDAY (VENUS): Love, friendship, reconciliation, and beauty.

SATURDAY (SATURN): Longevity, exorcism, endings, homes, and houses.

SUNDAY (SUN): Healing, spirituality, success, strength, and protection.

The Lunar Phase

The lunar phase is important in determining the best times for magic.

THE WAXING MOON (from the New Moon to the Full) is the ideal time for magic to draw things toward you.

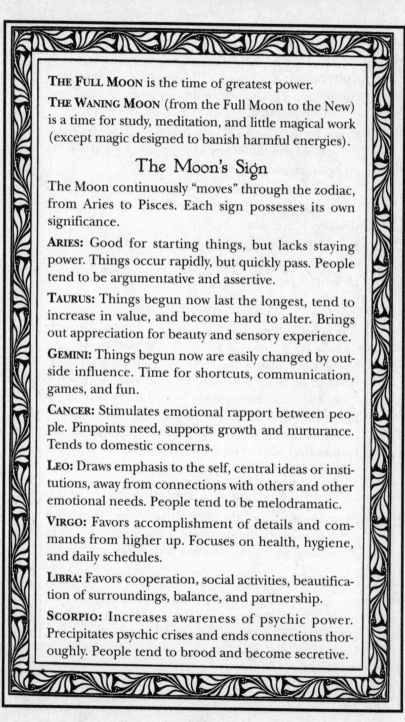

THE FULL MOON is the time of greatest power.

THE WANING MOON (from the Full Moon to the New) is a time for study, meditation, and little magical work (except magic designed to banish harmful energies).

The Moon's Sign

The Moon continuously "moves" through the zodiac, from Aries to Pisces. Each sign possesses its own significance.

ARIES: Good for starting things, but lacks staying power. Things occur rapidly, but quickly pass. People tend to be argumentative and assertive.

TAURUS: Things begun now last the longest, tend to increase in value, and become hard to alter. Brings out appreciation for beauty and sensory experience.

GEMINI: Things begun now are easily changed by outside influence. Time for shortcuts, communication, games, and fun.

CANCER: Stimulates emotional rapport between people. Pinpoints need, supports growth and nurturance. Tends to domestic concerns.

LEO: Draws emphasis to the self, central ideas or institutions, away from connections with others and other emotional needs. People tend to be melodramatic.

VIRGO: Favors accomplishment of details and commands from higher up. Focuses on health, hygiene, and daily schedules.

LIBRA: Favors cooperation, social activities, beautification of surroundings, balance, and partnership.

SCORPIO: Increases awareness of psychic power. Precipitates psychic crises and ends connections thoroughly. People tend to brood and become secretive.

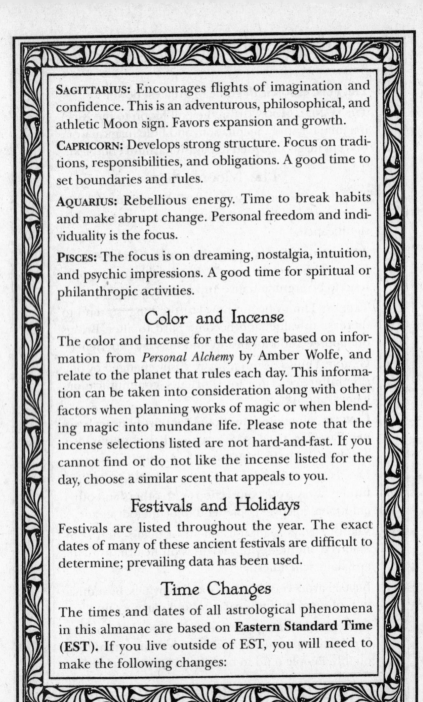

SAGITTARIUS: Encourages flights of imagination and confidence. This is an adventurous, philosophical, and athletic Moon sign. Favors expansion and growth.

CAPRICORN: Develops strong structure. Focus on traditions, responsibilities, and obligations. A good time to set boundaries and rules.

AQUARIUS: Rebellious energy. Time to break habits and make abrupt change. Personal freedom and individuality is the focus.

PISCES: The focus is on dreaming, nostalgia, intuition, and psychic impressions. A good time for spiritual or philanthropic activities.

Color and Incense

The color and incense for the day are based on information from *Personal Alchemy* by Amber Wolfe, and relate to the planet that rules each day. This information can be taken into consideration along with other factors when planning works of magic or when blending magic into mundane life. Please note that the incense selections listed are not hard-and-fast. If you cannot find or do not like the incense listed for the day, choose a similar scent that appeals to you.

Festivals and Holidays

Festivals are listed throughout the year. The exact dates of many of these ancient festivals are difficult to determine; prevailing data has been used.

Time Changes

The times and dates of all astrological phenomena in this almanac are based on **Eastern Standard Time (EST).** If you live outside of EST, you will need to make the following changes:

PACIFIC STANDARD TIME: Subtract three hours.

MOUNTAIN STANDARD TIME: Subtract two hours.

CENTRAL STANDARD TIME: Subtract one hour.

ALASKA: Subtract four hours.

HAWAII: Subtract five hours.

DAYLIGHT SAVING TIME: Add an hour. Daylight Saving Time runs from March 8, 2009, to November 1, 2009.

2009 Sabbats and Full Moons

January 10	Full Moon 10:27 pm
February 2	Imbolc
February 9	Full Moon 9:49 am
March 10	Full Moon 10:38 pm
March 20	Ostara (Spring Equinox)
April 9	Full Moon 10:56 am
May 1	Beltane
May 9	Full Moon 12:01 am
June 7	Full Moon 2:12 pm
June 21	Litha (Summer Solstice)
July 7	Full Moon 5:21 am
August 1	Lammas
August 5	Full Moon 8:55 pm
September 4	Full Moon 12:02 pm
September 22	Mabon (Fall Equinox)
October 4	Full Moon 2:10 am
October 31	Samhain
November 2	Full Moon 2:14 pm
December 2	Full Moon 2:30 am
December 21	Yule (Winter Solstice)
December 31	Full Moon 2:13 pm

January

1 **Thursday**
New Year's Day • Kwanzaa ends
Waxing Moon
Moon phase: First Quarter
Color: Purple

Moon sign: Pisces
Incense: Jasmine

---

2 **Friday**
First Writing (Japanese)
Waxing Moon
Moon phase: First Quarter
Color: Coral

Moon sign: Pisces
Incense: Vanilla

---

3 **Saturday**
St. Genevieve's Day
Waxing Moon
Moon phase: First Quarter
Color: Indigo

Moon sign: Pisces
Moon enters Aries 4:50 am
Incense: Sage

◑ **Sunday**
Frost Fairs on the Thames
Waxing Moon
Moon phase: Second Quarter 6:56 am
Color: Orange

Moon sign: Aries
Incense: Hyacinth

---

5 **Monday**
Epiphany Eve
Waxing Moon
Moon phase: Second Quarter
Color: Gray

Moon sign: Aries
Moon enters Taurus 10:46 am
Incense: Narcissus

---

6 **Tuesday**
Epiphany
Waxing Moon
Moon phase: Second Quarter
Color: Red

Moon sign: Taurus
Incense: Bayberry

---

7 **Wednesday**
Rizdvo (Ukranian)
Waxing Moon
Moon phase: Second Quarter
Color: Yellow

Moon sign: Taurus
Moon enters Gemini 1:11 pm
Incense: Lavender

8 Thursday
Midwives' Day
Waxing Moon
Moon phase: Second Quarter
Color: Green

Moon sign: Gemini
Incense: Myrrh

---

9 Friday
Feast of the Black Nazarene (Filipino)
Waxing Moon
Moon phase: Second Quarter
Color: White

Moon sign: Gemini
Moon enters Cancer 1:14 pm
Incense: Mint

Saturday
Business God's Day (Japanese)
Waxing Moon
Moon phase: Full Moon 10:27 pm
Color: Brown

Moon sign: Cancer
Incense: Pine

---

11 Sunday
Carmentalia (Roman)
Waning Moon
Moon phase: Third Quarter
Color: Yellow

Moon sign: Cancer
Moon enters Leo 12:41 pm
Incense: Eucalyptus

---

12 Monday
Revolution Day (Tanzanian)
Waning Moon
Moon phase: Third Quarter
Color: Lavender

Moon sign: Leo
Incense: Rosemary

---

13 Tuesday
Twentieth Day (Norwegian)
Waning Moon
Moon phase: Third Quarter
Color: White

Moon sign: Leo
Moon enters Virgo 1:33 pm
Incense: Ylang-ylang

---

14 Wednesday
Feast of the Ass (French)
Waning Moon
Moon phase: Third Quarter
Color: Brown

Moon sign: Virgo
Incense: Lilac

15 Thursday
Birthday of Martin Luther King, Jr. (actual)
Waning Moon
Moon phase: Third Quarter
Color: Turquoise

Moon sign: Virgo
Moon enters Libra 5:30 pm
Incense: Clove

16 Friday
Apprentices Day
Waning Moon
Moon phase: Third Quarter
Color: Pink

Moon sign: Libra
Incense: Rose

○ Saturday
St. Anthony's Day (Mexican)
Waning Moon
Moon phase: Fourth Quarter 9:46 pm
Color: Gray

Moon sign: Libra
Incense: Sandalwood

18 Sunday
Assumption Day
Waning Moon
Moon phase: Fourth Quarter
Color: Gold

Moon sign: Libra
Moon enters Scorpio 1:20 am
Incense: Juniper

19 Monday
Birthday of Martin Luther King, Jr. (observed)
Waning Moon
Moon phase: Fourth Quarter
Color: White

Moon sign: Scorpio
Incense: Hyssop

20 Tuesday
Inauguration Day
Waning Moon
Moon phase: Fourth Quarter
Color: Black

Moon sign: Scorpio
Moon enters Sagittarius 12:30 pm
Incense: Geranium

21 Wednesday
St. Agnes Day
Waning Moon
Moon phase: Fourth Quarter
Color: Topaz

Moon sign: Sagittarius
Incense: Bay laurel

22 **Thursday**
St. Vincent's Day (French)
Waning Moon
Moon phase: Fourth Quarter
Color: Crimson

Moon sign: Sagittarius
Incense: Nutmeg

---

23 **Friday**
St. Ildefonso's Day
Waning Moon
Moon phase: Fourth Quarter
Color: Rose

Moon sign: Sagittarius
Moon enters Capricorn 1:18 am
Incense: Thyme

---

24 **Saturday**
Alasitas Fair (Bolivian)
Waning Moon
Moon phase: Fourth Quarter
Color: Blue

Moon sign: Capricorn
Incense: Patchouli

---

25 **Sunday**
Burns' Night (Scottish)
Waning Moon
Moon phase: Fourth Quarter
Color: Amber

Moon sign: Capricorn
Moon enters Aquarius 1:56 pm
Incense: Frankincense

☽ **Monday**
Chinese New Year (ox)
Waning Moon
Moon phase: New Moon 2:55 am
Color: Silver

Moon sign: Aquarius
Incense: Lily

---

27 **Tuesday**
Vogelgruff (Swiss)
Waxing Moon
Moon phase: First Quarter
Color: Maroon

Moon sign: Aquarius
Incense: Ginger

---

28 **Wednesday**
St. Charlemagne's Day
Waxing Moon
Moon phase: First Quarter
Color: White

Moon sign: Aquarius
Moon enters Pisces 1:12 am
Incense: Marjoram

29 **Thursday**
Australia Day
Waxing Moon
Moon phase: First Quarter
Color: Green

Moon sign: Pisces
Incense: Carnation

30 **Friday**
Three Hierarchs' Day (Eastern Orthodox)
Waxing Moon
Moon phase: First Quarter
Color: Purple

Moon sign: Pisces
Moon enters Aries 10:25 am
Incense: Vanilla

31 **Saturday**
Independence Day (Nauru)
Waxing Moon
Moon phase: First Quarter
Color: Brown

Moon sign: Aries
Incense: Magnolia

Sabbats in the Southern Hemisphere

Because the Earth's Northern and Southern Hemispheres experience opposite seasons at any given time, the season-based sabbat dates listed in this almanac are not correct for those residing south of the equator. Listed here are the Southern Hemisphere sabbat dates for 2009:

February 2	Lammas
March 21	Mabon
May 1	Samhain
June 21	Yule
August 2	Imbolc
September 22	Ostara
November 1	Beltane
December 21	Litha

February

1   Sunday
St. Brigid's Day (Irish)
Waxing Moon
Moon phase: First Quarter
Color: Yellow

Moon sign: Aries
Moon enters Taurus 5:08 pm
Incense: Almond

2   Monday
Imbolc • Groundhog Day
Waxing Moon
Moon phase: Second Quarter 6:13 pm
Color: Gray

Moon sign: Taurus
Incense: Narcissus

3   Tuesday
St. Blaise's Day
Waxing Moon
Moon phase: Second Quarter
Color: Red

Moon sign: Taurus
Moon enters Gemini 9:14 pm
Incense: Cedar

4   Wednesday
Independence Day (Sri Lankan)
Waxing Moon
Moon phase: Second Quarter
Color: Yellow

Moon sign: Gemini
Incense: Bay laurel

5   Thursday
Festival de la Alcaldesa (Italian)
Waxing Moon
Moon phase: Second Quarter
Color: Turquoise

Moon sign: Gemini
Moon enters Cancer 11:05 pm
Incense: Apricot

6   Friday
Bob Marley's Birthday (Jamaican)
Waxing Moon
Moon phase: Second Quarter
Color: White

Moon sign: Cancer
Incense: Violet

7   Saturday
Full Moon Poya (Sri Lankan)
Waxing Moon
Moon phase: Second Quarter
Color: Black

Moon sign: Cancer
Moon enters Leo 11:43 pm
Incense: Ivy

February

8 **Sunday**
Mass for Broken Needles (Japanese)
Waxing Moon
Moon phase: Second Quarter
Color: Orange

Moon sign: Leo
Incense: Heliotrope

Monday
St. Marion's Day (Lebanese)
Waxing Moon
Moon phase: Full Moon 9:49 am
Color: Lavender

Moon sign: Leo
Incense: Neroli

10 **Tuesday**
Gasparilla Day (Florida)
Waning Moon
Moon phase: Third Quarter
Color: White

Moon sign: Leo
Moon enters Virgo 12:38 am
Incense: Cinnamon

11 **Wednesday**
Foundation Day (Japanese)
Waning Moon
Moon phase: Third Quarter
Color: Brown

Moon sign: Virgo
Incense: Honeysuckle

12 **Thursday**
Lincoln's Birthday (actual)
Waning Moon
Moon phase: Third Quarter
Color: Green

Moon sign: Virgo
Moon enters Libra 3:33 am
Incense: Balsam

13 **Friday**
Parentalia (Roman)
Waning Moon
Moon phase: Third Quarter
Color: Coral

Moon sign: Libra
Incense: Rose

14 **Saturday**
Valentine's Day
Waning Moon
Moon phase: Third Quarter
Color: Blue

Moon sign: Libra
Moon enters Scorpio 9:50 am
Incense: Rue

February

15 Sunday
Lupercalia (Roman)
Waning Moon
Moon phase: Third Quarter
Color: Gold

Moon sign: Scorpio
Incense: Marigold

◖ Monday
Presidents' Day (observed)
Waning Moon
Moon phase: Fourth Quarter 4:37 pm
Color: White

Moon sign: Scorpio
Moon enters Sagittarius 7:53 pm
Incense: Rosemary

---

17 Tuesday
Quinalia (Roman)
Waning Moon
Moon phase: Fourth Quarter
Color: Black

Moon sign: Sagittarius
Incense: Basil

---

18 Wednesday
Saint Bernadette's Second Vision
Waning Moon
Moon phase: Fourth Quarter
Color: Topaz

Moon sign: Sagittarius
Incense: Lavender

---

19 Thursday
Pero Palo's Trial (Spanish)
Waning Moon
Moon phase: Fourth Quarter
Color: Crimson

Moon sign: Sagittarius
Moon enters Capricorn 8:25 am
Incense: Mulberry

---

20 Friday
Installation of the new Lama (Tibetan)
Waning Moon
Moon phase: Fourth Quarter
Color: Pink

Moon sign: Capricorn
Incense: Mint

---

21 Saturday
Feast of Lanterns (Chinese)
Waning Moon
Moon phase: Fourth Quarter
Color: Indigo

Moon sign: Capricorn
Moon enters Aquarius 9:06 pm
Incense: Sage

February

22 Sunday
Caristia (Roman)
Waning Moon
Moon phase: Fourth Quarter
Color: Amber

Moon sign: Aquarius
Incense: Hyacinth

23 Monday
Terminalia (Roman)
Waning Moon
Moon phase: Fourth Quarter
Color: Silver

Moon sign: Aquarius
Incense: Hyssop

Tuesday
Mardi Gras (Fat Tuesday)
Waning Moon
Moon phase: New Moon 8:35 pm
Color: Gray

Moon sign: Aquarius
Moon enters Pisces 7:59 am
Incense: Ylang-ylang

25 Wednesday
Ash Wednedsay
Waxing Moon
Moon phase: First Quarter
Color: White

Moon sign: Pisces
Incense: Marjoram

26 Thursday
Zamboanga Festival (Filipino)
Waxing Moon
Moon phase: First Quarter
Color: Purple

Moon sign: Pisces
Moon enters Aries 4:24 pm
Incense: Myrrh

27 Friday
Threepenny Day
Waxing Moon
Moon phase: First Quarter
Color: Rose

Moon sign: Aries
Incense: Yarrow

28 Saturday
Kalevala Day (Finnish)
Waxing Moon
Moon phase: First Quarter
Color: Brown

Moon sign: Aries
Moon enters Taurus 10:33 pm
Incense: Sandalwood

March

1 Sunday
Matronalia (Roman)
Waxing Moon
Moon phase: First Quarter
Color: Gold

Moon sign: Taurus
Incense: Marigold

---

2 Monday
St. Chad's Day (English)
Waxing Moon
Moon phase: First Quarter
Color: Lavender

Moon sign: Taurus
Incense: Narcissus

---

3 Tuesday
Doll Festival (Japanese)
Waxing Moon
Moon phase: First Quarter
Color: Maroon

Moon sign: Taurus
Moon enters Gemini 2:59 am
Incense: Bayberry

---

4 Wednesday
St. Casimir's Day (Polish)
Waxing Moon
Moon phase: Second Quarter 2:46 am
Color: Brown

Moon sign: Gemini
Incense: Lavender

---

5 Thursday
Isis Festival (Roman)
Waxing Moon
Moon phase: Second Quarter
Color: Green

Moon sign: Gemini
Moon enters Cancer 6:07 am
Incense: Jasmine

---

6 Friday
Alamo Day
Waxing Moon
Moon phase: Second Quarter
Color: Pink

Moon sign: Cancer
Incense: Orchid

---

7 Saturday
Bird and Arbor Day
Waxing Moon
Moon phase: Second Quarter
Color: Blue

Moon sign: Cancer
Moon enters Leo 8:24 am
Incense: Magnolia

March

8	Sunday	
	Daylight Saving Time begins	Moon sign: Leo
	Waxing Moon	Incense: Juniper
	Moon phase: Second Quarter	
	Color: Amber	

9	Monday	
	Forty Saints' Day	Moon sign: Leo
	Waxing Moon	Moon enters Virgo 11:34 am
	Moon phase: Second Quarter	Incense: Neroli
	Color: Gray	

☻ Tuesday

	Purim	Moon sign: Virgo
	Waxing Moon	Incense: Basil
	Moon phase: Full Moon 10:38 pm	
	Color: Black	

11	Wednesday	
	Feast of the Gauri (Hindu)	Moon sign: Virgo
	Waning Moon	Moon enters Libra 2:46 pm
	Moon phase: Third Quarter	Incense: Lilac
	Color: Yellow	

12	Thursday	
	Receiving the Water (Buddhist)	Moon sign: Libra
	Waning Moon	Incense: Clove
	Moon phase: Third Quarter	
	Color: White	

13	Friday	
	Purification Feast (Balinese)	Moon sign: Libra
	Waning Moon	Moon enters Scorpio 8:22 pm
	Moon phase: Third Quarter	Incense: Alder
	Color: Coral	

14	Saturday	
	Mamuralia (Roman)	Moon sign: Scorpio
	Waning Moon	Incense: Rue
	Moon phase: Third Quarter	
	Color: Indigo	

March

15 Sunday
Phallus Festival (Japanese)
Waning Moon
Moon phase: Third Quarter
Color: Yellow

Moon sign: Scorpio
Incense: Almond

---

16 Monday
St. Urho's Day (Finnish)
Waning Moon
Moon phase: Third Quarter
Color: Ivory

Moon sign: Scorpio
Moon enters Sagittarius 5:21 am
Incense: Clary sage

---

17 Tuesday
St. Patrick's Day
Waning Moon
Moon phase: Third Quarter
Color: Red

Moon sign: Sagittarius
Incense: Ginger

☽ Wednesday
Sheelah's Day (Irish)
Waning Moon
Moon phase: Fourth Quarter 1:47 pm
Color: White

Moon sign: Sagittarius
Moon enters Capricorn 5:18 pm
Incense: Honeysuckle

---

19 Thursday
St. Joseph's Day (Sicilian)
Waning Moon
Moon phase: Fourth Quarter
Color: Purple

Moon sign: Capricorn
Incense: Carnation

---

20 Friday
Ostara • Spring Equinox • Int'l Astrology Day
Waning Moon
Moon phase: Fourth Quarter
Color: Rose

Moon sign: Capricorn
Incense: Cypress

---

21 Saturday
Juarez Day (Mexican)
Waning Moon
Moon phase: Fourth Quarter
Color: Black

Moon sign: Capricorn
Moon enters Aquarius 6:06 am
Incense: Pine

March

22 Sunday
Hilaria (Roman)
Waning Moon
Moon phase: Fourth Quarter
Color: Orange

Moon sign: Aquarius
Incense: Heliotrope

23 Monday
Pakistan Day
Waning Moon
Moon phase: Fourth Quarter
Color: Silver

Moon sign: Aquarius
Moon enters Pisces 5:08 pm
Incense: Lily

24 Tuesday
Day of Blood (Roman)
Waning Moon
Moon phase: Fourth Quarter
Color: White

Moon sign: Pisces
Incense: Geranium

25 Wednesday
Tichborne Dole (English)
Waning Moon
Moon phase: Fourth Quarter
Color: Topaz

Moon sign: Pisces
Incense: Bay laurel

☽ Thursday
Prince Kuhio Day (Hawaiian)
Waning Moon
Moon phase: New Moon 12:06 pm
Color: Crimson

Moon sign: Pisces
Moon enters Aries 1:03 am
Incense: Nutmeg

27 Friday
Smell the Breezes Day (Egyptian)
Waxing Moon
Moon phase: First Quarter
Color: Purple

Moon sign: Aries
Incense: Vanilla

28 Saturday
Oranges and Lemons Service (English)
Waxing Moon
Moon phase: First Quarter
Color: Blue

Moon sign: Aries
Moon enters Taurus 6:09 am
Incense: Patchouli

March

---

29 Sunday
Feast of St. Eustace's of Luxeuil
Waxing Moon
Moon phase: First Quarter
Color: Gold

Moon sign: Taurus
Incense: Eucalyptus

---

30 Monday
Seward's Day (Alaskan)
Waxing Moon
Moon phase: First Quarter
Color: White

Moon sign: Taurus
Moon enters Gemini 9:36 am
Incense: Rosemary

---

31 Tuesday
The Borrowed Days (Ethiopian)
Waxing Moon
Moon phase: First Quarter
Color: Gray

Moon sign: Gemini
Incense: Cedar

Angelica (*Angelica archangelica*)

This statuesque background plant can grow in full Sun, reaches up to five feet tall, and prefers rich soil. The candied stems make an excellent garnish for sweets. Magical powers include protection, cleansing, and exorcism. Angelica also brings psychic visions.

Borage (*Borago officinalis*)

Borage prefers partial shade, growing about eighteen inches high. It has large oval leaves covered in hairs, and star-shaped blue flowers. Candy the flowers for a garnish or dry them for use in crafts. Magically, borage strengthens courage and psychic powers.

–Elizabeth Barrette

April

♈

1 Wednesday
April Fools' Day
Waxing Moon
Moon phase: First Quarter
Color: Brown

Moon sign: Gemini
Moon enters Cancer 12:30 pm
Incense: Lavender

☾ Thursday
The Battle of Flowers (French)
Waxing Moon
Moon phase: Second Quarter 10:34 am
Color: Green

Moon sign: Cancer
Incense: Apricot

---

3 Friday
Thirteenth Day (Iranian)
Waxing Moon
Moon phase: Second Quarter
Color: White

Moon sign: Cancer
Moon enters Leo 3:32 pm
Incense: Violet

---

4 Saturday
Megalesia (Roman)
Waxing Moon
Moon phase: Second Quarter
Color: Indigo

Moon sign: Leo
Incense: Ivy

---

5 Sunday
Palm Sunday
Waxing Moon
Moon phase: Second Quarter
Color: Orange

Moon sign: Leo
Moon enters Virgo 7:01 pm
Incense: Frankincense

---

6 Monday
Chakri Day (Thai)
Waxing Moon
Moon phase: Second Quarter
Color: Lavender

Moon sign: Virgo
Incense: Hyssop

---

7 Tuesday
Festival of Pure Brightness (Chinese)
Waxing Moon
Moon phase: Second Quarter
Color: Red

Moon sign: Virgo
Moon enters Libra 11:22 pm
Incense: Ylang-ylang

April

8 Wednesday
Buddha's Birthday
Waxing Moon
Moon phase: Second Quarter
Color: Yellow

Moon sign: Libra
Incense: Honeysuckle

Thursday
Passover begins
Waxing Moon
Moon phase: Full Moon 10:56 am
Color: Turquoise

Moon sign: Libra
Incense: Mulberry

---

10 Friday
Good Friday
Waning Moon
Moon phase: Third Quarter
Color: Pink

Moon sign: Libra
Moon enters Scorpio 5:23 am
Incense: Thyme

---

11 Saturday
Heroes Day (Costa Rican)
Waning Moon
Moon phase: Third Quarter
Color: Blue

Moon sign: Scorpio
Incense: Rue

---

12 Sunday
Easter
Waning Moon
Moon phase: Third Quarter
Color: Yellow

Moon sign: Scorpio
Moon enters Sagittarius 2:00 pm
Incense: Almond

---

13 Monday
Thai New Year
Waning Moon
Moon phase: Third Quarter
Color: Gray

Moon sign: Sagittarius
Incense: Lily

---

14 Tuesday
Sanno Festival (Japanese)
Waning Moon
Moon phase: Third Quarter
Color: White

Moon sign: Sagittarius
Incense: Ginger

15 Wednesday
Plowing Festival (Chinese)
Waning Moon
Moon phase: Third Quarter
Color: Topaz

Moon sign: Sagittarius
Moon enters Capricorn 1:27 am
Incense: Bay laurel

---

16 Thursday
Passover ends
Waning Moon
Moon phase: Third Quarter
Color: Purple

Moon sign: Capricorn
Incense: Balsam

Friday
Orthodox Good Friday
Waning Moon
Moon phase: Fourth Quarter 9:36 am
Color: Rose

Moon sign: Capricorn
Moon enters Aquarius 2:19 pm
Incense: Mint

---

18 Saturday
Flower Festival (Japanese)
Waning Moon
Moon phase: Fourth Quarter
Color: Black

Moon sign: Aquarius
Incense: Magnolia

---

19 Sunday
Orthodox Easter
Waning Moon
Moon phase: Fourth Quarter
Color: Gold

Moon sign: Aquarius
Incense: Marigold

---

20 Monday
Drum Festival (Japanese)
Waning Moon
Moon phase: Fourth Quarter
Color: Silver

Moon sign: Aquarius
Moon enters Pisces 1:55 am
Incense: Clary sage

---

21 Tuesday
Tiradentes Day (Brazilian)
Waning Moon
Moon phase: Fourth Quarter
Color: Black

Moon sign: Pisces
Incense: Geranium

April

22 Wednesday
Earth Day
Waning Moon
Moon phase: Fourth Quarter
Color: Brown

Moon sign: Pisces
Moon enters Aries 10:09 am
Incense: Marjoram

23 Thursday
St. George's Day (English)
Waning Moon
Moon phase: Fourth Quarter
Color: White

Moon sign: Aries
Incense: Carnation

☽ Friday
St. Mark's Eve
Waning Moon
Moon phase: New Moon 11:22 pm
Color: Coral

Moon sign: Aries
Moon enters Taurus 2:46 pm
Incense: Rose

25 Saturday
Robigalia (Roman)
Waxing Moon
Moon phase: First Quarter
Color: Blue

Moon sign: Taurus
Incense: Sandalwood

26 Sunday
Arbor Day
Waxing Moon
Moon phase: First Quarter
Color: Amber

Moon sign: Taurus
Moon enters Gemini 5:02 pm
Incense: Hyacinth

27 Monday
Humabon's Conversion (Filipino)
Waxing Moon
Moon phase: First Quarter
Color: Ivory

Moon sign: Gemini
Incense: Neroli

28 Tuesday
Floralia (Roman)
Waxing Moon
Moon phase: First Quarter
Color: Gray

Moon sign: Gemini
Moon enters Cancer 6:38 pm
Incense: Cedar

29 **Wednesday**
Green Day (Japanese)
Waxing Moon
Moon phase: First Quarter
Color: White

Moon sign: Cancer
Incense: Lilac

---

30 **Thursday**
Walpurgis Night • May Eve
Waxing Moon
Moon phase: First Quarter
Color: Crimson

Moon sign: Cancer
Moon enters Leo 8:56 pm
Incense: Jasmine

Chervil (*Anthriscus cerefolium*)

Chervil prefers partial or dappled shade, does better in spring or fall plantings, and needs rich, moist soil. This plant reaches up to twenty inches in height. Magically, it promotes wisdom and spiritual growth.

Comfrey (*Symphytum officinalis*)

Large hairy leaves rise eighteen inches from a central crown, and blue bell-shaped flowers appear on taller stalks. The dried leaves make a charm for travel safety and are also good for money spells. Use them to stuff poppets for healing.

Corsican Mint (*Mentha requienii*)

Its tiny, low-growing leaves need dappled to dense shade, and moist rich soil. This plant attracts fairies. Magically, it improves psychic awareness and stimulates the mind.

–Elizabeth Barrette

May

○ Friday
Beltane • May Day
Waxing Moon
Moon phase: Second Quarter 4:44 pm
Color: Purple

Moon sign: Leo
Incense: Thyme

---

2 Saturday
Big Kite Flying (Japanese)
Waxing Moon
Moon phase: Second Quarter
Color: Gray

Moon sign: Leo
Incense: Pine

---

3 Sunday
Holy Cross Day
Waxing Moon
Moon phase: Second Quarter
Color: Gold

Moon sign: Leo
Moon enters Virgo 12:37 am
Incense: Heliotrope

---

4 Monday
Bona Dea (Roman)
Waxing Moon
Moon phase: Second Quarter
Color: Lavender

Moon sign: Virgo
Incense: Clary sage

---

5 Tuesday
Cinco de Mayo
Waxing Moon
Moon phase: Second Quarter
Color: Gray

Moon sign: Virgo
Moon enters Libra 5:51 am
Incense: Basil

---

6 Wednesday
Martyrs' Day (Lebanese)
Waxing Moon
Moon phase: Second Quarter
Color: Yellow

Moon sign: Libra
Incense: Bay laurel

---

7 Thursday
Pilgrimage of St. Nicholas (Italian)
Waxing Moon
Moon phase: Second Quarter
Color: Turquoise

Moon sign: Libra
Moon enters Scorpio 12:48 pm
Incense: Nutmeg

May

8 **Friday**
Liberation Day (French)
Waxing Moon
Moon phase: Second Quarter
Color: Rose

Moon sign: Scorpio
Incense: Violet

Saturday
Lemuria (Roman)
Waxing Moon
Moon phase: Full Moon 12:01 am
Color: Blue

Moon sign: Scorpio
Moon enters Sagittarius 9:49 pm
Incense: Sage

---

10 **Sunday**
Mother's Day
Waning Moon
Moon phase: Third Quarter
Color: Amber

Moon sign: Sagittarius
Incense: Juniper

---

11 **Monday**
Ukai Season Opens (Japanese)
Waning Moon
Moon phase: Third Quarter
Color: Silver

Moon sign: Sagittarius
Incense: Lily

---

12 **Tuesday**
Florence Nightingale's Birthday
Waning Moon
Moon phase: Third Quarter
Color: Red

Moon sign: Sagittarius
Moon enters Capricorn 9:09 am
Incense: Cinnamon

---

13 **Wednesday**
Pilgrimage to Fatima (Portugese)
Waning Moon
Moon phase: Third Quarter
Color: Brown

Moon sign: Capricorn
Incense: Honeysuckle

---

14 **Thursday**
Carabao Festival (Spanish)
Waning Moon
Moon phase: Third Quarter
Color: Purple

Moon sign: Capricorn
Moon enters Aquarius 10:01 pm
Incense: Clove

15 Friday
Festival of St. Dympna (Belgian)
Waning Moon
Moon phase: Third Quarter
Color: Coral

Moon sign: Aquarius
Incense: Vanilla

---

16 Saturday
St. Honoratus' Day
Waning Moon
Moon phase: Third Quarter
Color: Indigo

Moon sign: Aquarius
Incense: Patchouli

☽ Sunday
Norwegian Independence Day
Waning Moon
Moon phase: Fourth Quarter 3:26 am
Color: Yellow

Moon sign: Aquarius
Moon enters Pisces 10:17 am
Incense: Marigold

---

18 Monday
Las Piedras Day (Uraguayan)
Waning Moon
Moon phase: Fourth Quarter
Color: White

Moon sign: Pisces
Incense: Narcissus

---

19 Tuesday
Pilgrimage to Treguier (French)
Waning Moon
Moon phase: Fourth Quarter
Color: Black

Moon sign: Pisces
Moon enters Aries 7:30 pm
Incense: Geranium

---

20 Wednesday
Pardon of the Singers (British)
Waning Moon
Moon phase: Fourth Quarter
Color: White

Moon sign: Aries
Incense: Lavender

---

21 Thursday
Victoria Day (Canadian)
Waning Moon
Moon phase: Fourth Quarter
Color: Crimson

Moon sign: Aries
Incense: Myrrh

May

22 Friday
Heroes' Day (Sri Lankan)
Waning Moon
Moon phase: Fourth Quarter
Color: Pink

Moon sign: Aries
Moon enters Taurus 12:40 am
Incense: Alder

23 Saturday
Tubilustrium (Roman)
Waning Moon
Moon phase: Fourth Quarter
Color: Black

Moon sign: Taurus
Incense: Magnolia

Sunday
Culture Day (Bulgarian)
Waning Moon
Moon phase: New Moon 8:11 am
Color: Orange

Moon sign: Taurus
Moon enters Gemini 2:34 am
Incense: Hyacinth

25 Monday
Memorial Day (observed)
Waxing Moon
Moon phase: First Quarter
Color: Ivory

Moon sign: Gemini
Incense: Neroli

26 Tuesday
Pepys' Commemoration (English)
Waxing Moon
Moon phase: First Quarter
Color: Scarlet

Moon sign: Gemini
Moon enters Cancer 2:58 am
Incense: Ylang-ylang

27 Wednesday
St. Augustine of Canterbury's Day
Waxing Moon
Moon phase: First Quarter
Color: Topaz

Moon sign: Cancer
Incense: Marjoram

28 Thursday
St. Germain's Day
Waxing Moon
Moon phase: First Quarter
Color: Green

Moon sign: Cancer
Moon enters Leo 3:44 am
Incense: Carnation

May

---

29 Friday
Shavuot
Waxing Moon
Moon phase: First Quarter
Color: Purple

Moon sign: Leo
Incense: Yarrow

☽ **Saturday**
Memorial Day (actual)
Waxing Moon
Moon phase: Second Quarter 11:22 pm
Color: Blue

Moon sign: Leo
Moon enters Virgo 6:17 am
Incense: Ivy

---

31 Sunday
Flowers of May
Waxing Moon
Moon phase: Second Quarter
Color: Gold

Moon sign: Virgo
Incense: Almond

Chameleon Plant (*Houttuynia cordata* 'Chameleon')

Also known as "Hot Tuna," the Chamelion Plant thrives in
shady, wet areas. In fact, it will grow in water and at pond
edges. This herb has a hot spicy flavor. Its heart-shaped
leaves are a dramatic blend of green, yellow, cream, and
hot pink. Great for adding some "spice" to your love life!

Creeping Thyme (*Thymus serpyllum*)

This herb reaches three to six inches in height and likes
partial shade. Thyme relates to the planet Venus and the
element of water, so use it to focus personal energies, stir
up your courage, and enhance your psychic powers. A
pillow stuffed with thyme prevents nightmares.

–Elizabeth Barrette

June

1 **Monday**
National Day (Tunisian)
Waxing Moon
Moon phase: Second Quarter
Color: Lavender

Moon sign: Virgo
Moon enters Libra 11:17 am
Incense: Hyssop

---

2 **Tuesday**
Rice Harvest Festival (Malaysian)
Waxing Moon
Moon phase: Second Quarter
Color: Red

Moon sign: Libra
Incense: Bayberry

---

3 **Wednesday**
Memorial to Broken Dolls (Japanese)
Waxing Moon
Moon phase: Second Quarter
Color: Brown

Moon sign: Libra
Moon enters Scorpio 6:43 pm
Incense: Lavender

---

4 **Thursday**
Full Moon Day (Burmese)
Waxing Moon
Moon phase: Second Quarter
Color: Purple

Moon sign: Scorpio
Incense: Apricot

---

5 **Friday**
Constitution Day (Danish)
Waxing Moon
Moon phase: Second Quarter
Color: White

Moon sign: Scorpio
Incense: Mint

---

6 **Saturday**
Swedish Flag Day
Waxing Moon
Moon phase: Second Quarter
Color: Blue

Moon sign: Scorpio
Moon enters Sagittarius 4:23 am
Incense: Sage

☻ **Sunday**
St. Robert of Newminster's Day
Waxing Moon
Moon phase: Full Moon 2:12 pm
Color: Gold

Moon sign: Sagittarius
Incense: Frankincense

June

♊

8 Monday
St. Medard's Day (Belgian)
Waning Moon
Moon phase: Third Quarter
Color: Gray

Moon sign: Sagittarius
Moon enters Capricorn 3:59 pm
Incense: Lily

---

9 Tuesday
Vestalia (Roman)
Waning Moon
Moon phase: Third Quarter
Color: White

Moon sign: Capricorn
Incense: Ylang-ylang

---

10 Wednesday
Time-Observance Day (Chinese)
Waning Moon
Moon phase: Third Quarter
Color: Yellow

Moon sign: Capricorn
Incense: Bay laurel

---

11 Thursday
Kamehameha Day (Hawaiian)
Waning Moon
Moon phase: Third Quarter
Color: Green

Moon sign: Capricorn
Moon enters Aquarius 4:52 am
Incense: Clove

---

12 Friday
Independence Day (Filipino)
Waning Moon
Moon phase: Third Quarter
Color: Pink

Moon sign: Aquarius
Incense: Rose

---

13 Saturday
St. Anthony of Padua's Day
Waning Moon
Moon phase: Third Quarter
Color: Black

Moon sign: Aquarius
Moon enters Pisces 5:32 pm
Incense: Pine

---

14 Sunday
Flag Day
Waning Moon
Moon phase: Third Quarter
Color: Amber

Moon sign: Pisces
Incense: Juniper

June

☽ **Monday**
St. Vitus' Day Fires
Waning Moon
Moon phase: Fourth Quarter 6:14 pm
Color: Silver

Moon sign: Pisces
Incense: Rosemary

16 **Tuesday**
Bloomsday (Irish)
Waning Moon
Moon phase: Fourth Quarter
Color: Black

Moon sign: Pisces
Moon enters Aries 3:51 am
Incense: Geranium

17 **Wednesday**
Bunker Hill Day
Waning Moon
Moon phase: Fourth Quarter
Color: Topaz

Moon sign: Aries
Incense: Lilac

18 **Thursday**
Independence Day (Egyptian)
Waning Moon
Moon phase: Fourth Quarter
Color: Turquoise

Moon sign: Aries
Moon enters Taurus 10:20 am
Incense: Carnation

19 **Friday**
Juneteenth
Waning Moon
Moon phase: Fourth Quarter
Color: Purple

Moon sign: Taurus
Incense: Alder

20 **Saturday**
Flag Day (Argentinian)
Waning Moon
Moon phase: Fourth Quarter
Color: Indigo

Moon sign: Taurus
Moon enters Gemini 1:00 pm
Incense: Rue

21 **Sunday**
Father's Day • Litha • Summer Solstice
Waning Moon
Moon phase: Fourth Quarter
Color: Orange

Moon sign: Gemini
Incense: Almond

June

Monday
Rose Festival (English)
Waning Moon
Moon phase: New Moon 3:35 pm
Color: White

Moon sign: Gemini
Moon enters Cancer 1:12 pm
Incense: Narcissus

---

23 Tuesday
St. John's Eve
Waxing Moon
Moon phase: First Quarter
Color: Gray

Moon sign: Cancer
Incense: Ginger

---

24 Wednesday
St. John's Day
Waxing Moon
Moon phase: First Quarter
Color: White

Moon sign: Cancer
Moon enters Leo 12:50 pm
Incense: Honeysuckle

---

25 Thursday
Fiesta of Santa Orosia (Spanish)
Waxing Moon
Moon phase: First Quarter
Color: Crimson

Moon sign: Leo
Incense: Mulberry

---

26 Friday
Pied Piper Day (German)
Waxing Moon
Moon phase: First Quarter
Color: Coral

Moon sign: Leo
Moon enters Virgo 1:46 pm
Incense: Orchid

---

27 Saturday
Day of the Seven Sleepers (Islamic)
Waxing Moon
Moon phase: First Quarter
Color: Gray

Moon sign: Virgo
Incense: Ivy

---

28 Sunday
Paul Bunyan Day
Waxing Moon
Moon phase: First Quarter
Color: Yellow

Moon sign: Virgo
Moon enters Libra 5:24 pm
Incense: Marigold

June

○ **Monday**
Feast of Saints Peter and Paul
Waxing Moon
Moon phase: Second Quarter 7:28 am
Color: Silver

Moon sign: Libra
Incense: Clary sage

---

30 **Tuesday**
The Burning of the Three Firs (French)
Waxing Moon
Moon phase: Second Quarter
Color: Scarlet

Moon sign: Libra
Incense: Cedar

Ferns

Ferns come in many varieties, all of which require considerable shade. Use ferns in rain-making spells. They are also believed to grant eternal youth and health. Dry and carry unopened fiddleheads to attract fairies.

Foxglove (*Digitalis purpurea*)

Tolerates partial shade, but prefers deep shade and moist, rich soil. Oblong leaves form a low rosette surmounted by a dramatic flower spike reaching three to six feet high. This herb attracts fairies and is sacred to Druids. Magically, it grants protection and the ability to see invisible things.

Ginger (*Zingiber officinale*)

Needs rich, moist soil and open or deep shade. Magically, ginger brings success, power, and money. Try casting a love spell using gingersnaps or gingerbread!

–Elizabeth Barrette

July

1 Wednesday
Climbing Mount Fuji (Japanese)
Waxing Moon
Moon phase: Second Quarter
Color: White

Moon sign: Libra
Moon enters Scorpio 12:18 am
Incense: Bay laurel

2 Thursday
Heroes' Day (Zambian)
Waxing Moon
Moon phase: Second Quarter
Color: Purple

Moon sign: Scorpio
Incense: Jasmine

3 Friday
Indian Sun Dance (Native American)
Waxing Moon
Moon phase: Second Quarter
Color: Coral

Moon sign: Scorpio
Moon enters Sagittarius 10:10 am
Incense: Violet

4 Saturday
Independence Day
Waxing Moon
Moon phase: Second Quarter
Color: Black

Moon sign: Sagittarius
Incense: Sandalwood

5 Sunday
Tynwald (Nordic)
Waxing Moon
Moon phase: Second Quarter
Color: Orange

Moon sign: Sagittarius
Moon enters Capricorn 10:07 pm
Incense: Eucalyptus

6 Monday
Khao Phansa Day (Thai)
Waxing Moon
Moon phase: Second Quarter
Color: White

Moon sign: Capricorn
Incense: Rosemary

☺ Tuesday
Weaver's Festival (Japanese)
Waxing Moon
Moon phase: Full Moon 5:21 am
Color: Black

Moon sign: Capricorn
Incense: Cinnamon

July

---

8 Wednesday
St. Elizabeth's Day (Portugese)
Waning Moon
Moon phase: Third Quarter
Color: Brown

Moon sign: Capricorn
Moon enters Aquarius 11:03 am
Incense: Honeysuckle

---

9 Thursday
Battle of Sempach Day (Swiss)
Waning Moon
Moon phase: Third Quarter
Color: Crimson

Moon sign: Aquarius
Incense: Myrrh

---

10 Friday
Lady Godiva Day (English)
Waning Moon
Moon phase: Third Quarter
Color: Purple

Moon sign: Aquarius
Moon enters Pisces 11:44 pm
Incense: Yarrow

---

11 Saturday
Revolution Day (Mongolian)
Waning Moon
Moon phase: Third Quarter
Color: Gray

Moon sign: Pisces
Incense: Patchouli

---

12 Sunday
Lobster Carnival (Nova Scotia)
Waning Moon
Moon phase: Third Quarter
Color: Gold

Moon sign: Pisces
Incense: Hyacinth

---

13 Monday
Festival of the Three Cows (Spanish)
Waning Moon
Moon phase: Third Quarter
Color: Silver

Moon sign: Pisces
Moon enters Aries 10:40 am
Incense: Neroli

---

14 Tuesday
Bastille Day (French)
Waning Moon
Moon phase: Third Quarter
Color: Red

Moon sign: Aries
Incense: Basil

July

○ **Wednesday**
St. Swithin's Day
Waning Moon
Moon phase: Fourth Quarter 5:53 am
Color: Topaz

Moon sign: Aries
Moon enters Taurus 6:30 pm
Incense: Lavender

---

16 Thursday
Our Lady of Carmel
Waning Moon
Moon phase: Fourth Quarter
Color: Green

Moon sign: Taurus
Incense: Clove

---

17 Friday
Rivera Day (Puerto Rican)
Waning Moon
Moon phase: Fourth Quarter
Color: Rose

Moon sign: Taurus
Moon enters Gemini 10:41 pm
Incense: Cypress

---

18 Saturday
Gion Matsuri Festival (Japanese)
Waning Moon
Moon phase: Fourth Quarter
Color: Indigo

Moon sign: Gemini
Incense: Sage

---

19 Sunday
Flitch Day (English)
Waning Moon
Moon phase: Fourth Quarter
Color: Amber

Moon sign: Gemini
Moon enters Cancer 11:51 pm
Incense: Juniper

---

20 Monday
Binding of Wreaths (Lithuanian)
Waning Moon
Moon phase: Fourth Quarter
Color: Ivory

Moon sign: Cancer
Incense: Narcissus

☽ **Tuesday**
National Day (Belgian)
Waning Moon
Moon phase: New Moon 10:34 pm
Color: Scarlet

Moon sign: Cancer
Moon enters Leo 11:27 pm
Incense: Bayberry

July

22 Wednesday
St. Mary Magdalene's Day
Waxing Moon
Moon phase: First Quarter
Color: Yellow

Moon sign: Leo
Incense: Lilac

23 Thursday
Mysteries of Santa Cristina (Italian)
Waxing Moon
Moon phase: First Quarter
Color: Turquoise

Moon sign: Leo
Moon enters Virgo 11:22 pm
Incense: Nutmeg

24 Friday
Pioneer Day (Mormon)
Waxing Moon
Moon phase: First Quarter
Color: Pink

Moon sign: Virgo
Incense: Vanilla

25 Saturday
St. James' Day
Waxing Moon
Moon phase: First Quarter
Color: Blue

Moon sign: Virgo
Incense: Ivy

26 Sunday
St. Anne's Day
Waxing Moon
Moon phase: First Quarter
Color: Yellow

Moon sign: Virgo
Moon enters Libra 1:25 am
Incense: Frankincense

27 Monday
Sleepyhead Day (Finnish)
Waxing Moon
Moon phase: First Quarter
Color: White

Moon sign: Libra
Incense: Clary sage

☽ Tuesday
Independence Day (Peruvian)
Waxing Moon
Moon phase: Second Quarter 6:00 pm
Color: Black

Moon sign: Libra
Moon enters Scorpio 6:56 am
Incense: Ginger

July

29 Wednesday
Pardon of the Birds (French)
Waxing Moon
Moon phase: Second Quarter
Color: Brown

Moon sign: Scorpio
Incense: Marjoram

30 Thursday
Micman Festival of St. Ann
Waxing Moon
Moon phase: Second Quarter
Color: Purple

Moon sign: Scorpio
Moon enters Sagittarius 4:10 pm
Incense: Carnation

31 Friday
Weighing of the Aga Kahn
Waxing Moon
Moon phase: Second Quarter
Color: White

Moon sign: Sagittarius
Incense: Rose

Jupiter's Beard (*Centranthus ruber*)

Grows in partial or dappled shade. Leaves reach up to three feet tall and produce clusters of tiny pinkish to red flowers. Use this plant to symbolize the divine masculine, or for astrological workings involving Jupiter.

Lemon balm (*Melissa officinalis*)

These leaves tolerate partial, dappled, or open shade, reaching three feet in height. Associated with water and the Moon, this herb is sacred to Artemis and other Moon goddesses. Use it to connect with your emotions, for love and friendship spells, and for healing.

–Elizabeth Barrette

August

1 **Saturday**
Lammas
Waxing Moon
Moon phase: Second Quarter
Color: Brown

Moon sign: Sagittarius
Incense: Rue

---

2 **Sunday**
Porcingula (Native American)
Waxing Moon
Moon phase: Second Quarter
Color: Orange

Moon sign: Sagittarius
Moon enters Capricorn 4:08 am
Incense: Almond

---

3 **Monday**
Drimes (Greek)
Waxing Moon
Moon phase: Second Quarter
Color: Gray

Moon sign: Capricorn
Incense: Lily

---

4 **Tuesday**
Cook Islands Constitution Celebration
Waxing Moon
Moon phase: Second Quarter
Color: Red

Moon sign: Capricorn
Moon enters Aquarius 5:08 pm
Incense: Geranium

☻ **Wednesday**
Benediction of the Sea (French)
Waxing Moon
Moon phase: Full Moon 8:55 pm
Color: Yellow

Moon sign: Aquarius
Incense: Bay laurel

---

6 **Thursday**
Hiroshima Peace Ceremony
Waning Moon
Moon phase: Third Quarter
Color: Green

Moon sign: Aquarius
Incense: Apricot

---

7 **Friday**
Republic Day (Ivory Coast)
Waning Moon
Moon phase: Third Quarter
Color: Purple

Moon sign: Aquarius
Moon enters Pisces 5:34 am
Incense: Thyme

8 Saturday
Dog Days (Japanese)
Waning Moon
Moon phase: Third Quarter
Color: Blue

Moon sign: Pisces
Incense: Pine

---

9 Sunday
Nagasaki Peace Ceremony
Waning Moon
Moon phase: Third Quarter
Color: Yellow

Moon sign: Pisces
Moon enters Aries 4:23 pm
Incense: Heliotrope

---

10 Monday
St. Lawrence's Day
Waning Moon
Moon phase: Third Quarter
Color: Lavender

Moon sign: Aries
Incense: Rosemary

---

11 Tuesday
Puck Fair (Irish)
Waning Moon
Moon phase: Third Quarter
Color: White

Moon sign: Aries
Incense: Ylang-ylang

---

12 Wednesday
Fiesta of Santa Clara
Waning Moon
Moon phase: Third Quarter
Color: Brown

Moon sign: Aries
Moon enters Taurus 12:49 am
Incense: Lavender

◖ Thursday
Women's Day (Tunisian)
Waning Moon
Moon phase: Fourth Quarter 2:55 pm
Color: Turquoise

Moon sign: Taurus
Incense: Balsam

---

14 Friday
Festival at Sassari
Waning Moon
Moon phase: Fourth Quarter
Color: Pink

Moon sign: Taurus
Moon enters Gemini 6:25 am
Incense: Alder

August

15 Saturday
Assumption Day
Waning Moon
Moon phase: Fourth Quarter
Color: Gray

Moon sign: Gemini
Incense: Ivy

16 Sunday
Festival of Minstrels (European)
Waning Moon
Moon phase: Fourth Quarter
Color: Gold

Moon sign: Gemini
Moon enters Cancer 9:13 am
Incense: Marigold

17 Monday
Feast of the Hungry Ghosts (Chinese)
Waning Moon
Moon phase: Fourth Quarter
Color: White

Moon sign: Cancer
Incense: Neroli

18 Tuesday
St. Helen's Day
Waning Moon
Moon phase: Fourth Quarter
Color: Black

Moon sign: Cancer
Moon enters Leo 9:56 am
Incense: Cedar

19 Wednesday
Rustic Vinalia (Roman)
Waning Moon
Moon phase: Fourth Quarter
Color: White

Moon sign: Leo
Incense: Lilac

Thursday
Constitution Day (Hungarian)
Waning Moon
Moon phase: New Moon 6:01 am
Color: Crimson

Moon sign: Leo
Moon enters Virgo 10:00 am
Incense: Mulberry

21 Friday
Consulia (Roman)
Waxing Moon
Moon phase: First Quarter
Color: Purple

Moon sign: Virgo
Incense: Vanilla

22 Saturday
Ramadan begins   Moon sign: Virgo
Waxing Moon   Moon enters Libra 11:12 am
Moon phase: First Quarter   Incense: Patchouli
Color: Indigo

---

23 Sunday
National Day (Romanian)   Moon sign: Libra
Waxing Moon   Incense: Juniper
Moon phase: First Quarter
Color: Amber

---

24 Monday
St. Bartholomew's Day   Moon sign: Libra
Waxing Moon   Moon enters Scorpio 3:16 pm
Moon phase: First Quarter   Incense: Narcissus
Color: Silver

---

25 Tuesday
Feast of the Green Corn (Native American)   Moon sign: Scorpio
Waxing Moon   Incense: Basil
Moon phase: First Quarter
Color: Gray

---

26 Wednesday
Pardon of the Sea (French)   Moon sign: Scorpio
Waxing Moon   Moon enters Sagittarius 11:16 pm
Moon phase: First Quarter   Incense: Marjoram
Color: Topaz

◑ Thursday
Summer Break (English)   Moon sign: Sagittarius
Waxing Moon   Incense: Jasmine
Moon phase: Second Quarter 7:42 am
Color: White

---

28 Friday
St. Augustine's Day   Moon sign: Sagittarius
Waxing Moon   Incense: Yarrow
Moon phase: Second Quarter
Color: Rose

August ♍

29 Saturday
St. John's Beheading
Waxing Moon
Moon phase: Second Quarter
Color: Blue

Moon sign: Sagittarius
Moon enters Capricorn 10:44 am
Incense: Magnolia

30 Sunday
St. Rose of Lima Day (Peruvian)
Waxing Moon
Moon phase: Second Quarter
Color: Orange

Moon sign: Capricorn
Incense: Almond

31 Monday
Unto These Hills Pageant (Cherokee)
Waxing Moon
Moon phase: Second Quarter
Color: Ivory

Moon sign: Capricorn
Moon enters Aquarius 11:43 pm
Incense: Hyssop

Lily-of-the-Valley (*Convallaria majalis*)

This herb prefers dappled or open shade. Magically, it promotes peace, harmony, and love. Use lily-of-the-valley to soothe troubled relationships and create a pleasant domestic atmosphere. Sprinkle flowers in sacred space to draw a protective circle.

Lovage (*Levisticum officinale*)

Grows in partial, dappled, or open shade towering up to six feet tall. Its celery-like flavor makes it popular in soups and stocks. In bath water, the leaves are deodorizing and antiseptic. Use this herb in love spells.

–Elizabeth Barrette

September ♍

1 **Tuesday**
Greek New Year
Waxing Moon
Moon phase: Second Quarter
Color: Red

Moon sign: Aquarius
Incense: Ginger

---

2 **Wednesday**
St. Mamas' Day
Waxing Moon
Moon phase: Second Quarter
Color: Brown

Moon sign: Aquarius
Incense: Honeysuckle

---

3 **Thursday**
Founder's Day (San Marino)
Waxing Moon
Moon phase: Second Quarter
Color: Turquoise

Moon sign: Aquarius
Moon enters Pisces 11:58 am
Incense: Clove

☺ **Friday**
Los Angeles' Birthday
Waxing Moon
Moon phase: Full Moon 12:02 pm
Color: Pink

Moon sign: Pisces
Incense: Orchid

---

5 **Saturday**
Roman Circus
Waning Moon
Moon phase: Third Quarter
Color: Indigo

Moon sign: Pisces
Moon enters Aries 10:14 pm
Incense: Rue

---

6 **Sunday**
The Virgin of Remedies (Spanish)
Waning Moon
Moon phase: Third Quarter
Color: Gold

Moon sign: Aries
Incense: Marigold

---

7 **Monday**
Labor Day
Waning Moon
Moon phase: Third Quarter
Color: White

Moon sign: Aries
Incense: Lily

8 Tuesday
Birthday of the Virgin Mary
Waning Moon
Moon phase: Third Quarter
Color: Black

Moon sign: Aries
Moon enters Taurus 6:17 am
Incense: Bayberry

---

9 Wednesday
Chrysanthemum Festival (Japanese)
Waning Moon
Moon phase: Third Quarter
Color: Yellow

Moon sign: Taurus
Incense: Marjoram

---

10 Thursday
Festival of the Poets (Japanese)
Waning Moon
Moon phase: Third Quarter
Color: Green

Moon sign: Taurus
Moon enters Gemini 12:17 pm
Incense: Carnation

☽ Friday
Coptic New Year
Waning Moon
Moon phase: Fourth Quarter 10:16 pm
Color: Rose

Moon sign: Gemini
Incense: Cypress

---

12 Saturday
National Day (Ethiopian)
Waning Moon
Moon phase: Fourth Quarter
Color: Blue

Moon sign: Gemini
Moon enters Cancer 4:19 pm
Incense: Sandalwood

---

13 Sunday
The Gods' Banquet (Roman)
Waning Moon
Moon phase: Fourth Quarter
Color: Amber

Moon sign: Cancer
Incense: Eucalyptus

---

14 Monday
Holy Cross Day
Waning Moon
Moon phase: Fourth Quarter
Color: Silver

Moon sign: Cancer
Moon enters Leo 6:39 pm
Incense: Rosemary

15 Tuesday
Birthday of the Moon (Chinese)
Waning Moon
Moon phase: Fourth Quarter
Color: Gray

Moon sign: Leo
Incense: Cedar

---

16 Wednesday
Mexican Independence Day
Waning Moon
Moon phase: Fourth Quarter
Color: Topaz

Moon sign: Leo
Moon enters Virgo 7:56 pm
Incense: Bay laurel

---

17 Thursday
Von Steuben's Day
Waning Moon
Moon phase: Fourth Quarter
Color: White

Moon sign: Virgo
Incense: Balsam

☽ Friday
Dr. Johnson's Birthday
Waning Moon
Moon phase: New Moon 2:44 pm
Color: Pink

Moon sign: Virgo
Moon enters Libra 9:26 pm
Incense: Violet

---

19 Saturday
Rosh Hashanah
Waxing Moon
Moon phase: First Quarter
Color: Blue

Moon sign: Libra
Incense: Pine

---

20 Sunday
St. Eustace's Day
Waxing Moon
Moon phase: First Quarter
Color: Yellow

Moon sign: Libra
Incense: Hyacinth

---

21 Monday
Ramadan ends
Waxing Moon
Moon phase: First Quarter
Color: Lavender

Moon sign: Libra
Moon enters Scorpio 12:52 am
Incense: Hyssop

September

22 Tuesday
Mabon • Fall Equinox
Waxing Moon
Moon phase: First Quarter
Color: Scarlet

Moon sign: Scorpio
Incense: Basil

---

23 Wednesday
Shubun no Hi (Chinese)
Waxing Moon
Moon phase: First Quarter
Color: White

Moon sign: Scorpio
Moon enters Sagittarius 7:43 am
Incense: Lilac

---

24 Thursday
Schwenkenfelder Thanksgiving (Germ.-Amer.)
Waxing Moon
Moon phase: First Quarter
Color: Green

Moon sign: Sagittarius
Incense: Myrrh

---

25 Friday
Doll's Memorial Service (Japanese)
Waxing Moon
Moon phase: First Quarter
Color: Purple

Moon sign: Sagittarius
Moon enters Capricorn 6:19 pm
Incense: Rose

☾ Saturday
Feast of Santa Justina (Mexican)
Waxing Moon
Moon phase: Second Quarter 12:50 am
Color: Black

Moon sign: Capricorn
Incense: Magnolia

---

27 Sunday
Saints Cosmas and Damian's Day
Waxing Moon
Moon phase: Second Quarter
Color: Gold

Moon sign: Capricorn
Incense: Frankincense

---

28 Monday
Yom Kippur
Waxing Moon
Moon phase: Second Quarter
Color: White

Moon sign: Capricorn
Moon enters Aquarius 7:06 am
Incense: Clary sage

29 **Tuesday**
Michaelmas
Waxing Moon
Moon phase: Second Quarter
Color: Red

Moon sign: Aquarius
Incense: Ginger

30 **Wednesday**
St. Jerome's Day
Waxing Moon
Moon phase: Second Quarter
Color: Brown

Moon sign: Aquarius
Moon enters Pisces 7:26 pm
Incense: Lavender

Mandrake (*Mandragora officinarum*)

Prefers partial shade and light, deep soil. The leaves grow upright for one foot, then spread out to lie flat. This herb can grant protection, health, and wealth. Mandrake is associated with love and fertility due to the humanoid shape of its roots, which are used as charms.

Moss

Needs deep to full shade for best results. Moss conveys luck and attracts money and is especially good for recovering from misfortune because it rejuvinates after a dry spell as soon as water touches it. In Celtic tradition, moss is harvested with a silver knife, and used for blessings and protection.

Patchouli (*Pogostemon cablin*)

Grows well in moist, shady sites and reaches three to four feet tall. Its powerful scent makes it ideal for invoking lust and fertility. This herb can also be used in divination.

–Elizabeth Barrette

October

1 Thursday
Armed Forces Day (South Korean)
Waxing Moon
Moon phase: Second Quarter
Color: Green

Moon sign: Pisces
Incense: Nutmeg

2 Friday
Old Man's Day (Virgin Islands)
Waxing Moon
Moon phase: Second Quarter
Color: Pink

Moon sign: Pisces
Incense: Mint

3 Saturday
Sukkot begins
Waxing Moon
Moon phase: Second Quarter
Color: Brown

Moon sign: Pisces
Moon enters Aries 5:20 am
Incense: Sage

☺ Sunday
St. Francis' Day
Waxing Moon
Moon phase: Full Moon 2:10 am
Color: Gold

Moon sign: Aries
Incense: Heliotrope

5 Monday
Republic Day (Portugese)
Waning Moon
Moon phase: Third Quarter
Color: Gray

Moon sign: Aries
Moon enters Taurus 12:33 pm
Incense: Clary sage

6 Tuesday
Dedication of the Virgin's Crowns (English)
Waning Moon
Moon phase: Third Quarter
Color: Black

Moon sign: Taurus
Incense: Ylang-ylang

7 Wednesday
Kermesse (German)
Waning Moon
Moon phase: Third Quarter
Color: Brown

Moon sign: Taurus
Moon enters Gemini 5:46 pm
Incense: Lilac

8   Thursday
Okunchi (Japanese)
Waning Moon
Moon phase: Third Quarter
Color: Turquoise

Moon sign: Gemini
Incense: Apricot

---

9   Friday
Sukkot ends
Waning Moon
Moon phase: Third Quarter
Color: Rose

Moon sign: Gemini
Moon enters Cancer 9:48 pm
Incense: Thyme

---

10   Saturday
Health Day (Japanese)
Waning Moon
Moon phase: Third Quarter
Color: Gray

Moon sign: Cancer
Incense: Pine

◓   Sunday
Medetrinalia (Roman)
Waning Moon
Moon phase: Fourth Quarter 4:56 am
Color: Amber

Moon sign: Cancer
Incense: Eucalyptus

---

12   Monday
Columbus Day (observed)
Waning Moon
Moon phase: Fourth Quarter
Color: Lavender

Moon sign: Cancer
Moon enters Leo 1:02 am
Incense: Rosemary

---

13   Tuesday
Fontinalia (Roman)
Waning Moon
Moon phase: Fourth Quarter
Color: Gray

Moon sign: Leo
Incense: Geranium

---

14   Wednesday
Battle Festival (Japanese)
Waning Moon
Moon phase: Fourth Quarter
Color: Yellow

Moon sign: Leo
Moon enters Virgo 3:45 am
Incense: Honeysuckle

15 Thursday
The October Horse (Roman)
Waning Moon
Moon phase: Fourth Quarter
Color: Crimson

Moon sign: Virgo
Incense: Mulberry

16 Friday
The Lion Sermon (British)
Waning Moon
Moon phase: Fourth Quarter
Color: Purple

Moon sign: Virgo
Moon enters Libra 6:29 am
Incense: Vanilla

17 Saturday
Pilgrimage to Paray-le-Monial
Waning Moon
Moon phase: Fourth Quarter
Color: Blue

Moon sign: Libra
Incense: Sandalwood

18 Sunday
Brooklyn Barbecue
Waning Moon
Moon phase: New Moon 1:33 am
Color: Orange

Moon sign: Libra
Moon enters Scorpio 10:22 am
Incense: Hyacinth

19 Monday
Our Lord of Miracles Procession (Peruvian)
Waxing Moon
Moon phase: First Quarter
Color: Silver

Moon sign: Scorpio
Incense: Narcissus

20 Tuesday
Colchester Oyster Feast
Waxing Moon
Moon phase: First Quarter
Color: Maroon

Moon sign: Scorpio
Moon enters Sagittarius 4:49 pm
Incense: Cinnamon

21 Wednesday
Feast of the Black Christ
Waxing Moon
Moon phase: First Quarter
Color: Topaz

Moon sign: Sagittarius
Incense: Marjoram

22 **Thursday**
Goddess of Mercy Day (Chinese)
Waxing Moon
Moon phase: First Quarter
Color: Green

Moon sign: Sagittarius
Incense: Balsam

---

23 **Friday**
Revolution Day (Hungarian)
Waxing Moon
Moon phase: First Quarter
Color: Coral

Moon sign: Sagittarius
Moon enters Capricorn 2:39 am
Incense: Alder

---

24 **Saturday**
United Nations Day
Waxing Moon
Moon phase: First Quarter
Color: Indigo

Moon sign: Capricorn
Incense: Patchouli

☽ **Sunday**
St. Crispin's Day
Waxing Moon
Moon phase: Second Quarter 8:42 pm
Color: Yellow

Moon sign: Capricorn
Moon enters Aquarius 3:08 pm
Incense: Juniper

---

26 **Monday**
Quit Rent Ceremony (England)
Waxing Moon
Moon phase: Second Quarter
Color: Ivory

Moon sign: Aquarius
Incense: Neroli

---

27 **Tuesday**
Feast of the Holy Souls
Waxing Moon
Moon phase: Second Quarter
Color: Red

Moon sign: Aquarius
Incense: Bayberry

---

28 **Wednesday**
Ochi Day (Greek)
Waxing Moon
Moon phase: Second Quarter
Color: Brown

Moon sign: Aquarius
Moon enters Pisces 3:45 am
Incense: Bay laurel

October ♏

29 Thursday
Iroquois Feast of the Dead
Waxing Moon
Moon phase: Second Quarter
Color: Turquoise

Moon sign: Pisces
Incense: Jasmine

---

30 Friday
Meiji Festival (Japanese)
Waxing Moon
Moon phase: Second Quarter
Color: Purple

Moon sign: Pisces
Moon enters Aries 1:56 pm
Incense: Yarrow

---

31 Saturday
Halloween • Samhain
Waxing Moon
Moon phase: Second Quarter
Color: Blue

Moon sign: Aries
Incense: Magnolia

Pineapple Sage (*Salvia elegans*)

Requires protection from intense midday and afternoon Sun and needs more water than most sage varieties. This herb has a pineapple scent and its bright-red flowers attract hummingbirds. Magically, use it to connect with your animal guides and to promote wisdom.

Peppermint (*Mentha spp.*)

Likes partial shade and rich, moist, well-drained soil. This herb reaches up to two feet in height. Magically, peppermint promotes love, lust, and all kinds of energy. Dried leaves may be used to stuff poppets in love or healing spells.

–Elizabeth Barrette

November ♏

1 Sunday
All Saints' Day • Daylight Saving Time ends
Waxing Moon
Moon phase: Second Quarter
Color: Orange

Moon sign: Aries
Moon enters Taurus 7:44 pm
Incense: Frankincense

☺ Monday
All Souls' Day
Waxing Moon
Moon phase: Full Moon 2:14 pm
Color: Lavender

Moon sign: Taurus
Incense: Neroli

3 Tuesday
Election Day (general)
Waning Moon
Moon phase: Third Quarter
Color: Maroon

Moon sign: Taurus
Moon enters Gemini 11:53 pm
Incense: Ylang-ylang

4 Wednesday
Mischief Night (British)
Waning Moon
Moon phase: Third Quarter
Color: Brown

Moon sign: Gemini
Incense: Lavender

5 Thursday
Guy Fawkes Night (British)
Waning Moon
Moon phase: Third Quarter
Color: White

Moon sign: Gemini
Incense: Clove

6 Friday
Leonard's Ride (German)
Waning Moon
Moon phase: Third Quarter
Color: Purple

Moon sign: Gemini
Moon enters Cancer 2:42 am
Incense: Orchid

7 Saturday
Mayan Day of the Dead
Waning Moon
Moon phase: Third Quarter
Color: Indigo

Moon sign: Cancer
Incense: Ivy

November

8 Sunday
The Lord Mayor's Show (English)
Waning Moon
Moon phase: Third Quarter
Color: Yellow

Moon sign: Cancer
Moon enters Leo 5:23 am
Incense: Almond

◐ Monday
Lord Mayor's Day (British)
Waning Moon
Moon phase: Fourth Quarter 10:56 am
Color: Gray

Moon sign: Leo
Incense: Narcissus

10 Tuesday
Martin Luther's Birthday
Waning Moon
Moon phase: Fourth Quarter
Color: Black

Moon sign: Leo
Moon enters Virgo 8:30 am
Incense: Geranium

11 Wednesday
Veterans Day
Waning Moon
Moon phase: Fourth Quarter
Color: White

Moon sign: Virgo
Incense: Honeysuckle

12 Thursday
Tesuque Feast Day (Native American)
Waning Moon
Moon phase: Fourth Quarter
Color: Green

Moon sign: Virgo
Moon enters Libra 12:22 pm
Incense: Apricot

13 Friday
Festival of Jupiter
Waning Moon
Moon phase: Fourth Quarter
Color: Rose

Moon sign: Libra
Incense: Alder

14 Saturday
The Little Carnival (Greek)
Waning Moon
Moon phase: Fourth Quarter
Color: Black

Moon sign: Libra
Moon enters Scorpio 5:24 pm
Incense: Rue

15 Sunday
St. Leopold's Day
Waning Moon
Moon phase: Fourth Quarter
Color: Gold

Moon sign: Scorpio
Incense: Heliotrope

☽ Monday
St. Margaret of Scotland's Day
Waning Moon
Moon phase: New Moon 2:14 pm
Color: Silver

Moon sign: Scorpio
Incense: Lily

---

17 Tuesday
Queen Elizabeth's Day
Waxing Moon
Moon phase: First Quarter
Color: White

Moon sign: Scorpio
Moon enters Sagittarius 12:22 am
Incense: Ginger

---

18 Wednesday
St. Plato's Day
Waxing Moon
Moon phase: First Quarter
Color: Yellow

Moon sign: Sagittarius
Incense: Marjoram

---

19 Thursday
Garifuna Day (Belizian)
Waxing Moon
Moon phase: First Quarter
Color: Turquoise

Moon sign: Sagittarius
Moon enters Capricorn 10:00 am
Incense: Mulberry

---

20 Friday
Revolution Day (Mexican)
Waxing Moon
Moon phase: First Quarter
Color: Coral

Moon sign: Capricorn
Incense: Cypress

---

21 Saturday
Repentance Day (German)
Waxing Moon
Moon phase: First Quarter
Color: Blue

Moon sign: Capricorn
Moon enters Aquarius 10:11 pm
Incense: Sage

22 Sunday
St. Cecilia's Day
Waxing Moon
Moon phase: First Quarter
Color: Yellow

Moon sign: Aquarius
Incense: Marigold

---

23 Monday
St. Clement's Day
Waxing Moon
Moon phase: First Quarter
Color: Ivory

Moon sign: Aquarius
Incense: Rosemary

Tuesday
Feast of the Burning Lamps (Egyptian)
Waxing Moon
Moon phase: Second Quarter 4:39 pm
Color: Red

Moon sign: Aquarius
Moon enters Pisces 11:07 am
Incense: Cedar

---

25 Wednesday
St. Catherine of Alexandria's Day
Waxing Moon
Moon phase: Second Quarter
Color: Topaz

Moon sign: Pisces
Incense: Lilac

---

26 Thursday
Thanksgiving Day
Waxing Moon
Moon phase: Second Quarter
Color: Green

Moon sign: Pisces
Moon enters Aries 10:10 pm
Incense: Myrrh

---

27 Friday
Saint Maximus' Day
Waxing Moon
Moon phase: Second Quarter
Color: Purple

Moon sign: Aries
Incense: Vanilla

---

28 Saturday
Day of the New Dance (Tibetan)
Waxing Moon
Moon phase: Second Quarter
Color: Indigo

Moon sign: Aries
Incense: Sandalwood

29 Sunday
Tubman's Birthday (Liberian)
Waxing Moon
Moon phase: Second Quarter
Color: Amber

Moon sign: Aries
Moon enters Taurus 5:34 am
Incense: Juniper

30 Monday
St. Andrew's Day
Waxing Moon
Moon phase: Second Quarter
Color: Lavender

Moon sign: Taurus
Incense: Hyssop

Roman Chamomile (*Chamaemilum nobile*)

Needs partial or dappled shade, grows four to twelve feet high, and has feathery leaves and daisy-like flowers. Ruled by the Sun, chamomile is sacred to Ra and Cernunnos. Chamomile tea soothes digestion, relaxes the nerves, and brings sleep. It also makes a brightening rinse for blonde hair. This herb's magical applications include love, purification, and money.

Sweet Woodruff (*Gallium odoratum*)

Enjoys dappled to deep shade. The leaves form rosettes along the stems, and tiny white flowers appear at the stem ends. The crucial ingredient in May Wine, its magical powers include victory, protection, and wealth. Its other name, "Forest Master," hints at a connection to woodland gods such as Cernunnos; it can grant understanding of and influence over the woods.

–Elizabeth Barrette

December

1   **Tuesday**
Big Tea Party (Japanese)
Waxing Moon
Moon phase: Second Quarter
Color: Red

Moon sign: Taurus
Moon enters Gemini 9:23 am
Incense: Cinnamon

☻   **Wednesday**
Republic Day (Laotian)
Waxing Moon
Moon phase: Full Moon 2:30 am
Color: Yellow

Moon sign: Gemini
Incense: Lavender

3   **Thursday**
St. Francis Xavier's Day
Waning Moon
Moon phase: Third Quarter
Color: Green

Moon sign: Gemini
Moon enters Cancer 11:00 am
Incense: Nutmeg

4   **Friday**
St. Barbara's Day
Waning Moon
Moon phase: Third Quarter
Color: Rose

Moon sign: Cancer
Incense: Violet

5   **Saturday**
Eve of St. Nicholas' Day
Waning Moon
Moon phase: Third Quarter
Color: Blue

Moon sign: Cancer
Moon enters Leo 12:07 pm
Incense: Pine

6   **Sunday**
St. Nicholas' Day
Waning Moon
Moon phase: Third Quarter
Color: Gold

Moon sign: Leo
Incense: Eucalyptus

7   **Monday**
Burning the Devil (Guatemalan)
Waning Moon
Moon phase: Third Quarter
Color: Gray

Moon sign: Leo
Moon enters Virgo 2:05 pm
Incense: Clary sage

◑ **Tuesday**
Feast of the Immaculate Conception
Waning Moon
Moon phase: Fourth Quarter 7:13 pm
Color: White

Moon sign: Virgo
Incense: Basil

---

9 Wednesday
St. Leocadia's Day
Waning Moon
Moon phase: Fourth Quarter
Color: Brown

Moon sign: Virgo
Moon enters Libra 5:47 pm
Incense: Honeysuckle

---

10 Thursday
Nobel Day
Waning Moon
Moon phase: Fourth Quarter
Color: Turquoise

Moon sign: Libra
Incense: Balsam

---

11 Friday
Pilgrimage at Tortugas
Waning Moon
Moon phase: Fourth Quarter
Color: Pink

Moon sign: Libra
Moon enters Scorpio 11:31 pm
Incense: Thyme

---

12 Saturday
Hanukkah begins
Waning Moon
Moon phase: Fourth Quarter
Color: Indigo

Moon sign: Scorpio
Incense: Sage

---

13 Sunday
St. Lucy's Day (Swedish)
Waning Moon
Moon phase: Fourth Quarter
Color: Yellow

Moon sign: Scorpio
Incense: Hyacinth

---

14 Monday
Warriors' Memorial (Japanese)
Waning Moon
Moon phase: Fourth Quarter
Color: Lavender

Moon sign: Scorpio
Moon enters Sagittarius 7:25 am
Incense: Hyssop

15 Tuesday
Consualia (Roman)
Waning Moon
Moon phase: Fourth Quarter
Color: Maroon

Moon sign: Sagittarius
Incense: Bayberry

☽ Wednesday
Posadas (Mexican)
Waning Moon
Moon phase: New Moon 7:02 am
Color: White

Moon sign: Sagittarius
Moon enters Capricorn 5:32 pm
Incense: Bay laurel

---

17 Thursday
Saturnalia (Roman)
Waxing Moon
Moon phase: First Quarter
Color: Purple

Moon sign: Capricorn
Incense: Myrrh

---

18 Friday
Islamic New Year
Waxing Moon
Moon phase: First Quarter
Color: White

Moon sign: Capricorn
Incense: Mint

---

19 Saturday
Hanukkah ends
Waxing Moon
Moon phase: First Quarter
Color: Gray

Moon sign: Capricorn
Moon enters Aquarius 5:38 am
Incense: Sandalwood

---

20 Sunday
Commerce God Festival (Japanese)
Waxing Moon
Moon phase: First Quarter
Color: Orange

Moon sign: Aquarius
Incense: Almond

---

21 Monday
Yule • Winter Solstice
Waxing Moon
Moon phase: First Quarter
Color: White

Moon sign: Aquarius
Moon enters Pisces 6:42 pm
Incense: Lily

December ♑

22 Tuesday
Saints Chaeremon and Ischyrion's Day
Waxing Moon
Moon phase: First Quarter
Color: Black

Moon sign: Pisces
Incense: Ylang-ylang

---

23 Wednesday
Larentalia (Roman)
Waxing Moon
Moon phase: First Quarter
Color: Topaz

Moon sign: Pisces
Incense: Lilac

◖ **Thursday**
Christmas Eve
Waxing Moon
Moon phase: Second Quarter 12:36 pm
Color: Crimson

Moon sign: Pisces
Moon enters Aries 6:39 am
Incense: Nutmeg

---

25 Friday
Christmas Day
Waxing Moon
Moon phase: Second Quarter
Color: Purple

Moon sign: Aries
Incense: Rose

---

26 Saturday
Kwanzaa begins
Waxing Moon
Moon phase: Second Quarter
Color: Blue

Moon sign: Aries
Moon enters Taurus 3:26 pm
Incense: Pine

---

27 Sunday
Boar's Head Supper (English)
Waxing Moon
Moon phase: Second Quarter
Color: Amber

Moon sign: Taurus
Incense: Heliotrope

---

28 Monday
Holy Innocents' Day
Waxing Moon
Moon phase: Second Quarter
Color: Silver

Moon sign: Taurus
Moon enters Gemini 8:13 pm
Incense: Rosemary

December

---

29 **Tuesday**
Feast of St. Thomas à Becket
Waxing Moon
Moon phase: Second Quarter
Color: White

Moon sign: Gemini
Incense: Ginger

---

30 **Wednesday**
Republic Day (Madagascar)
Waxing Moon
Moon phase: Second Quarter
Color: Yellow

Moon sign: Gemini
Moon enters Cancer 9:45 pm
Incense: Marjoram

Thursday
New Year's Eve
Waxing Moon
Moon phase: Full Moon 2:13 pm
Color: Green

Moon sign: Cancer
Incense: Clove

Violet (*Viola pedata*)

Enjoys partial to deep shade. The heart-shaped leaves reach two to five inches high. The flowers may be candied as a garnish, or used to make floral water, perfume, or potpourri. Use violet when working with your animal guides. It also brings luck and protection where it grows.

Wild Bergamot (*Monarda fistulosa*)

Wild Bergamot likes partial shade in rich, well-drained soil. The bushy plant reaches three to four feet tall. Its pink to red trumpet-shaped flowers attract bees and hummingbirds, and the leaves make excellent hot or cold tea. Magically, bergamot ends money problems and breaks hexes.

–Elizabeth Barrette

Fire Magic

Dark Culture,
the Gothic Current,
and Magical Spirituality

by Raven Digitalis

Dark culture has been weaving its way into Paganism at an increasing rate since its inception in the late 1970s. Though many people would like to think that all Witches and "true magicians" are dark, dark, dark creatures, that idea is anything but true. At the same time, I suppose it entirely depends on a person's definition of darkness. In the case of "dark Witches" and "dark magicians," (terms I use to describe magical folk who are attracted to darker energies and aesthetics), the definition is aligned with positive, progressive spirituality rather than so-called "black magic" or an equal hindrance.

In reality, a minor percentage of Witches, Wiccans, and Pagans are heavily involved with or interested in dark culture, including the Gothic-industrial subculture, the vampyre lifestyle, and the fetish scene. However, looking around at any good-sized Pagan gathering makes obvious the fact that the "darkly inclined" are some of the most predominant alternative people drawn to magical spirituality.

La Magie de Culture Gothique

Gothic culture, in particular, is constructed around an ideology that embraces the beauty in darkness. Sadness is a common theme but isn't generally felt to an unhealthy degree. Dark art differs from other art forms in the sense that it expresses the shadowy and mysterious. Subtle forces align through the wearing of dark clothing, mournful makeup, listening to or creating dark music, writing eerie poetry, and creating dark art. Dark art is an outlet of personal transformation—that can occur on both a conscious and subconscious level. Expressive arts of any kind serve as magical acts to stimulate personal growth, and many artists channel divine energies, tapping into vibrations stored somewhere in the collective unconscious. The natural need to come to terms with humanity's dark nature is immense.

There are a number of reasons for the overlap between dark culture and magical spirituality. For one, Earth-based practitioners are some of the last people to cast a harmful judgment against this subculture. Pagan acceptance of alternative lifestyles is a blessing to those who are so often condemned for striding their own expressive/philosophical path. Renaissance styles, artistic flair, an appreciation for unique music, as well as liberal political views are all embraced by a good number of non-Gothic Pagans, allowing for an acceptance of alternative lifestyles not found in other religious systems.

Many individuals who are drawn to dark culture—whether the extent be great or small—feel assured when darkness is openly honored in celebrations such as Samhain (in the Celtic system) and New/Dark Moon esbats. It's a sad-but-true fact that many people—even followers of the Pagan path—avoid the reality of "the dark side," hence the rise of the dreaded modern "fluffy bunny New Age Wiccan" stereotype! Yes, our path seeks progression from the depths of unhappiness and unawareness, but that doesn't mean that darkness is its cause. The association between darkness and "evil" stems from an obsolete, fear-based ideology. This view is held in varying degrees in modern Western society. The majority of the population is diurnal, sleeping the solemn night away without venturing exploration of any sort. When a person's visual darkness is associated with sinister motives, discrimination results for those who quite literally wear it on their sleeve. Luckily, this unfortunate stereotype is subsiding more every day.

Celebrating Darkness

For centuries, there was little if no separation between magic and religion. This view is still widely held by indigenous or

tribal Pagan cultures across the globe. The division between these two elements occurred much later and was greatly due to Judeo-Christianity's influence. Because modern magic persevered under ancient Western spiritual concepts, modern magical spiritualists of all sorts combine the two, letting them dance in unison to a song of active global and personal change. As already mentioned, Pagan spiritual systems honor the reality of darkness—and all it encompasses—to provide a holistic and balanced structure of worship. Witches, celebrating the lunar tides just as much as the solar (ideally), understand the unique magical force that nighttime holds. This same force is channeled in dark culture.

Without darkness, celebrations of light would be meaningless. Likewise, celebrations of darkness are meaningless without their corresponding equal opposites. The force of darkness includes aspects of the natural world such as destruction, death, and decay. Without question, these darker aspects of Mama Nature's cycle are in place to provide fluidity; a constant change, renewal, and rebirth of all things. Just the same, the darker portions of our psyche (sorrow, anger, and apathy) exist for the same reasons . . . the microcosm embodying the macrocosm: As Above, So Below. If these forces are understood, honored, and worked with, a special type of spiritual understanding quite naturally follows.

Dark Witches basically work magic like every other Witch (and generally have similar ethical views), but tend to keep focused on darker currents, certainly not dismissing things like blood magic, body modification, fasting, and emotional introspection. When dark forces are recognized for what they are—as well as the role they play in our day-to-day lives—these energies can be objectively honed and worked with accordingly, *for positive means*. Emotion and intention are the fuel of magical work, and the dark Witch or shadow magician seeks to bring these aspects to a balanced state. Magic focused on emotional transformation is a strong point of interest for darkly inclined Pagans. Without inner transformation, how can external change occur? Our inner world creates our outer world, and personal darkness cannot be pushed aside.

External forces are also worked with by dark Witches and magicians. The emptiness and profound nature of night itself is something for any magical person to consider and perhaps use frequently. External reality is a mirror for internal reality, and vice versa. The darkness of night correlates with the darkness of the mind. It can represent the subconscious, the unseen, the hidden. Just as nocturnal animals and spirits make their presence known in the nighttime, so does our consciousness shift and enter a different mode of operation in these hours—a fact that is, unsurprisingly, both physiological and metaphysical.

Death Energy

I believe that, for the dark Witch or magician, there exists a natural attunement of sorts to death energy. For Goth types who prefer to express themselves visually, this is easily noticeable. In terms of dark art and philosophy, there seems to often be an underlying or overt focus on death. Death is the

Great Unknown, and as such, its visceral reality is a point of focus in serious spirituality of any type.

Death is the dark side of a full cycle, and this energy can be utilized for spiritual means alongside the dark lunar and solar tides—for death is the ultimate dark tide of life. Necromancy is a mystical, mysterious, and magical art that inherently appeals to many dark Witches and magicians. This has nothing to do with human or animal sacrifice (hey, many of us are vegetarian or vegan!), but with the harnessing of death energy. Goths and other dark culturists are not morbidly fascinated by death, but choose to recognize its power. Death represents the Supreme Unknowable and is therefore aligned to dark, abyss-like vibrations. Though some forms of High Necromancy actually require working with the discarded shell (a corpse) of a person or animal who died of natural causes, more common Necromantic practices are concerned with the magician aligning to chthonic energies in a much less potentially dangerous manner through deep meditation, similar to shamanic journeying. Necromancy and other dark arts confront raw, undeniable energies of existence.

As darker lifestyles and magical spiritual paths grow individually, they will also continue to grow together. For those of us with a foot in each of these spheres, or even those of us who simply dabble in either, we must actively claim our role as alchemists of the dark. Consciousness is rapidly evolving on Earth, and it's up to those unafraid to face darkness, both of the mind and of the world, to help change the plane in which we find ourselves for the better.

The Elements Enshrouded

Here is an idea for an exercise to help you in connecting with darkness. A simple activity such as this can be beneficial for any practicing magician or Witch. If you work with "darker" energies on a regular basis, this can help keep you connected to them. Otherwise, it can serve as a pleasant introduction to the beauty and profundity of nocturnal energy. Keep in mind, however, that simply connecting to the energy of nighttime is only one form of that which can be called "shadow magic." Because there are so many ways that darkness can be perceived, it follows that there are many ways to spiritually integrate with such energy. Nocturnal energy is lulling and soporific, making an exercise like this perfect to perform under shroud of night.

Before this exercise, do some research into the metaphysical properties of the mineral kingdom; ideal reference guides for doing so include *Love is in the Earth* by Melody, and *Cunningham's Encyclopedia of Crystal, Gem, and Metal Magic* by Scott Cunningham. Discover which stones align to which element, and let your intuition guide you to make a selection of four stones, one as an offering to each element. You may have these stones on hand or you may have to purchase them from a supplier. Make sure to select good-sized stones rather than pebbles. Also, it's best to ensure that the stones were not harvested in an unethical way, such as strip mining.

Find a black candle. Make sure that it's a true black candle—not a white candle dipped in a black shell. The darker the color the better, as the color energy is released into the atmosphere as the candle burns. It's also a good idea to inscribe various symbols on the wax and to anoint it with an essential oil of your choice.

During the dead of night, bring the stones and candle with you to a serene, natural, and unpolluted area, even if you have to travel to get there. Ensure that the area is relatively private and secluded, and that it has a stream, lake, beach, or other body of water.

Put yourself in a sacred and slowed frame of mind by walking very, very slowly in your chosen location. If there are any cars, lights, or people around, try not to pay too much attention; allow yourself to enter your own little world. Allow this walking meditation to bring your focus to the nature that surrounds you. Observe what you can of the natural world in the darkness. Look at the details of the natural world, admiring the intricate and immaculate side of nature herself.

Still walking slowly, with much peace and calm, discover an area that calls to you. Sit down and bring your attention to the ground beneath your body. Run your hands through the grass, the dirt, the sand, or whatever is beneath you. Softly and slowly feel the grass, the plants, the trees, or whatever surrounds you. Fully bring your attention to the element of earth, recognizing its presence all around you. When you feel truly connected to the element, speak directly to it in a whisper. Tell earth, as an element, that you appreciate, admire, and revere it for all that it is. Here, bury the stone you selected as an offering to earth.

Continue in a similar manner with the other elements. Take plenty of time to stay "in the zone" and fully experience yourself in the darkness with the elements. Next, stand up to experience the element air. Gaze above you, to the heavens. Observe the beauty of the starry (or overcast!) sky. Contemplate infinity. The cosmos stretches forever, and astronomers say that space itself is expanding. Reflect on the grandness of this. Inhale deeply and slowly multiple times, in through your nose and out through your mouth. Smell the air, twirl around a bit, and get to know this most sustaining element. When you feel a connection, grab the stone you selected for air, and throw it as far as you can. As long as it lands somewhere in nature (i.e., not rocketed through someone's window), the offering has been made. Whisper to air your reasons for loving it as an element.

Next is fire. Find a spot to sit down and light the wick of your candle. Let it burn for a few minutes as you meditate and connect to the energies radiating from the sacred flame. Hold your hand above the fire, wave the candle around your aura, hold it high; do whatever you like in order to connect to the flame itself as a representative of fire. When ready, whisper to the flame your admiration to the element and, for a few seconds, char the fire stone in the candle flame. Blow out the candle, sending admiration through the wick's smoke, and put both the candle and stone back in your pocket or bag. Burn this candle down when you get home (keep an eye on it) with the stone at its base, doing with the remnants what you please.

Finally, approach the nearby body of water. Connect to it as much as possible; if it's seasonal and you're a competent swimmer, take a night swim! Or, simply soak your hands or feet in the water. Play with the water and let it play with you. Feel its serene fluidity, recognizing it as another mystery of existence, and one that both sustains and feeds life. Spend plenty of time connecting to water and reflect on what it represents, both physically and metaphysically. When ready, whisper your fond words to the element and throw your offering stone so that it will sink deep within the watery womb.

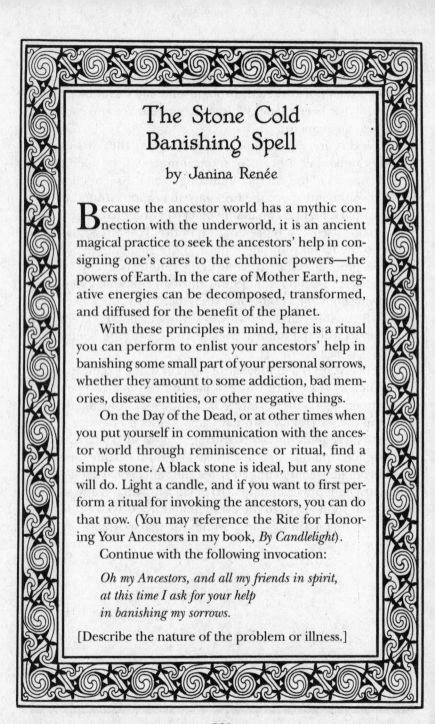

The Stone Cold Banishing Spell

by Janina Renée

Because the ancestor world has a mythic connection with the underworld, it is an ancient magical practice to seek the ancestors' help in consigning one's cares to the chthonic powers—the powers of Earth. In the care of Mother Earth, negative energies can be decomposed, transformed, and diffused for the benefit of the planet.

With these principles in mind, here is a ritual you can perform to enlist your ancestors' help in banishing some small part of your personal sorrows, whether they amount to some addiction, bad memories, disease entities, or other negative things.

On the Day of the Dead, or at other times when you put yourself in communication with the ancestor world through reminiscence or ritual, find a simple stone. A black stone is ideal, but any stone will do. Light a candle, and if you want to first perform a ritual for invoking the ancestors, you can do that now. (You may reference the Rite for Honoring Your Ancestors in my book, *By Candlelight*).

Continue with the following invocation:

Oh my Ancestors, and all my friends in spirit,
at this time I ask for your help
in banishing my sorrows.

[Describe the nature of the problem or illness.]

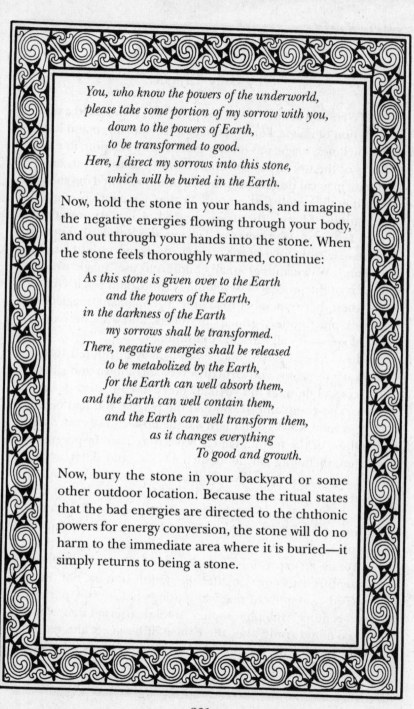

You, who know the powers of the underworld,
please take some portion of my sorrow with you,
down to the powers of Earth,
to be transformed to good.
Here, I direct my sorrows into this stone,
which will be buried in the Earth.

Now, hold the stone in your hands, and imagine the negative energies flowing through your body, and out through your hands into the stone. When the stone feels thoroughly warmed, continue:

As this stone is given over to the Earth
and the powers of the Earth,
in the darkness of the Earth
my sorrows shall be transformed.
There, negative energies shall be released
to be metabolized by the Earth,
for the Earth can well absorb them,
and the Earth can well contain them,
and the Earth can well transform them,
as it changes everything
To good and growth.

Now, bury the stone in your backyard or some other outdoor location. Because the ritual states that the bad energies are directed to the chthonic powers for energy conversion, the stone will do no harm to the immediate area where it is buried—it simply returns to being a stone.

Centuries of Magic

by Sally Cragin

No culture at any time at any place on Earth lacked a tradition of magic. For those of us in the northern and European climes, magic was quickly grafted into religion; in many areas of the world, the spiritual tradition continues to incorporate magical rituals and symbols. In the so-called developed world in the twenty-first century, "magic" has a variety of interpretations. There's the magic evoked in literary traditions such as fantasy (the works of Tolkien and Rowling). There's stage magic or street magic, usually involving cards or sleight of hand. We encourage small children to use "magic words" as part of the process of developing civility (and yes, it's magical when they remember to say them!). Shamans, magicians, priests, practitioners, griots, storytellers, midwives, herbalists, astrologers—it's all a grand continuum.

In medieval times, magic was usually attributed to the work of the saints, and virtually every small town and village had a local deity, as did virtually every disease, disorder, ailment, and complaint. If you had the plague, you had better pray to Saint Roch. Saint Clare was the protector of eyes; Saint Apolline, of the teeth. Magical relics were used by pregnant women, including garments such as coats and skirts, which were kept at the local church. During labor, mothers called upon Saint Margaret and the Virgin Mary for help for the pain. (Millennia earlier, Greek mothers prayed to Diana the Huntress, thought to govern one's ability to withstand difficult physical activities.)

We see an expansion of magic and astrological references in scientific works written after the twelfth century, but there are vivid examples of magical writings before this period. Ninth-century Arab philosopher Al-Kindi asserted that words spoken aloud could alter the course of heavenly and earthbound bodies, the purpose being, of course, celestial harmony. Magic was invariably worked in pursuit of knowledge

or power. Think of the alchemist experimenting with base metals in hopes of creating pure gold.

Magic as prescribed by the established religion was acceptable, but alongside the veneration of saints were older traditions. These would now fall under the rubric of herbalism, folk wisdom, and Witchcraft. Interestingly, Witchcraft was tolerated for centuries and didn't become the focus of the church until a bull from Pope Innocent VIII in 1484. Witchcraft was not a serious crime in Britain until 1542. The era of Witch-hunts was most vehement during the sixteenth and seventeenth centuries.

Magic Words and the Efficacy of Cursing

The most famous magic word that has survived into the present day is *abracadabra*, which has a variety of possible origins, although the historical record notes that Serenus Sammonicus—a second-century physician in the court of the Roman emperor Caracalla—first used the term. Caracalla, a vicious despot now remembered for constructing the Baths at Caracalla in Rome, suffered from mental and physical disease and

Serenus suggested he wear an amulet with *abracadabra* written in a pyramid pattern. This magical object would weaken the disease. Other theories for the origins include Aramaic *avra kedabra* for "I create as I speak," and the Hebrew *abrakha adabra* for "I shall bless, I shall speak." *Hocus pocus*, another all-purpose magician's chant, may have been derived from the Eucharistic phrase, *hoc est poculum*, or "this is the cup."

In the sixteenth century, the use of prayers, pater nosters, aves, and the Creed were the "magical" ingredients for a prayer of healing. These would not be performed by the person suffering, but by a hired hand, a cunning man or wise woman well versed in the power of healing and divination. The practitioner might write these words on a piece of paper to be attached to the patient or burned after the words had been spoken. One "White Paternoster" survives in the form of a nighttime children's prayer: "Matthew, Mark, Luke, and John / Bless the bed that I lie on."

Yes, some words are magical indeed, and the tradition of the curse, usually hurled at someone who has done the curser wrong, is an ancient tradition throughout Great Britain. Curses could include a colorful variety of vengeful wishes, including the pox, pile, and plagues of Egypt. As Keith Thomas wrote in *Religion and the Decline of Magic* (Charles Scribner's Sons, 1971), "Curses were employed by the weak against the strong, never the other way around." Cursing was a dangerous business from the Middle Ages forward and could lead to an appearance in court or even an accusation of Witchcraft.

Writing letters or words on a piece or bread or fruit and feeding it to animals that had been bitten by mad dogs was a widely accepted magical practice. Of course, herbs, salves, and various other substances could also be used in the practice of magic, and were even given to animals.

The Magic Touch

Royalty was said to have the "magic touch," and both British and French monarchs were thought to have a supernatural power to cure scrofula, or "the King's evil." This term encompassed various skin ailments as well as a tuberculous inflammation of the lymph glands thought to come from consuming tainted milk. Unlike many magical customs whose origins are lost in the mists of time, Edward the Confessor (reigned AD 1042–1066) was the first practitioner of "the king's touch." This power was instantly conferred upon coronation, when the ruler was anointed with holy oil.

The ritual grew in complexity and formality during the time of Henry VII (reigned 1485–1509). Its popularity waxed and waned. Edward averaged some thousand sufferers a year. The subsequent royal family, the Plantagenets, continued the practice though they saw fewer petitioners. Charismatic Charles II (reigned 1660–1685) and the later Stuart kings treated numerous patients. Charles attended to more than 90,000 sufferers in 19 years and is also said to have cured 60 people. This ritual was made official with an entry in the Book of Common Prayer and was extremely trendy with the populace (supporters claimed that Charles touched "near half the nation").

Queen Anne (reigned 1702–1714), was the last English sovereign to heal by royal touch. (Bonnie Prince Charlie, also used the royal touch as late as 1745.) Her most famous visitor was author Samuel Johnson during his infancy. Since Johnson, Boswell, and others of his circle frequently wrote about Johnson's ailments and pockmarked visage, the efficacy of Queen Anne's touch is questionable.

In France, the practice began even earlier, with Clovis (AD 481), and continued through the monarchy of Louis XVI (reigned 1774–1792, beheaded in 1793). One Easter Sunday, Louis XIV (reigned 1643–1715), touched some 1,600 persons at Versailles. The custom continued until the scientific enlightenment of the eighteenth century. Still, it remains a lingering belief well into the present day, if you consider the "healing touch" ascribed to the late Princess Diana when visiting the ill, the injured, and those in other dire straits.

The Rise of Astrology and Enochian Magic

After the Reformation, historical record shows that astrologers became more and more prevalent, and they used a variety of methods to produce cures or answers to questions. Astrologers would provide information on everything from political matters to the best time to make a request for money, fight a duel, get married, or conceive a child of a particular sex. Astrologer John Case counseled: "If thou want'st an heir, or man-child to inherit thy land, observe a time when the masculine planets and signs ascend, and [are] in full power and force, then take thy female, and cast in thy seed, and thou shalt have a man-child."

My favorite astrologer/magician is a fellow named Dr. John Dee. He was astrologer to Queen Elizabeth I (reigned 1558–1603), and he practiced his trade in a time when astrology was the only science (mathematics was still considered magic) and casting a monarch's horoscope was treason. He actually practiced his arts during a magical period for astrologers, a time when Saturn and Jupiter (the Markers of Time)

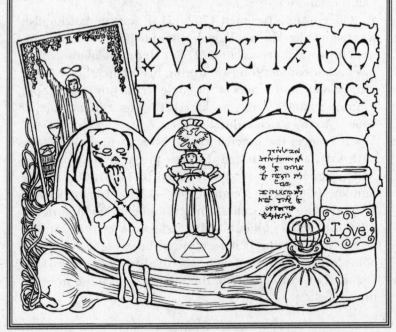

were conjunct. This happens every 20 years, but his lifespan also coincided with the ends of two longer cycles. A trigonalis is a roughly 200-year cycle in which the conjunction takes place in the same element—in this case, water (Pisces). The Saturn-Jupiter conjunction recurs in a particular sign only every 800–960 years. During Dee's life, these two significant cycles were coming to a close and a new era was about to begin, fueled by the conjunction's move into a new sign (Aries, the first sign of the zodiac) *and* into a new element (air).

Heady times for everyone, and among Dee's feats was choosing the time of Elizabeth's coronation—he selected an hour when Virgo (the queen's Sun sign) was in the ascendant. When she was in her mid-forties, he counseled her against her courtship with the Duke of Anjou. Dee replied with *biothanatos*, a Greek word meaning a "violent death." (The duke died of typhoid a year later.)

But Dee wasn't just an astrologer, he was also influential in the fields of navigation, astronomy, and medicine. Among his friends were cartographer Gerard Mercator and some of the leading seers of Europe. You know this story won't have a happy ending, despite Dee's innate survival skills as a Cancer (born July 13, 1527). Dee practiced the crab's specialty, the sideways move, with aplomb. When he fell under the spell of "skryer"(spirit medium) Edward Kelley, whom he met in 1582, he really got into trouble. Kelley convinced him they could talk to angels, and the resulting transmissions were known as "Enochian Magic."

"I have from my youth up," wrote Dee, "desired and prayed unto God for pure and sound wisdom and understanding of truths natural and artificial, so that God's wisdom, goodness, and power bestowed in the frame of the world might be brought in some bountiful measure under the talent of my capacity." Yet, Dee was also mindful of the difference between astrology—which was the leading science of the day, encompassing disciplines ranging from medical, financial, psychological, mathematical, and political aspects—and what were called the "black arts."

"I have always had a great regard and care to beware of the filthy abuse of such as willingly or wittingly invoke or consult with spiritual creatures of the damned sort: angels of darkness, forgers, patrons of lies and untruths. Instead I have flown unto God through hearty prayer, full oft and in sundry manners," Dee wrote in the 1580s, when he was beginning his own experiments and realizing he did not have the personal ability to "skry."

Kelley wanted to work with Dee because he thought that the combination of Dee's scientific abilities and his own "skrying" might allow them to discover the philosophers' stone, which would transform lead to gold. Dee and Kelley had an intense relationship, including Dee's insistence that Kelley perform magical rituals nearly every day for lengthy periods of time. *The Enochian Magick of Dr. John Dee* (Llewellyn, 1998) presents Dee's notebooks of these experiments and includes sketches, magic words, symbols, and a lexicon of the "angelic language." No matter how much skepticism one might bring to the table, the relationship between Dee and Kelley and the sheer volume of data that emerged in a short time isn't easily explained. As author Geoffrey James notes, "It took Tolkien, a professor of philology, years to fabricate the Elvish tongue that figures so largely in his work; if Kelley fabricated the keys, he would have had to do so in a matter of days."

Here is some sample text from the first "key" (there are forty-eight in all). "Ol sonf vorsg goho Iad balt lansh calz vonpho." Dee translated this to "I raygne over you sayeth the God of Justice in power exalted above the firmaments of wrath." Dee's interest in magic did not go unnoticed by those at the top of government. In a diary he kept in Greek at his home in Mortlake, he noted the arrival of courtiers who were close to the queen.

Dee himself was not capable of seeing visions in the crystal used for skrying, thus he needed assistance from a medium. Author Benjamin Wooley explores Dee's experiments in skrying at great length in his splendid volume *The Queen's Conjurer* (Henry Holt, 2000). Among the tools in Dee's study were crystal balls, a lump of obsidian, and a "great perspective glass," which Elizabeth I had stood before. "Anyone who 'foined' or lunged at it with a dagger or a sword found their reflection, 'with like hand, sword or dagger' lunging back at them, an effect so unsettling that many had claimed that it must have magical powers," writes Wooley. "Dee used it to demonstrate how such effects could all be explained by the mathematics of perspective."

Now middle-aged, Dee fled to Prague, where he was under the protection of Holy Roman Emperor Rudolf for a time. But the English suspected him of spying, and his return home was fraught with travail. He lost most of his library and quietly died in England in 1608, his reputation in shreds, his connections with royalty long lost. But other astrologers flourished during the same period, notably William Lilly, who specialized in horary astrology, which purports to answer questions by using data derived from analyzing a chart drawn up for the moment the query is posed.

Until the 1960s and the rise of the daily newspaper horoscopes, astrology pretty much went into decline during the Enlightenment and the gradual widespread acceptance of Copernican theory. Edward Halley's prediction of the regular transit of the comet that bears his name was also another blow to astrological beliefs, which had opined that comets, like eclipses, signaled a shift in power or a fall from grace.

Nowadays, both despite and in tandem with the proliferation of science, the spirit of magic lives everywhere—from the card-trick specialist in Vegas to the herbalist quietly gathering weeds in the woods. And one suspects that two thousand years from now, we'll still be talking about magical rituals.

Clock Magic

by Elizabeth Hazel

Clocks bring the magical essence of time into daily use. Horology, the study of clocks, follows the history and variations on clocks and time. Generally, clocks measure the movement of the Sun and/or Moon, and divide time into units (hours, minutes, seconds).

The most ancient timekeeping device was a standing stick. Egyptians built tall timekeeping pillars, called Cleopatra's Needles, in 1500 BC. Sundials were the next leap in time-technology. Sun dials are able to give a more accurate measure of time by being oriented to north and parallel to the angle of Earth's axis. Su Sung's eleventh-century water clock (a clepsydra), oil clocks, and hour glasses were subsequent advances in timekeeping.

Advancements in early clock building led to progress in other sciences, and the specialized machines and tools used in clock making quietly contributed to other technologies from the Middle Ages until the Industrial Revolution. Clocks are a part of economic and social history, transportation, commerce, astronomy, physics, mathematics, and philosophy. Early European clocks were wonders of primitive gear-and-cog technology, hand-carved of wood.

Home clocks were one of the first personal gizmos people could own. Craftsmen designed table clocks, wall clocks, lantern and carriage clocks, chiming and musical clocks; clocks with month dials, Sun and Moon dials, and even barometers. Special clocks called marine chronometers were designed for sea travel, compensating for the motion of the ship. Long case pendulum clocks became popular, yielding the beloved grandfather and grandmother clocks, with lower and higher chimes, respectively. So-called skeleton clocks, with all inner workings visible under a glass dome, later became very popular in the nineteenth century.

Before the twentieth century, clocks were a microcosm of design and ingenuity. Clocks had enormous regional variation; they were handmade in small, local shops, and the maker's name was usually inscribed on the dial or face of the clock. Highly ornamented Bavarian cuckoo clocks with pendulums and weights contrast dramatically with the simple, almost primitive early-American banjo or lyre clocks. The nineteenth century was the golden age of clockmaking, and many of the clocks most desired by collectors come from this period.

In addition to varying designs, clockmakers made forays into alternative sources of power. In 1843, Alexander Bain patented his clock powered by an "earth battery," which drove the pendulum with electrically induced magnets. Quartz crystals and gravity were more and less successful power sources. The Atmos

clock runs perpetually and can be powered for 48 hours by a 2-degree temperature change. The most accurate clocks are the Caesium Atomic clocks, which were invented in the 1950s.

The Magic of Time

Time is a magical substance. Sometimes it seems to go quickly, sometimes it drags by. Human perception of time is quite different from the measurement of it, but people are always aware that time passes. Time represents the aging phenomenon, and is an unavoidable bullet in this sense. Certain things happen at certain times. Often people wish they had more time. Time is often compared to a circle or a spiral, and astrology is the study of the cyclic nature of time and subsequent events on our Earth.

The Pagan year is based on the division of Earth's yearly orbit into eight parts, which are noted by eight high sabbats. One way to ritually honor and recognize the principle of time is to erect a time stick or create a time pillar on Litha (Summer Solstice), when the Sun is at its greatest power.

It is fairly easy to acquire the supplies for making a battery-powered wall clock. Making clocks with goddess faces, rings of zodiac signs, tarot cards, or other symbols is a fun coven craft project. A "blessing clock" can be made with photographs of family members and friends at each of the hours.

Enchanting Dial Clocks

A "Time Heals All Wounds" Charm: Cut a bundle of comfrey, yarrow, St. John's wort, or some other healing herb, and suspend the bundle from a long string or ribbon. Take the clock off the wall, hang the bundle from the nail or hook that supports the clock, and replace the clock while saying a short incantation such as: "Healing time, soothe my friend; in time she'll be well and happy again."

Prosperity Clock Spell: Decide on the exact amount of time needed for a prosperity spell to manifest. Perform the prosperity spell, and then complete the ritual by taping a piece of parchment with the "due date" on the back of the clock. Rehang the clock and chant: "By hands and face, with this time there will be / By six, nine, twelve, and three, wealth flowing toward me / So mote it be."

Daily Time Spell: A similar procedure is to create specific results by saying a chant or a prayer at the exact same time every day. For example, resolve to say a chant every day at 6:00 pm for five days, and the result will arrive on the sixth day. This kind of magical procedure is similar to the same-time-every-day mandate of mantras. The discipline and focus needed to carry out this kind of spell greatly improves outcomes.

Time Reversal: To reverse bad luck or the outcome of an event, take a dial clock and turn the hands backward while saying, "Hour by hour, back it goes / back to where the trouble flows / Returning to the sorrow there / and by the Goddess, bring healing and repair / So mote it be."

Time Stands Still: Set a particular goal—to make a difficult phone call, accomplish some important deed, or finish some uncomfortable task. Write a magical contract that agrees to have that goal accomplished by a specific time, X days in the future. Sign the contract and note the time. Stop the clock. After the goal is

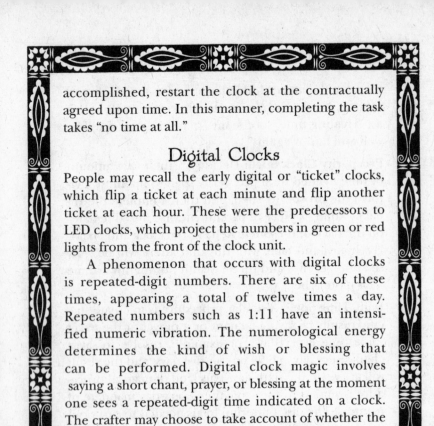

accomplished, restart the clock at the contractually agreed upon time. In this manner, completing the task takes "no time at all."

Digital Clocks

People may recall the early digital or "ticket" clocks, which flip a ticket at each minute and flip another ticket at each hour. These were the predecessors to LED clocks, which project the numbers in green or red lights from the front of the clock unit.

A phenomenon that occurs with digital clocks is repeated-digit numbers. There are six of these times, appearing a total of twelve times a day. Repeated numbers such as 1:11 have an intensified numeric vibration. The numerological energy determines the kind of wish or blessing that can be performed. Digital clock magic involves saying a short chant, prayer, or blessing at the moment one sees a repeated-digit time indicated on a clock. The crafter may choose to take account of whether the digital event he or she sees is before or after noon and adjust the wish accordingly.

1:11 – Represents the Triple Goddess

Chant "By Maid, Mother and Crone, blessings to this home."

2:22 – Represents duality, yin/yang

Chant "By the day and by the night, perfect in the Goddess' sight."

3:33 – Sum of nine; karma, resolving patterns

Chant "Three times three, wisdom comes to me."

4:44 – Seasons, cosmic axis points, material reality

Chant "Four by four, there's time for more."

5:55 – Chaos, magic, power, and will

> Chant "By Sun, Moon, and stars, good spirits, give thy charms."

11:11 – Master number, other dimensions, the mind of God

> Chant at 11:11 am "By Lord and Lady and faeries sweet, blessed be throughout the day, and to all merry meet"

> Chant at 11:11 pm "Goodly gods of dark and light, keep us safe throughout the night."

Original chants or prayers can be written for each of these special digital times. When a person happens to look at a digital clock at the moment a triple-digit number appears, it may be regarded as an omen, a warning, or a call for a moment of meditation to gain a nugget of wisdom.

Power Pendant Watch

Before the advent of wrist watches, men's fashions included a vest with room for a pocket watch, often connected to the vest with a watch fob. Watch fobs are chains with an anchor; usually some little charm (the fob) was attached to the chain. Ladies also wore small watches on necklaces or watches designed as brooches to be pinned to a blouse.

Time is a magical substance, and a pendant watch is an awesome power tool. Either obtain a pendant watch or suspend a pocket watch from a sturdy necklace chain. Consecrate the watch as one would a pendulum or other magical tool. Smudge it with sage and place it on a patten (a plate with a pentagram on it). Chronos is the god of time, and it is to this god that watches should be dedicated. When the watch has been ritually cleansed, chant:

> *Lord of Time, Lord of Power,*
> *Increase my wisdom, hour by hour.*
> *Of passing time, ever mindful,*
> *Of minutes passing, ever watchful;*
> *Of days and years, of here and now,*
> *Of all the things I make and grow;*
> *I will be the master of my time,*
> *As I so will and charge, this thing be mine.*

Wear the power pendant during rituals and ceremonies, especially the four solar sabbats (Ostara, Litha, Mabon, and Yule). One may also use this pendant when performing the time spells mentioned earlier, which are performed at a particular time every day. Wearing the pendant watch is an easy reminder. The power pendant can also be used when creating a timed magical contract, and it could be the clock that is stopped and restarted when the spell is completed. Hang it in a conspicuous place as a reminder that time is passing and the goal must be met.

Clock Divination

Mystics have long known that *the moment in which a question is asked contains the answer.*

Horary astrology, a technique used since the Middle Ages, answers specific questions by interpreting a chart erected for the exact moment a question is asked. Horary methods are useful for finding lost items, pets, and people. These methods are also consulted for outcomes (e.g., will I win my court case?). Both of these methods are complex and take a long time to learn. The eighteenth-century astrologer/tarotist Etteilla invented a shortcut horary method by assigning astrological attributions to tarot cards.

Tarot can be used in a simpler way for time divination. The best results come when the question is sincere and clearly stated. Questions asked on behalf of a second party (e.g., will my boyfriend get a job?) are more difficult to answer. Practice on yourself first, then move on to second-party questions. This method can also be used to interpret dreams by noting the time a dream awakens you.

There are two ways to perform this sort of divination. Here's a sample question: "I dreamed I drove a car into the Sun or a fireball; woke at 2:49 am." Shuffle the deck and flip through the cards from the top. Pull out the first "two" card. This may be a pip card, a court card (see below), or a major arcana card—i.e., the High Priestess (2), Strength (11), or Judgement (20). Continue to flip through the deck until the first "four" card and "nine" cards are located. Spread out the cards in order. In this example, the cards are: Two of Swords, Four of Wands, Hermit (9). One possible interpretation for this dream: a search for information (Two of Swords) will successfully lead the seeker (Four of Wands) to a secret source of light, a wise man, a particular book, or an advisor (Hermit). [According to tarot scholar David Allen Hulse, the Knight cards are twos, Queens are threes, Kings are sixes, and Page/Princesses are tens.]

It is possible to use one card to represent double-digit times. Tens, Pages, and the Wheel of Fortune can represent 10:00, or ten minutes past the hour. The Strength card (or Justice, depending on the deck) may represent 11:00, or eleven minutes past the hour, etc. If a question is posed at 5:21, and the World card (21) appears before a "two" card, then the World card should be used.

The second method is to shuffle the deck and pull the cards that match the digits. For the sample question posed at 2:49, take the second, fourth, and ninth cards from the deck and read them. If the question was asked at 12:48, take the first, second, fourth, and eighth cards. As with most techniques, the more one experiments with time divination, the easier it becomes to interpret the answers.

Wild Justice:
The Bounty of Themis

by Gail Wood

She stands in stillness, holding the scales of justice. Before our courthouses and places of administration, she is blindfolded and silent. Themis, the Greek goddess of order and justice, is alive and vibrant in our lives. She is depicted as a stern-looking woman, sometimes blindfolded, holding scales and either a sword or a cornucopia. Holding the scales, she balances and weighs the opposing forces so that order is maintained in the universe. As a magical being, she steps down from the courthouse stairs and becomes an energetic divine force in our lives.

The Greeks revered Themis with many praiseworthy names: Venerable, Holy Reverend, Good Counselor, Savior, Soteria, August, Protectoress, and Highborn. Her very name, Themis, means "order." She is the goddess of divine right order as sanctioned by laws, customs, and the rules established by the gods. Even the gods were expected to abide by her edicts. She was also a goddess of wisdom called Ebolous or "good counselor."

Themis maintained and regulated the ceremonies of the gods. She invited them to the festivals and prepared their feasts. As the gods decreed, she became the goddess of Justice to the humans, interpreting the will of the gods as well as protecting the just and punishing the guilty. It was her divine voice that first instructed humans in the laws of justice, morality, piety, rules of hospitality, good governance, the conduct of assembly, and the pious and proper offerings to the gods. Judges called themselves *themistopoloi*, "the servants of Themis." Her devotees from all walks of life tried to lead virtuous and charitable lives.

Themis presided over the proper relationship between men and women, the basis for an ordered family and society. Mirroring the order found on Mount Olympus, the abode of

the gods, Themis maintained the order of family. She was the one who handed Hera the cup of nectar upon Hera's arrival on Olympus. All the gods revered her and always referred to her as Lady Themis. She was an advisor to Zeus, and all the gods were expected to follow her rules.

As in life, so in death, and Themis took part in deciding the afterlife for a human being's immortal soul. Hades always consulted her before making the final judgment. This formalized and civilized role in death probably indicates that Themis was at one time, before the advent of the Olympian gods, a powerful dark goddess, working with the dark and light energies.

Themis was also accorded a mystical side. Her gift of insight came directly from Gaia (titan of Earth), and it is said that Themis is the one who built the oracle of Delphi to interpret the will of the gods. It was she who passed on the gift for prophecy and prediction to Phoebe, the famed Sybil of Delphi. This oracular ability coupled with her wise counseling skills gives Themis a magical and numinous persona, perhaps at odds with the more ordered and civilized stern-faced goddess.

From a twenty-first-century perspective, we can see that the need for order and the proper running of society was a deep concern for the Greek civilization. The Greek society became more patriarchal and ordered as time went on, and their gods and goddesses reflected that change, often being re-worked from more chthonic and magical gods and goddess of the localities the Greeks conquered.

Themis is still with us today, transmuted with the Roman goddess Justitia into Lady Justice. She can be found in statues at courthouses, law schools, and other places where criminal punishment occurs and where justice is meted out. We see her image in tarot in the Justice card of the major arcana, where it means impartiality, fairness, and equality.

To modern Pagans, the Themis of today is more than the stillness of statues erected as symbols. Just as humans continue to evolve and grow over time, so does the goddess. Who she was in Greek times is different than who she is today, just as you are different from who you were years ago. So who is she today, and how can we interact and work with her?

I experience Themis as an abundant, generous, loving, somewhat stern goddess of justice, forgiveness, and mercy with a very mysterious, mystical side. In my experiences with her, she is most concerned with my progress, understanding, and learning. She also holds me to the promises I make, even when those promises are made only to myself.

There is a deep, eternal power to Themis that goes beyond the civilized images inherited through ancient Greek culture. She stands in the surging powers of the universal life force directing those energies of darkness and light. She balances these energies, not precariously, but with solid, loving purpose. Themis sees much both with intuition and with sharp vision, and she is not blinded by the glamour we often use on ourselves.

Her sword is used for both defense and to cut away that which does not serve us. Oftentimes, it's the latter that pains us the most. Sometimes our most cherished beliefs are the ones that cause us the most harm. As humans, we have a bad habit of cherishing or nurturing what is not actually good for us; sometimes it is a relationship that is unhealed or broken, sometimes it is our own faults. Themis makes us examine these things and demands that we do the work needed for our own benefit and order.

Themis' symbol is the cornucopia, which connects her deeply to the bounty and abundance of the fertile ground, feeding and healing others, and the more agricultural aspects of life. There are two tales about the beginning of the cornucopia, both from Greek legends. The first and older of the two concerns Zeus and his childhood nanny. Fearing that his father (Cronos) would devour him, his Titan mother (Rhea) sent Zeus to be raised in Crete. The daughters of the king hung him from a cradle in a tree so he could not be found in heaven, Earth, or sea. The she-goat Amalthea provided milk to him. Eventually, Zeus broke off one of Amalthea's horns and endowed it with magic, ever filling the desires of the possessor. He gave it to the daughters of the king in thanks. So this horn became the symbol of plenty, and the word *cornucopia* means "horn of plenty."

A later legend tells us of a feud between Hercules and the river god Achelous. The two males vied for the affections of one woman. They engaged in a wrestling match, each changing shapes many times. While Achelous was a bull, Hercules broke off one of his horns and threw it into the river. The water nymphs, Naiads, treated it as a sacred object, filling it with beautiful flowers and gifts. The horn was adopted by the goddess of Plenty, Copia, and it was called the cornucopia—the Horn of Plenty.

I believe it is this horn of plenty, the cornucopia, that links Themis to the ancient goddesses of Earth, abundance, and bounty. There is not scholarly evidence to trace Themis from those early chthonic goddesses to her personification of justice and the will of the gods, yet the presence of the cornucopia and its vision of thanksgiving, generosity, and abundant nourishment link Themis to this strong, nurturing energy. The cornucopia tempers the rather cold, stern, aridness of

Themis as the goddess of Justice. It brings understanding, compassion, and love into the picture.

The mystical attributes of Themis connect her to us on a soul level. She has the gift of prophecy and is able to balance the need for justice and truth with the flowing perspective of bountiful forgiveness. As Themis leads the souls of the dead to their final destination, she doesn't look only at the facts of a life but also at the heart of a person. In our twenty-first-century world, Themis is alive and well for all of us, and we can journey in meditation to work with her and seek her wisdom.

Meditation to the Goddess Themis

Make yourself comfortable and remove as many disturbances as possible from your meditation area. You may wish to set up an altar and offering to Themis reflecting her affinity for balance, discernment, fairness, bounty, impartiality, forgiveness, and order. Settle yourself into the space and take a long, deep breath. Take a second long, deep breath and close your eyes. Take another deep breath that fills you from the top of your head to the tips of your fingers and the bottoms of your feet.

As you breathe deeply, feel your connection to the sustaining solidity of Mother Earth.

Envision yourself standing in your favorite outdoor place in the whole world. You drink in the wonder and love of this place. As you breathe deeply, you see a pathway moving into the woods and you begin to follow it. Deeper and deeper you go into the forest, unafraid and steadily moving deeper. You begin to hear laughter and drumming. You emerge from the woods into a clearing. There's a fire circle in the center with a low-burning fire and a cauldron set upon it. There are many people around, chatting and talking. One of the women looks up and sees you. You know it is Themis and you move toward her as she moves to you. She stands before you and you drink in her appearance.

She places her hands on your shoulders and looks deep into your eyes. You know she sees all your mistakes, joys, concerns, celebrations, needs, and contentment. She looks long and hard. She smiles slightly and leads you over to a bench. She seats you there. She reaches out to her altar and picks up a pair of scales, and says, "These are the things in your life." She holds the scales by the fulcrum, the balancing point and you watch as the areas of you life appear on either side of the scale. You note whether the scale is balanced or tilted to one side or the other. You listen carefully as she tells you how and what needs to be changed. (Pause here until she finishes.)

When Themis is finished, she smiles more broadly. She hands you a blindfold and says, "This is the blindfold of justice. Use this when you need to view things impartially. Also beware not to overuse it, or you will become blinded to what you need to know." You take the blindfold and tie it around your wrist.

She hands you her sword and says, "Take this and use it when you need to defend yourself and when you need to cut away things that no longer serve you well. Be aware that you need to exercise wisdom when using this sword in order to not punish harshly or cut away what is essential." You take the sword and strap it to your back.

She hands you the cornucopia and says, "Take this horn of plenty and use it freely and happily. From this flows all that you need and it is not for you to be stingy in receiving. This horn teaches you that generosity flows without ceasing and whatever you need is always, always with you." You take the cornucopia and fasten it to your waist.

You stand before her, tall and straight. You look for a gift to give her and realize you have none, and so you look into her eyes. She smiles even more broadly now and says, "Go with my gifts and live your life to the fullest of your ability. Live in honor, fairness, order, bounty, and love. That will be the tribute to gifts and my love for you."

With a hug, she spins you around and sets you back on the path to your favorite place. You swear she gave you a slap on the bottom as you walked away. As you enter into your favorite place again, the echo of her laughter remains in the air.

Take a deep breath and return to the here and now. Take another deep breath and open your eyes. Take a third deep breath and renew your connection to the grounding power of Mother Earth. Blessed Be.

Magic in Times of Trouble

by Dallas Jennifer Cobb

When we are rested, peaceful, and content, it is easy to gracefully practice the tenet "An it harm none." But what about situations fraught with fear, stress, anger, and panic? Don't most of us revert to the use of domination and force when we feel cornered?

How do you tap into deeper spiritual reserves and inner strength when you are really up against the wall? Can you reach deep down to find ways to see even the most evil and attacking person through a peaceful, Pagan perspective? Are you able to ground yourself spiritually and practice magic in times of trouble?

Three years ago, a shocking incident took place that forced me to find these strengths and develop these skills. I want to share what I learned and practiced in case you have a situation or a person with whom these skills might become necessary. I want to remind you how to use simple magic to protect yourself, practical ways to cultivate good energy, and the natural laws that inform the Pagan practice of "What goes around comes around."

The Troubled Times

Three years ago, my neighbor sued me over a trivial and frivolous incident. Prior to the incident, we had shared a neighborly relationship. I helped her with shopping, we traded food across the street, and I minded her kids every now and then. Two women at home alone with kids, we empathized, laughed, and sometimes cried about life. I thought this woman and I were friends.

One morning a process server arrived at my gate and handed me a $400,000 lawsuit. It was from my friend and neighbor across the road. And yet, the night before when I had taken soup over to her house, she didn't mention the lawsuit. Strange.

My first response was disbelief, which was quickly overtaken by shock, and then anger. Overnight, I went from thinking of her as a friend and neighbor to considering her a danger and a threat—an enemy and attacker. Her actions threatened my home and savings, my possessions, and my security. She was a threat not just to me but to my family and my homestead.

Now, if I lived in a big city, blocks away from this woman, it might have been easy to put her out of sight, out of mind. Or, to just let the issue go and let my lawyer handle it. But I live in a rural village of 1,700 people, and this woman lived directly across a small street. Unable to avoid her, I had to learn how to manage my feelings and responses when I saw her. I also needed to counteract the attacking, negative energy that I perceived from her directed at me. When encountering her in the grocery store, in front of the school, or at the post office, I needed ways to stay safe. This meant not only shielding myself from attack, but also not losing my own self-control.

While I often had the impulse to shout at her across the street to vent my anger and fear, and I thought about placing a curse on her and casting negative spells, in my heart I knew that the eventual outcome would be negative for me, too. So I focused instead on transformation. Transformation of my feelings, her attacking energy, and the situation.

Transforming Troubled Feelings

As a practitioner of transformative magic, I believe that the best way to deal with evil is to transform it, not to attempt to fight it or destroy it. I would prefer evil passed me by or went around me, rather than engage me head-on.

My Pagan practice, based on natural law, told me that "What goes around comes around" and it usually returns via the Threefold Law: everything you do comes back to you three times. That meant that anything I did, said, or sent to my neighbor would come back to me abundantly. And since I already had a lot of troubles, I couldn't risk stirring up any more.

Ideally, if I were a highly evolved spiritual being, I would have sent this woman positive energy, blessings, and good wishes. But I am not so highly evolved, and initially, I wasn't capable of positive thoughts toward my attacker. Still reeling from the betrayal and attack, I was off balance and felt really vulnerable.

Realizing that I have a lot more influence in my own realm and over my own feelings than I had over someone else's, my first step was to work with and transform my own feelings. I needed to move myself away from fear, anger, and pain toward confidence, safety, and security—a pretty radical transformation.

My early efforts focused on self-protection and employed a huge cast of magical helpers. I hired a lawyer to protect me legally, and a psychotherapist to help me process the feelings of betrayal and hurt and protect myself emotionally. I used my journal to record feelings, express my negativity, and transform it. My magical circle helped by cleansing and blessing me, and I did a lot of protection and transformation magic in ritual. My partner became a deeper ally with whom I shared my fears and processed my feelings of betrayal.

By processing the energy in a variety of ways, I came to realize that I hadn't done anything mean, bad, or stupid to anyone. I held my head up and spoke my truth. While I refrained from speaking negatively about my attacker, I didn't silence myself. I spoke about what happened and how I felt. I let the power of my emotions be my medium. I spoke only about what had happened to me and how I felt about it.

While there is no quick fix for traumatic events, even fear, anger, and pain can be transformed through self-care and protective practices. With regular practice, negative energy can be neutralized, dispelled, and deflected. And once that healing has started and your feelings are being transformed, you can continue on to perform some simple self-protection.

Simple Self-Protection

When we are under attack, even from only one person, it can often feel like the whole world is against us. Bad magic, or negative energy, feeds on feelings of vulnerability and fear. So it is important to cleanse and protect yourself. By neutralizing, dispelling, and deflecting negative energy, you protect yourself from being charged with negativity or simply having your good energy sucked out of you. Some of the most effective methods of spiritual and psychic protection are also the easiest.

With your feet planted on the ground, draw Earth's energy up through your body and envision it cascading out the top of your head, showering you with golden light. Use a deep breath to draw the energy up, and exhale to shower it out and around. Continue to breathe deeply until you can feel a perceptible shift in your energy—perhaps a tightening of the scalp or a chill up the back of the neck. Know that you are enveloped in the energy of Earth, where natural law governs and protects.

Each morning, take a cleansing shower or bath. Use salts to consciously scrub away old, bad energy. Let the negativity be absorbed by the salt and carried off. As you rinse, bid the negative energy farewell, suggesting it go back to where it came from. After you dry yourself, anoint your body with sacred oils to protect and uplift. (Always dilute essential oils before applying them to your skin.) Uplifting oils include lavender, orange, or lemon balm. Protecting oils include

magnolia and sandalwood. You can use whatever you feel good about, whatever gives you a good vibe. I used jasmine through my troubled times, because it is reputed to be the healer of broken hearts, and that is what betrayal felt like to me.

Adorn yourself with sacred or consecrated jewelry or symbols at all times. Imbued with the good magic of your circle, solitary practice, and craft, their energy is always with you and can be drawn on in times of trouble. Remember to use the consecrated jewelry as a touchstone—something you can touch and be reminded of goodness and protection.

Use dried sage and sweet grass and smudge yourself, clearing your aura. As you fan the cleansing smoke around your body, think about what you seek to release. Let the smoke absorb the negative energy and take it away, dissipating as the smoke disappears.

Make up your own cleansing ritual that removes the negativity, restores your sense of worth and value, and helps you to maintain equilibrium—even in times of stress.

Protecting Your Property

My home felt threatened both because of the lawsuit and because of the proximity of my negative neighbor. I went to great lengths to protect my physical space from her energy. Some of my techniques might work for you.

Because my garage and parking spot were the closest parts of my property to her property, I started with a simple protection spell for my car. I smudged her and told her how much I valued her. I washed her and then rubbed wax onto her, giving her a shiny exterior to deflect negative energy. Finally, I placed a bumper sticker on the back bumper—the one that faced directly toward my neighbor's house—reading "Follow Your Bliss." I chose this because it was a wish and it was positive. I hoped that every time my neighbor read it she would be uplifted and reminded to think about what really made her happy. I hoped that it would subtly transform her negativity toward me.

Plants and flowers possess magical qualities and can be allies in protection. Because I felt vulnerable in my backyard, which was overlooked by my attacking neighbor, I planted a lot of plants that grow tall. I hoped to create a webbed mesh of greenery that would limit visibility, sound, and energy transference and help me to feel safe.

Because I consider them to be guardians, I planted Russian helianthus—giant sunflowers. They grew to be valiant guardians standing eight to fourteen feet tall, their faces turning with the Sun to watch over my garden, car, and home. Thick fibrous stalks created an impenetrable physical boundary and helped establish a firm psychic boundary.

For color, joy, and inspiration, I planted hollyhocks in a variety of colors. Their flowered stalks grew tall and cascaded brilliant flowers all around. When I looked at them, I felt light and blessed. Beauty can uplift and transform emotions instantly. The hollyhocks also drew birds, bees, and insects to the garden, adding to my sense of abundance and rightness with the natural world. And within the garden I felt safe, protected, and nurtured, even though I was still in close proximity to my negative neighbor.

Garden ornaments can be employed to deflect negative energy around the perimeter of your property. Children's toys such as windmills, spinning rainbows, and whirl-a-gigs are ideal for deflecting energy because the movement disperses and deflects negative energy. Mounted at the corners of the property, and in the usual line of sight or contact, they can help to dispel any bad wishes or harm intended for you. I used large, rainbow-colored ornaments that looked happy and cheery when they spun in the wind hoping that they would both dispel any bad energy directed toward me or my property, and inspire happy thoughts and actions. When I recognized that I was hoping my negative neighbor would be inspired to happiness, I realized that even my pain was being transformed.

To feel safe inside your home after a violation, use an herbal smudge or a candle to cleanse the area. Let all the negativity be carried away in the flame of the candle or dissipating smoke. From the door of your home, walk clockwise throughout the space, pausing by each door and window where you can wave extra smoke or draw a protective pentagram. Envision the space lightening and know you are making it safe. Use an incantation for conscious clearing and protection, repeating it often as you smudge. You can draft your own or borrow mine:

> *I clear this space*
> *and let it be known*
> *goodness and mercy*
> *bless this home.*

After clearing and cleansing your space, place at your doors, windows, and gates small protective objects imbued with the magic of protection. Charge them to only allow good people, energy, and ideas in and to deflect, neutralize, or dispel anything with negative intent.

Preparing Yourself for Peril and Bad People

Once you feel safe and have taken the steps to protect your home and property, you can start to think of ways to prepare yourself for meeting bad people or peril in other, more public places.

If you are going somewhere you think you might encounter negative people, prepare yourself beforehand. Use some simple practices for self-protection to cleanse negative energy off of you, and envelop yourself in protective energy. Also, take the time to preview what could happen. Decide in advance how you want to behave and how you want to be perceived—not just by the negative person, but by those who might witness the interaction. Remind yourself of your deepest magical beliefs and how you choose to be in the world. With this preparation, you have a greater opportunity to act rather than react.

Many times when I have encountered my attacker in public, I have opted for silence for a variety of reasons. Initially, it was because I feared if I opened my mouth, only bad things would come out. Later, I chose to simply walk by her as if she did not exist, because negativity was all I could perceive coming from her, and I chose to deflect it. If you don't engage with an angry person, then the anger rests with them.

Choosing to be silent in certain situations should not be confused with being forced into silence. Remember, if you haven't done anything bad, then you haven't done anything bad. And even if someone is trying to shame you, you can hold onto your deep knowledge of natural law and social norms. Good will come to good people, and good actions bring goodness back to you.

Remember: the world is not blind, and people remember. Rest assured that whether it is a few days or a few decades from now, you will be known by your reputation. So, even if you are feeling attacked, remember that many people in your community will see you for who you are in action and deed, just as they will clearly see your attacker. This is especially true in a small town or tight-knit community.

Seeing Through Magical Eyes

You will know that magic is at work in your life on a very deep level when you start to be surprised by the transformation of your own thoughts and feelings. For me, there came a time when I started to look across the street at my neighbor and not feel threatened, but feel saddened by how weak and fearful this woman seemed to be.

One day, I saw my neighbor and former friend hauling groceries out of her car, and I caught of glimpse of her energy. She appeared to be empty, flattened, and hollow. I felt a touch of pity for her. I knew then that the lawsuit wasn't something she had done to hurt me, but something she did to try to fill some void inside of her, perhaps with money and a sense of power. That I was the target of her actions was mere coincidence, and perhaps just a result of our proximity.

As I stood there watching her, I recognized the huge shift of perception within me. My attacker was no longer a strong, menacing force, but a weary soul to be quietly pitied. And at that moment, I no longer felt fear or hurt.

The Natural Order of the Magical Universe

There is a natural order to the universe and the cycles of nature govern everything, especially magical work. Whether it is in the physical, psychic, spiritual, or magical realm, what

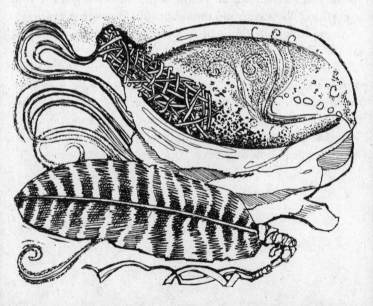

you plant grows and comes to fruition, and that is what you shall reap. After the harvest, what remains is plowed under to compost and regenerate.

Holding an awareness of the cycle of birth, life, death, and resurrection can help you keep moving through times of trouble, knowing they won't last forever. When you expect transformation, your eyes and soul seek it and are more attuned to it; you can call it to you and make space for it in your life. By choosing to flow with the cycle of nature, you may even hasten the passage of the times of trouble, by letting go of resistance and not welcoming further negativity or attack. When everything is said and done, the residue from the times of trouble may just compost and fertilize the soil and soul.

I know that the magical realm is not an instantaneous one. And the rule "What goes around comes around" doesn't promise instant payback or the return of energy in the same form. But natural law and experience have taught me that everything comes around energetically. Through my practice of using magic in times of trouble, I have come to understand how this can work in my life.

Three years have passed. My home is secure and my garden is abundant. I have a deep sense of the magic at work in my life and a stronger appreciation for times of trouble. My neighbor moved about five months ago after a long period of increasing alienation. I hope that she plants better things in her new garden, because everyone reaps what they sow!

Shamanic Magic:
Ancient Becomes New Again

by Abby Willowroot

Since the release of the first Harry Potter book in 1997, the young wizard has become a part of millions of readers' lives. And a big part of the ongoing Harry Potter craze is our need as a society to connect with the mystical and transcendent. As hectic and techno-filled as life has become, our deep need and longing for the wisdom and guidance of a shaman has not changed. We live in a modern world that has lost its way and its confidence in the powers of magic and of the universe.

From the earliest of times, the secrets, rituals, and practices of the shaman have been with us. Shamanism is woven tightly into the threads of the human tapestry. We have relied on the shaman to bring us into contact with worlds other than our own and with the spirit realms of the ancestors, both human and animal. Shamanic wisdom has always provided the context for our sacred experiences.

Many look to Harry Potter as we once looked to our shaman to restore our sense of wonder. Harry fits all the criteria: He communicates with animals, namely, a magical owl; he has been through a great personal trial and defeated death; he is on a kind of vision quest and fights dark forces; and he at times enters trancelike states and accesses Voldemort's evil mind and world. Harry is a shaman, and people all over the world, both young and old, understand this even if they do not describe it in shamanic terms.

We have lost our sense of wonder and have floundered spiritually, both personally and as a culture. Today, some of us look to conventional religions, others to celebrities, others to musicians, and others to athletes, always seeking to find

the shaman's secrets of power and insight. We end up feeling confused because we cannot recognize that the shaman is there, hiding right among us.

Modern shamanism *is* alive in our world, but many of us don't know where to find it. We look to shamanic ways of the distant past, but they cannot serve us as we need them to. Just as the ancient buffalo was a totem animal, a symbol for food, security, and power, today's equivalent beast of power is an 18-wheeler. Owl and raven carried messages; today, the cell phone and the Internet carry the messages. We are an urban people, and our cultural icons and power symbols reflect that fact.

Animals and their magical spirits have become scarce in our everyday lives, and the domesticated animals we know have forgotten much of their own ancient animal wisdom. The animal wisdom of the shaman comes through in powerful ways, amplified by a new knowing of hidden powers of the animal world. As we have become a global people, so the animals of all continents have become spirit totems for us, even as their numbers decrease, they teach us. We learn compassion from the elephant, keen observation from the hawk and eagle, quiet from the panda, endurance from the rat, patience from the penguin, stealth from the cheetah. Soon our modern shaman will weave all this information together, with spiritual and techno insights, visions and inspiration and present it to us in many ways.

Many of our friends, family, allies, and teachers have become virtual. They come to us as highly charged electronic impulses, instantly flashing across space and time. We have access to our ancestor's lives via genealogical resources, always present, saved digitally in archives. Yet, we may have trouble spiritually connecting with these ancestors. Our stories and songs are recorded in digital libraries. We can go online and find prayers, blessings, rituals, and others who seek what we seek. With a wealth of information available to us, we still crave guidance.

Where once we lived on the wild land, now we live in cities, towns, and even in the Internet. Where once we interacted with a handful of people, now we interact with thousands of people. Where once we lived into our thirties, now we live decades longer. Our families are smaller and our circle of friends is larger. We're aware of more spiritual facts and less experienced in spiritual ecstasy than were our ancestors. We are a people between worlds and elements; between the natural world and the electrical impulse world. We have experiences in both worlds and a true home in neither. We're not yet integrated, not yet fully immersed in the "Naturotronic" world that is coming into being.

Today's world is not necessarily better or worse than the old ways, just different. Thus, today's shamans will have different roles, less obvious than in the past. A healing, positive world is possible in our age, and it is the shaman who will guide our spirits as we make this happen.

Our spirits await the opportunity to embrace shamanic wisdom and the rituals and teachings we so deeply need and desperately seek. Many step up to fill this need, but seldom do they feed the hunger within us. Hollow rituals and manufactured wisdom are often offered in place of what is sought. Too often, workshops, classes, and retreats, devoid of much value, promise instant shamanic wisdom, yours for the price of admission.

We are learning to see, think, and hear digitally and express ourselves digitally and visually in a way that is powerful and magical. We are in a time as powerful and as revolutionary as the time when the wheel was invented. Everything is affected, and our world is in rapid flux. We cannot yet see all the wonders that will unfold before humanity, as a result of this changing time. We are the ancestors of the next great chapter of human history. Just as the history of culture is measured as pre-literate, pre-agriculture, pre-Renaissance, and pre–Industrial Revolution, it will also be measured as pre-digital. We are the first generation of that new age, the Naturotronic Age.

In this time of change, new shamans are emerging, and we are just now discovering who they are. Visionary artists, spiritual Webmasters, original code writers, research scientists, and original musicians are today's shamans; they are the keepers of secrets, the creators of transcendental experience through their disciplines. These are the walkers between worlds, communicators of hidden knowledge.

To see these modern shamans, we must take the time to stop moving, look around, slow down, and listen to the voice within us that seeks. The location of shamanic wisdom will become clear, allowing you to bring the needed rituals and renewals of body and spirit to you. In past generations, there was only one way of the shaman in a culture; today there are several. Because our society is so large and so complex; there are different types of shaman, each with unique gifts and insights.

• **Techno shamans** are skilled walkers of electrons and information packets. Their special gift is that of integration of diverse information and the sacred language of mathematics. They access animal energies through both spirit and scientific knowledge of the animal's makeup.

• **Cultural shamans** are skilled in the visual, auditory, and tactile arts of symbols and signs. Artistic communication across both time and space is their domain. These shamans access animal energies primarily through visual and sound paths into the animals' psyche.

• **Spirit shamans** are skilled in the integration of the heart, spirit, and mind. Their special talent is in the identification and manifestation of cohesive action through sacred balance. They access animal powers primarily through the spirit energy and heart essence of the animal.

• **Enviro shamans** are skilled in hearing the voices and rumblings of the lands and seas. Their special gifts include the ability to expand our conscious kinship to the eternal tides of Mother Nature. They access animal powers through the habitat of the creatures and the elemental forces that shape the animals' essential nature and habits.

Although these paths to the magic of animal powers are different, the essential truths of the animals' nature are expressed in each. All are necessary, all are uniquely powerful. And the function of the shaman is the same: to bridge the chasms between body, spirit, animals, humans, other worlds and our own. Shamans are still the most essential and powerful walkers between worlds. All four types of shamans have the power to access traditional shamanic skills, but they also have additional skills and insights in specific areas.

It is our generation's task to begin the process of translating the old ways into their more urban, contemporary equivalent. Harry Potter and his journey have become a valuable part of our urban psyche that helps to form our bridge to the future. Over the din of modern life, we can still hear the voice of the river, the howl of the wind, the rustle of the leaves, and the sounds of a summer meadow or desert. It is in these things that we will be able to gain access to the animal powers of these environments. Wind brings creatures of the air, the waters bring creatures of the depths and shore. Earth's land brings the creatures of the fields, forests, deserts, and mountains. In working through and with the environment to find shamans, we benefit ourselves and our world.

We are the ancestors of the future, and our wisdom, or lack thereof, will have a powerful impact for generations to come. We must be reminded to look to the world around us for today's shamans and listen for their spiritual guidance to connect us in an often disconnected world.

Magic Squares

by K. D. Spitzer

With the advent of computers, ancient magic squares went mainstream and became recreational mathematics. When that happened, they lost their magical connotation and a centuries-long esoteric link to spirituality and the supernatural.

Sacred grids are found all over the ancient world. They are comprised of boxes with an equal number of items going across and down. Some were the basis of land use, some for the layout of buildings, and others were used as magical amulets. The boxes were filled with a pattern of repeating letters. Committed to paper or clay, the magic was given physical form. By keeping this small piece of paper or clay tablet about his person, the wearer could protect himself, variously, from dangers when traveling, diseases contracted in crowded souks or marketplaces, or the long hand of the deity reaching out to torment or punish the unwary. Other squares feature boxes filled with numbers, each row or column adding up to the same number.

The Chinese claim that their magic squares are the most ancient, dating from 3000 BC. A link with the spiritual world, which is known to be a colony of female seers, is at the source of this legend.

It was a sacrifice to the river god that brought the river turtle, which had a magic square of three on its back. (Turtles hold a sacred place among the world's earliest peoples.) The Chinese people call it the Lo Shu square—*Lo Shu* means "river map." Here in the West, we call it the Saturn square (three squares across and three down).

Later, a holy and wise man, Fu Hsi, noticed the pattern on the shell of a tortoise; as legend tells it, it had interlocking squares amid concentric circles. As it happened, Chinese legends contend there were sixty-four squares (eight by eight) and thus the turtle inspired the sixty-four hexagrams of the I Ching. The connection between the first turtle to the second is lost in the mists of time.

The symbolism of the squares was quite stimulating. The sacred grid was used to lay out a town, temple, fairgrounds, and even game boards. We know the first turtle of note had a magic square of three on its back because a nearby temple was laid out in that pattern. The magic of this mathematical puzzle thus lent itself to the sacredness of the temple.

Land was also divided into a magic square of three. Perimeter boxes were allocated to farmers. The center box was communal land to be shared and worked by the surrounding eight peasants.

In another example of the prevalence of squares, the market fairs of Europe were laid out in grids—a microcosm of the kingdom at large. Merchants from the north were given the northern squares, vendors from eastern towns were given the eastern squares. The king and his councilors were given the center of the grid. Saints (or deities) were given specific squares to infuse with their special powers. The elements themselves had their own assigned places (fire, air, earth, and water—with perhaps wood, metal, or spirit also being considered elements at the time).

A magic grid is a vehicle for many spiritual mysteries. One grid incorporated the elements and was elevated to a high art form by tweaking a theory here and an interconnectedness there. Out spun Feng Shui, which is now used all over the world as a method of physical placement.

It is likely that these mathematical puzzles traveled to India and thence to Babylonia, Persia, and all of the ancient Mediterranean world. India's mathematicians developed the theories from China before their work inevitably found its way to the Middle East. The Babylonians and Sumerians were also sharp number theorists and applied much of what they knew to establishing the science of astrology with its basis in math.

They devised further numerological grids and understood their mathematical connection to the planets. The mysterious energies of the planets were then physically available to clients, not just floating around in the ethers, but manifested into something small enough to hold in the hand or wear around the neck.

Modern mathematicians deplore the whole ambiguity of legend and folklore, desiring evidence more factual for the origin of the squares. Some theorize that magic squares did not appear in the West until the twelfth century (the ninth century in Baghdad) when written documentation appears; actually, a very famous alphabetical magic square was found scratched twice on walls in Pompeii, covered with lava and ash in AD 79.

The Sator Square

One particular magic square survived quite famously and was a favorite among alchemists in the fifteenth and sixteenth centuries. The sator square is still studied today by language experts, code breakers, Latinists, and magicians.

S	A	T	O	R
A	R	E	P	O
T	E	N	E	T
O	P	E	R	A
R	O	T	A	S

There is a great cacophony of argument regarding the sator square. Some go to great lengths to reveal its Christian roots and show the connection to the prayerful pater noster. Others link it to Paganism, the worship of Mithras in particular, which was the religion of choice of the Roman legions. Many believe in its magical properties; in the eighteenth century, the Pennsylvania Dutch painted it on their barns to protect their cattle from Witchcraft.

Square of Three

4	9	2
3	5	7
8	1	6

In 1510, Cornelius Agrippa—astrologer, magician, writer, and occultist—reports that magic squares are assigned to the classical planets in perceived reverse order from Earth. Thus, the Magic Square of three is ruled by Saturn (the outmost planet that was known at the time) and is reputed to protect a mother from dangerous childbirth. The rows and columns add up to 15 and the square totals 45.

Square of Four

16	3	2	13
5	10	11	8
9	6	7	12
4	15	14	1

The magic square of four was made famous by Albrecht Durer, a Renaissance artist whose works show the link between math and art. His engraving, *Melancholia I,* is a self-portrait and full of alchemical symbols. The rows and columns total 34 (there are reputedly 86 ways to do it), and the entire grid adds up to 136. The bottom two center boxes reveal the date of the engraving. This square is ruled by Jupiter and will bring luck to business enterprise.

Square of Five

11	24	7	20	3
4	12	25	8	16
17	5	13	21	9
10	18	1	14	22
23	6	19	2	15

The five-by-five square is ruled by Mars; the rows and columns total 65, which reduces to 11, a mystical number. The grid totals 325, and you can wear it to protect against aggression or bolster your courage.

Square of Six

6	32	3	34	35	1
7	11	27	28	8	30
19	14	16	15	23	24
18	20	22	21	17	13
25	29	10	9	26	12
36	5	33	4	2	31

Six-by-six grids take us into the controversial realm of the triple sixes. Columns and rows add up to 111, and the entire grid totals 666. In Western Paganism and astrology, six is the ancient, powerful number of the Sun. For the modern world, 666 is the feared "Number of the Beast" or Satan. The Sumerians had 36 lesser gods and one supreme god. To protect themselves from their power, the mathematician/priests created this grid to wear as an amulet, adding 1 + 2 + 3 through 36 to add up to 666. The six-by-six grid, pecked into a clay tablet, could be worn around the neck.

Square of Seven

22	47	16	41	19	35	4
5	23	48	17	42	11	29
30	6	24	49	18	36	12
13	31	7	25	43	19	37
38	14	32	1	26	44	20
21	39	8	33	2	27	45
46	15	40	9	34	3	28

Seven by seven belongs to Venus, bringing her influence to all matters of love and cold, hard cash. The column/rows add to 175 and the grid to 1,225.

Square of Eight

8	58	59	5	4	62	63	1
49	15	14	52	53	11	10	56
41	23	22	44	48	19	18	45
32	34	35	29	25	38	39	28
40	26	27	37	36	30	31	33
17	47	46	20	21	43	42	24
9	55	54	12	13	51	50	16
64	2	3	61	60	6	7	57

This square belongs to Mercury; column and rows total 260 and the grid totals 2,080. This evolved as a game board for checkers and chess.

Square of Nine

37	78	29	70	21	62	13	54	5
6	38	79	30	71	22	63	14	46
47	7	39	80	31	72	23	55	15
16	48	8	40	81	32	64	24	56
57	17	49	9	41	73	33	65	25
26	58	18	50	1	42	74	34	66
67	27	59	10	51	2	43	75	35
36	68	19	60	11	52	3	44	76
77	28	69	20	61	12	53	4	45

The last magic square is nine by nine, and it is ruled by the Moon. Columns and rows total 369 and the entire grid adds up to 3,321. Mathematicians and magicians love this important lunar grid as it is a square of a square ($3 \times 3 \times 3 \times 3$).

How to Create
Your Own Magic Square

It's really quite simple to create a magic square. Looking at the Saturn square, we see nine empty boxes arranged in three rows and three columns. Starting with the middle box in the top row, place the number 1. We can move consecutively through the other eight numbers. Move diagonally up and to the right when placing the next number. Think of the grid as being wraparound or continuous and place the number 2 in the bottom row on the right; then continue by moving up and to the right again. If this move is not possible (when you try to place the number 4, for instance), then you need to move down one square from the previous number you placed (the 3), place the next number, and begin moving up and to the right again. You will have to use the alternate down movement again when placing the number 7. Keep placing the digits until you have completed your own Saturn square.

8	1	6
3	5	7
4	9	2

Magic squares can be worn or placed on the altar to lend their powerful and ancient energy to your magic.

Kali: Mother, Warrior, and Cosmic Consciousness

by Abel R. Gomez

Kali is perhaps one of the most demonized and misunderstood goddess in Western spirituality. Originally from the tribal cultures of India, her infamous appearance has made her the center of a demonic cult in *Indiana Jones and the Temple of Doom* and landed her as a goddess to be feared or avoided. Kali, meaning "black" or "time" has been revered as a loving goddess by Hindus for thousands of years. In the West, she has been either feared or "watered down" by New Age concepts of goddess worship. Her mysterious origins, frightening iconography, and untamed persona have drawn many modern Witches to study and experience her transcendent and healing mysteries.

Like most Hindu divinities, there are a number of myths recounting the birth of Kali. In one popular myth, Kali was born from the third eye of the goddess Durga. The gods and their assistants had tried to defeat the demon Raktabija, but to no avail. They decided to join forces and combined into an exploding star to create the fierce warrior goddess Durga. But the demon was also fierce and, according to myth, a thousand new demons were created with every drop of its blood that touched the floor. Durga could not defeat the demon, and the goddess Kali was born out of her frustration and anguish.

When Kali appeared, she brought with her a ferocity unlike any other. She savagely slew the demon and drank every drop of his blood in order to defeat him. According to myth, her lust for blood became so intense that she would have destroyed the entire universe had it not been for her lover, Shiva, laid before her. This pose, known as Daks(h)inakali, typically depicted Kali dancing on Shiva, and it is one of the most common and popular icons of the goddess Kali.

In Hindu art, Kali is typically portrayed as an Indian woman with black skin and four arms. In one hand, she holds the head of a demon she killed; she holds a sword in another; and she beckons worshipers to her with her other two arms. Kali wears a necklace of human skulls and two dead men as earrings. Unlike most Hindu deities, she is completely nude except for a girdle made from the arms of dead men.

Though her appearances may be frightening to most in the West, there are significant reasons for such a manifestation. Like other Hindu deities, Kali's multilayered image is highly symbolic.

Kali's nudity symbolizes her open-minded and her all-embracing nature. Her skin is black, the color from which all other colors are formed and into which all colors are absorbed. Kali's hue represents lack of color, what Hindus would call *Nirguna*, or pure Shakti, the transcendent force of the universe. She is the Dark Goddess, the void from which all beings are born and to whom all must return.

Though Eastern culture tends to be conservative about nudity, there is a deep tolerance for spiritual antinomianism, consciously engaging in taboo behavior for spiritual attainment. Many devotees of Shiva and Kali in India and South Asia wear little clothing, particularly devotees to Shiva and Kali as a divine couple. In her nakedness, Kali is free from all illusions, from all attachments to this world. On a deeper level, Kali's nudity represents a shift away from materialism toward the concept of Cosmic Consciousness and greater self-realization. She is free from the mundane world to experience the rapture and fullness of existence.

In Hindu Shaktism, or Goddess worship, Kali is worshipped both as an aspect of the Goddess and the Supreme Goddess, from which all goddesses originate, much like Dione Fortune's idea, "All Gods are One God, All Goddesses are One Goddess." Kali is said to be a fire that burns away all untruths. She is fully breasted as a symbol of her role as a mother goddess and the endless creation she initiates. Kali's necklace of fifty human heads symbolizes the fifty letters of the Sanskrit language and her role as the patron of mantras and worshipful chanting. She wears a girdle of human hands

representing the cycles of karma that reside within her and her aspect as the Primordial Goddess in whom we live, move, and have our being.

There are a number of diverse spiritual traditions that honor Kali. In addition to the Goddess worship of Shaktism, there are traditions of Hindu Tantra, or sexual mysticism, that honor Kali as Adi-shakti, or ultimate energy, the companion to the ultimate reality of Shiva. Companionship is demonstrated in the highly sexualized images of Kali and Shiva that convey the union of energy and reality. Other groups, particularly devotees in Tamil, may cross-dress in order to more easily allow Kali to possess them to create ecstatic experiences. Perhaps the path most similar to Western Paganism is Shakti Bhakti, or "Goddess Devotion," for which worshippers offer flowers, water, and light to the benign manifestations of the Goddess.

Witches and Neopagans have their own ways of worshiping Kali, which is, at times, strikingly different than the Hindu practices. According to some traditions, it is customary to offer blood sacrifices during Kali worship, a practice many modern Pagans would shun even though it has historical and spiritual significance. Interestingly, scholarly researchers have compared Wiccan esbat rituals with the highly mystical Tantric Chakra-Puja rites in which participants engage in ritual sexual intercourse, similar to the Great Rite.

There is still much to be learned from her rituals and myths, some of which have yet to be translated or discovered. As with most Pagan traditions, there are those who insist on relying on uncovered mythology, while others rely more on personal experience. Perhaps it is even wiser still to employ both ideologies. Learn Kali's myths and rituals and let her come alive in whatever manner feels most natural to you.

When we combine ancient teachings and Western goddess spirituality, we see that Kali is not a terrifying satanic monster, but a Dark Mother who insists that we face the shadowy aspects of nature. She is the slayer of inner demons—our thoughts, worries, and inhibitions that restrict us from our highest potential. Though she can be harsh, she is a loving mother, with her arms outstretched, encompassing the entire universe. When we chant her mantra, "Om Krim Kalyai Namah," we are released from the ignorance of the seemingly mundane world into the essence of Kali, the ultimate reality of existence.

Water Magic

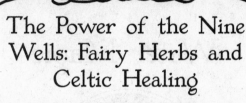

The Power of the Nine Wells: Fairy Herbs and Celtic Healing

by Sharynne MacLeod NicMhacha

Throughout the Celtic world, ancient folk healing practices survived well into the twentieth century and were widely practiced in the various Celtic lands. (The Celtic "nations" include Brittany, Cornwall, Galicia, Ireland, Isle of Man, Scotland, and Wales.) Some of these healing rites were associated with elements of the natural world, including natural plants and herbs, holy water, and sacred stones. In addition to the use of herbal lore and preparations, many healing ceremonies included the use of charms, spells, incantations, and other ritualistic practices.

In earliest times, the Druids in Gaul—the ancient name for a large area in Western Europe—were said to have gathered mistletoe in a solemn ceremony, for this plant was known as "All-Heal" in the ancient Gaulish language. Other ancient accounts, which are almost two thousand years old, tell how the Gauls ritually gathered other healing plants as well. Club moss (or *Selago*) was gathered by a person clad in white with their bare feet washed clean. An offering of bread and wine was made before gathering the

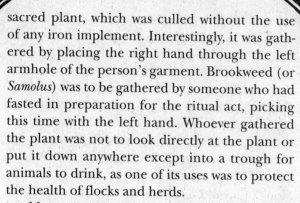

sacred plant, which was culled without the use of any iron implement. Interestingly, it was gathered by placing the right hand through the left armhole of the person's garment. Brookweed (or *Samolus*) was to be gathered by someone who had fasted in preparation for the ritual act, picking this time with the left hand. Whoever gathered the plant was not to look directly at the plant or put it down anywhere except into a trough for animals to drink, as one of its uses was to protect the health of flocks and herds.

Many centuries later in Gaelic Scotland, healing plants were also gathered according to certain magical principles. A number of plants were said to be gathered with a specific hand (including yarrow and ivy), and one Scottish charm outlining the correct procedure for gathering St. John's wort stated that it should be plucked with the right hand but preserved with the left. In addition, the Druids of Gaul stated that club moss warded off all harm from the person who possessed it and that it was also good for eye troubles. This same belief still existed in early-twentieth-century Scotland, where the plant was used to treat eye disease and as a powerful protecting plant.

Other healing plants that were used in Celtic healing magic in Scotland included figwort, bog violet, pearlwort, catkins, reeds, shamrocks (*seamrag*), bog myrtle, primrose and juniper. In Ireland, nettles, rowan, vervain, yarrow, and mugwort were widely gathered for healing purposes. Irish folk healers were said to use chamomile, tansy, loosestrife, lichen, dandelion, plantain, cleavers, mullein, ivy, hazel, and apple in their highly specialized herbal healing magic. Healing herbs were sometimes burned in a flame or used in conjunction with sacred water. Often, special charms or spells were recited while using these healing plants. Here are some excerpts from several versions of an old Scottish healing charm that was recited when gathering yarrow:

I will cull the fair yarrow
So that my hand will be more brave
So that my foot will be more swift
And my speech as the beams of the sun

May I be an island in the ocean
May I be a hill on the shore
May I be a star in the waning moon

May I be a rock in the sea
May I be a staff to the weak
I can wound, but none can wound me.

In some of these Celtic healing charms, mythological elements or characters are mentioned. For example, in one Scottish charm recited when gathering figwort, the person mentions the "ninth wave," a Celtic mythological element that refers to the magical boundary between this world and the otherworld.

> *I will gather the figwort*
> *Of a thousand blessings*
> *Of a thousand virtues*
>
> *The nine joys*
> *Came with the nine waves*
> *To gather the figwort . . .*

Pagan deities are mentioned in certain healing charms and spells, even into the Christian era. More than one thousand years ago, well after the introduction of the new religion, ancient texts recorded healing charms and incantations in Ireland that still invoked the physician god Dian

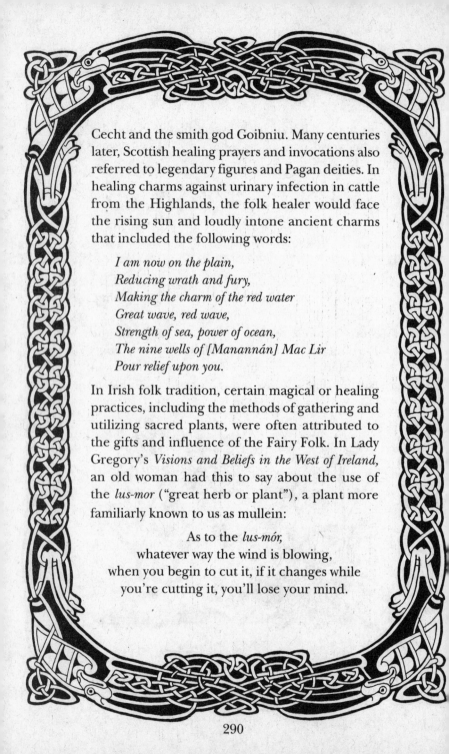

Cecht and the smith god Goibniu. Many centuries later, Scottish healing prayers and invocations also referred to legendary figures and Pagan deities. In healing charms against urinary infection in cattle from the Highlands, the folk healer would face the rising sun and loudly intone ancient charms that included the following words:

> *I am now on the plain,*
> *Reducing wrath and fury,*
> *Making the charm of the red water*
> *Great wave, red wave,*
> *Strength of sea, power of ocean,*
> *The nine wells of [Manannán] Mac Lir*
> *Pour relief upon you.*

In Irish folk tradition, certain magical or healing practices, including the methods of gathering and utilizing sacred plants, were often attributed to the gifts and influence of the Fairy Folk. In Lady Gregory's *Visions and Beliefs in the West of Ireland*, an old woman had this to say about the use of the *lus-mor* ("great herb or plant"), a plant more familiarly known to us as mullein:

> As to the *lus-mór*,
> whatever way the wind is blowing,
> when you begin to cut it, if it changes while
> you're cutting it, you'll lose your mind.

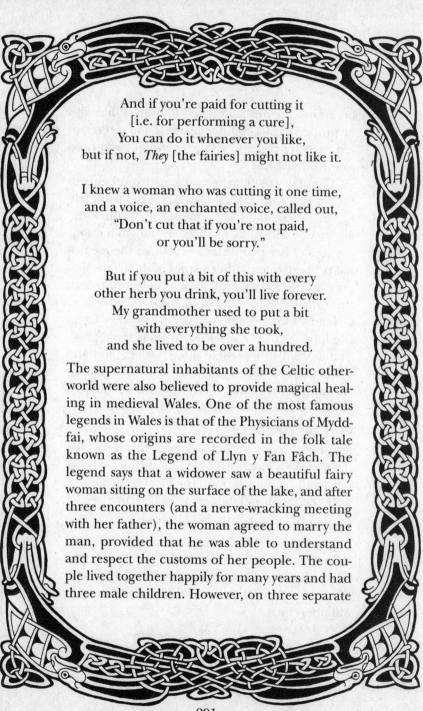

And if you're paid for cutting it
[i.e. for performing a cure],
You can do it whenever you like,
but if not, *They* [the fairies] might not like it.

I knew a woman who was cutting it one time,
and a voice, an enchanted voice, called out,
"Don't cut that if you're not paid,
or you'll be sorry."

But if you put a bit of this with every
other herb you drink, you'll live forever.
My grandmother used to put a bit
with everything she took,
and she lived to be over a hundred.

The supernatural inhabitants of the Celtic other-world were also believed to provide magical healing in medieval Wales. One of the most famous legends in Wales is that of the Physicians of Myddfai, whose origins are recorded in the folk tale known as the Legend of Llyn y Fan Fâch. The legend says that a widower saw a beautiful fairy woman sitting on the surface of the lake, and after three encounters (and a nerve-wracking meeting with her father), the woman agreed to marry the man, provided that he was able to understand and respect the customs of her people. The couple lived together happily for many years and had three male children. However, on three separate occasions, the husband failed to fully understand or properly react to his wife's reaction to certain life experiences, and so she eventually returned to the otherworld.

The fairy woman reappeared from beneath the waters of the lake and spoke to her sons, telling them that she was bestowing upon them the knowledge and gift of healing. She taught her sons the lore of her people and explained the medicinal properties and other virtues of the plants that grew in their area, and, as she had prophesied, the sons became well-known healers. The fairy woman's sons became physicians to Rhys Gryg, the lord of a local castle, and their fame grew. The descendants of these three healers (and ultimately, of the fairy woman of Llyn y Fan Fâch), are still known in Wales. Here are some examples of their magic-derived healing charms and lore:

Cure for Headache

For those frequently afflicted with headaches, let them make a lotion from vervain, betony, chamomile, and red fennel; wash the head three times a week therewith, and the person will be cured.

Charm for Toothache

Engrave the following words on an iron nail: *Agla, Sabaoth, Athanatos*, and put the nail under the affected tooth. Then, drive the nail into an oak tree, and while it remains there, the toothache will not return.

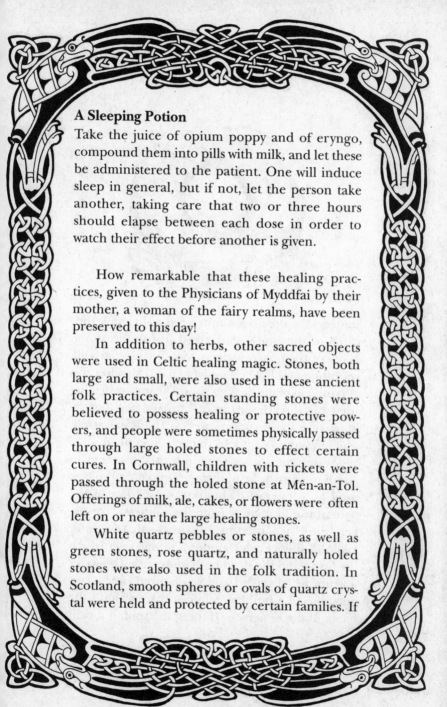

A Sleeping Potion

Take the juice of opium poppy and of eryngo, compound them into pills with milk, and let these be administered to the patient. One will induce sleep in general, but if not, let the person take another, taking care that two or three hours should elapse between each dose in order to watch their effect before another is given.

How remarkable that these healing practices, given to the Physicians of Myddfai by their mother, a woman of the fairy realms, have been preserved to this day!

In addition to herbs, other sacred objects were used in Celtic healing magic. Stones, both large and small, were also used in these ancient folk practices. Certain standing stones were believed to possess healing or protective powers, and people were sometimes physically passed through large holed stones to effect certain cures. In Cornwall, children with rickets were passed through the holed stone at Mên-an-Tol. Offerings of milk, ale, cakes, or flowers were often left on or near the large healing stones.

White quartz pebbles or stones, as well as green stones, rose quartz, and naturally holed stones were also used in the folk tradition. In Scotland, smooth spheres or ovals of quartz crystal were held and protected by certain families. If

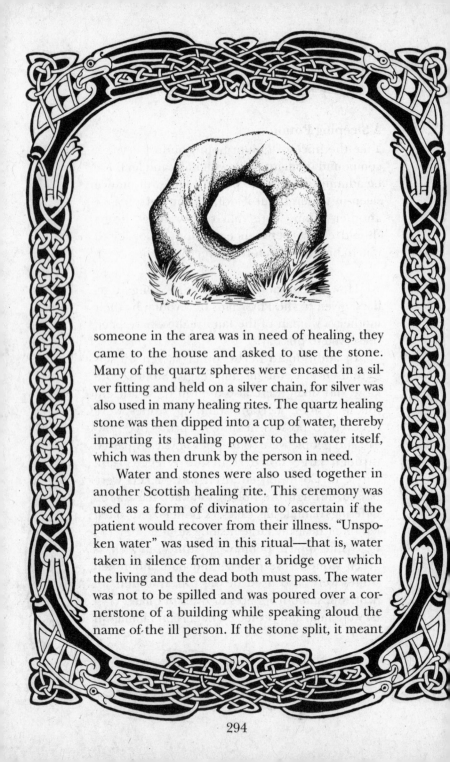

someone in the area was in need of healing, they came to the house and asked to use the stone. Many of the quartz spheres were encased in a silver fitting and held on a silver chain, for silver was also used in many healing rites. The quartz healing stone was then dipped into a cup of water, thereby imparting its healing power to the water itself, which was then drunk by the person in need.

Water and stones were also used together in another Scottish healing rite. This ceremony was used as a form of divination to ascertain if the patient would recover from their illness. "Unspoken water" was used in this ritual—that is, water taken in silence from under a bridge over which the living and the dead both must pass. The water was not to be spilled and was poured over a cornerstone of a building while speaking aloud the name of the ill person. If the stone split, it meant

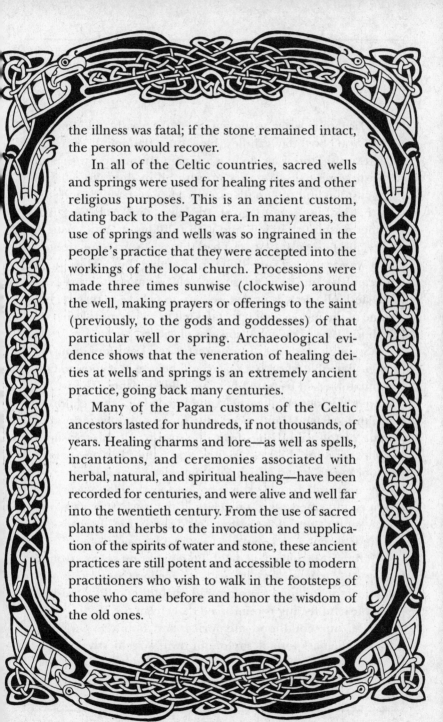

the illness was fatal; if the stone remained intact, the person would recover.

In all of the Celtic countries, sacred wells and springs were used for healing rites and other religious purposes. This is an ancient custom, dating back to the Pagan era. In many areas, the use of springs and wells was so ingrained in the people's practice that they were accepted into the workings of the local church. Processions were made three times sunwise (clockwise) around the well, making prayers or offerings to the saint (previously, to the gods and goddesses) of that particular well or spring. Archaeological evidence shows that the veneration of healing deities at wells and springs is an extremely ancient practice, going back many centuries.

Many of the Pagan customs of the Celtic ancestors lasted for hundreds, if not thousands, of years. Healing charms and lore—as well as spells, incantations, and ceremonies associated with herbal, natural, and spiritual healing—have been recorded for centuries, and were alive and well far into the twentieth century. From the use of sacred plants and herbs to the invocation and supplication of the spirits of water and stone, these ancient practices are still potent and accessible to modern practitioners who wish to walk in the footsteps of those who came before and honor the wisdom of the old ones.

Wild Wishes

by Gail Wood

Wish upon a star, wishing wells, make a wish and blow out your birthday candles, blow on a dandelion puff and make a wish, throw a coin in a fountain and make a wish, and a wish come true. We grew up with all of these are charming customs and still do them, even when our adult minds tell us that wishing is not logical. We have come to believe that wishes, wishful thinking, and wish fulfillment are a waste of time and energy at best, and bad things at worst. We are told that we cannot get something for nothing, but wishes mean we can have our heart's desire merely by stating it. Every fairy tale and folktale tells us that we have to believe to receive, but some of the more cautionary tales tell us to be careful what we wish for. We've become suspicious of wishes.

Stating our desires is a powerful act. I am in a group of magical people who work magic and believe in its power. Our facilitator asked us to tell her our wildest wishes. The wishes flowed in, eloquent, heartfelt, and needed. Jobs for children, health for friends, and success for spouses and partners were some of the wild wishes from the group. All the treasured wishes were for children, friends, and family; not one person in our group stated a wish for themselves. Was it because we were nearly all women? Was it because we do a lot of work for others and often place ourselves last? Or was it because we truly weren't sure these wishes would come true? Perhaps our attitude is that *wishes come true for others, but not for me.*

Often, our beliefs and subsequent actions come from a place of scarcity, and we live with the feeling that there is only so much of anything to go around, including fulfilled wishes. That fearful feeling is reinforced daily from the media, other people, our childhood memories, and family experience. Rather than ask for a desire of our own, we selflessly and generously ask for what our loved ones want and need. Because it is scarce, we make ourselves the last to reap the bounty. Then, thinking nothing will be left, we leave our wishes unspoken. When we wish, we are beginning to realize we want change; and often the first thing we have to change is our ability to trust that we live in an abundant and loving universe. We need to trust and believe that the flow of change, benefit, and wishes comes from an endlessly deep, rich well.

Another reason we may be reluctant to state our wishes is because, on some deep level, we don't believe we are worthy of this abundance. Again, this is based on a sense of scarcity. This time, we wonder if forgiveness and worth are scarce, and, if it is, then we definitely do not deserve what is meagerly portioned out. Most of us are our own harshest judges and constantly deem ourselves undeserving. We look at our past transgressions and current faults and judge ourselves to be unworthy of change, abundance, and the forgiveness that brings freedom.

Forgiveness is an incredible emotional issue, and it can be one of the biggest obstacles to our sense of worthiness for wish fulfillment. How can I forgive people who have done heinous things to me and to others? Does forgiving mean forgetting? Living in an unforgiving state is an emotionally charged one that creates a strong, angry, hurtful connection to the other person, even when that "other" person is yourself. That connection remains alive and full of negative energy that damages you. As long as that connection sparks with this negative energy, healing is postponed or incomplete. Moreover, you remain tied to the other person in a way that causes both of you damage. To stop the energy flow and disconnect the exchange of negativity, you must forgive. Once that energy flow ceases, the healing energy begins its work. Forgiveness is really more about you than it is about the other person.

Often, the first place to seek forgiveness is with your own true self. Your past mistakes, vulnerabilities, and situations will often continue to haunt you until you really forgive yourself for them. When you do, you free yourself from those bindings that held you away from perceiving and receiving the abundance of the universe.

Forgiving others has a similar effect. You can forgive others in a variety of ways. By saying "I forgive you" to the person either in this world or through a meditation to their higher selves is a simple and effective way to move your heart to forgiveness. If the forgiveness is difficult, you can ask your gods to help you with it by saying words to the effect of, "Dear Goddess, I wish to forgive X for what was done to me. It is my fear that I will not be able to do it. Please help me forgive X. I forgive X. Blessed Be." Then, thank your gods and let them assist you.

Forgiving does not mean you have to forget what was done to you or that you put yourself into similar situations that could cause you harm. That would not be smart—and the magical life is all about being smart! The forgetting part of "forgive and forget" is that you disconnect from that negatively charged energy. The charge no longer has any power, including power over your emotions and reactions. Once that charge is gone, you can take back that power and use it to heal and to change . . . and so to wish.

When you are whole and energized, you are able to tap into the ecstatic energy of the living, loving, breathing universe. Being able to move in that ecstatic flow of energy is part of our birthright as spiritual beings. Unfettered by the negative power of ongoing and unforgiving anger, we can tap into our wild, wonderful center.

Then we begin to see our own worth and, beyond ourselves, into the abundance of the universe. We are liberated from our miserly fear of wishing, and we are free to live our lives from a place where there is no scarcity. No longer are we tight-fisted with our desires and our dreams. Now we can dance with the universe and say honestly and emphatically, "I deserve this." Once we realize that we are valuable, we then realize that we have the power and the magic to make our wishes come true.

Wishing is akin to living in the moment. It frees us from brooding and worrying about what comes next. Wishing allows the Goddess to give us what we want and what we deserve; in wishing, we live in the realization that what we deserve is joy. It's fun, it's happy, it's the beauty of wishes come true. It's the wonder of getting the larger half of the wishbone and blowing out all our birthday candles. Wishing is recapturing our faith that magic can and will happen just for us. It is grace, a gift from our gods because they love us. I believe that the Goddess and the God very much want love and joy for us; they enjoy the happy, fun, loving energy we create when we fully feel the marvel of wishes come true.

Let all wishes out and free!
Goddess greets them with great glee.

Wishing is not a passive activity. It is something active and magical in our lives. We fully participate in the process of directing energy toward our desires when we wish. To achieve active and successful wishing, we just need to keep a few fundamental things in mind:

• Speak your wish out loud in strong, positive, and present-tense terms.

• Have a positive attitude of successful wishing. When we wish, the universe starts sending its energy toward our desire. If we follow up with negative statements, the universe will draw back, assuming that we didn't really mean it. Allow the universe to work.

• Be willing to accept the gift of the wish. If the opportunity you wish for comes your way, embrace and accept that it is yours and you were meant to accept it with joy.

• Be attentive for signs that your wish is being fulfilled, and then be alert for opportunities to balance and give back. Perhaps when you wish for the perfect puppy and you find each other, you donate a bag of dog food to the local animal shelter.

• Express thankfulness. Be grateful for your wish come true and express it, say it out loud.

We can add wishing to our spiritual practice through rituals and spells. Wishing rituals are wonderful for springtime, as well as waxing and Full Moon rituals. The core of the working is told below and you can set it into a spell or the ritual framework of your spiritual path. It can be a solitary ritual or used for group work. This is a great ritual to do outdoors or indoors. Since fire is involved, be sure to take appropriate safety precautions.

Wild Wishes Magical Working

Gather together writing utensils and easily burned small bits of paper. You can use regular ink and paper or specially prepared inks and parchment. You will also need a fireproof bowl or pot, lighter or matches, and kindling, if appropriate.

Take some time to create a sacred space. Burn some incense, make sure that the space is clean, and clear enough room for burning paper and for dancing, either around the center or in place. Place your burning bowl and accoutrements in the center of the circle. When your space is properly cleansed and consecrated, spend some time with each other. Talk, sing, and listen. Let go of expectations and connect with the grounding energy of Mother Earth. Then begin to chant and meld your energies together. Separate yourself from the everyday world and move between the worlds. Create the ritual framework that you desire, calling in the energies of the sacred world and the Goddess and the God. Make yourself comfortable for a meditation.

Take a deep, cleansing breath and let go of expectations. Breathe in peace and serenity and keep breathing deeply. You are standing at night in your favorite outdoor place, filled with the wonder and joy of that space. The sky is full of stars and you feel a deep intimate connection to the whole universe. There is no separation. The stars twinkle, dance, and twirl as you watch the sky. You feel cradled in Earth and surrounded by love. As you watch the stars, you see them begin to shoot across the sky. One or two or more capture your attention, and you make a wish. Each wishing star moves past you and bursts into a spectacular sight of color and light. The stars keep moving until you are done wishing. Take a deep breath and reconnect with your special place. Take another deep breath and come back to your sacred circle. Open your eyes, remembering your starry wishes.

Write your wishes down on the pieces of paper, one per piece. When everyone is finished, stand in the center of the circle surrounding the burning bowl. Start circling the bowl, toning and chanting. Put your wish in the bowl, ending with an emphatic statement, such as "I wish for a sweet-tempered puppy, BLESSED BE!" Have everyone echo your "BLESSED BE." Continue until all the wishes are said and acclaimed. Then light fire to the papers and, as the fire burns all the way down, raise a cone of power with this chant.

Blessed Goddess, hear my call!
Hear my wishes, wild and free.
Wishes for the good of all
Grant these wishes three times three.

After the cone of power is raised, ground the excess energy into Earth for healing and gratitude. Finish your ritual and close the sacred space. Take the ashes from the burnt wishes and bury them in the ground. If you don't live in a place where you can dig, you can place the ashes in a planter and cover it with soil. As you cover the ashes, say, "Thank you for the work that's done, Magic born with harm to none."

Go joyfully into your life expecting all your wishes to come true. May you always blow out all the candles on your cake with a wish. Blessed Be!

Cauldrons: Myth and Magic

by Lily Gardner

Double, double, toil and trouble;
Fire burn, and cauldron bubble.
Fillet of a fenny snake,
In the cauldron boil and bake;
Eye of newt and toe of frog,
Wool of bat and tongue of dog,
Adder's fork and blindworm's sting,
Lizard's leg and howlet's wing;
For a charm of pow'rful trouble
Like a hell-broth boil and bubble.

     –William Shakespeare, *Macbeth*, Act 4, Scene 1

The three Witches in Shakespeare's *Macbeth* have stirred Western imagination for four hundred years, placing the cauldron next to the broom as the tool most associated with Witchcraft. Inside the theater, actors will not refer to *Macbeth* by name for fear of injury to themselves or bad luck for the production. The reason behind the superstition is that Shakespeare is said to have used a real spell in his play.

I know what you're thinking: Shakespeare's depiction of the Weird Sisters is just the kind of demonization of Witches that contributed to the persecution of Pagans for centuries. But wait—Shakespeare, that great cribber of myth and legend, got a few things right. The Weird Sisters are a malevolent version of the Scandinavian Norns, also known as the Wyrd, the goddesses of destiny. At the base of the Tree of Life, they peered into a great cauldron and witnessed unmanifest potential, everything in our world that *could* be. They also witnessed that which can be surmised. In the same way a meteorologist studies weather patterns to make a forecast given the present indications, the Norns witnessed what *should* be. Finally, the Norns divined that which is at the present moment coming into being, everything that *is*. All possibilities that failed to come into being fell back into the cauldron to become unmanifest potential again. Unlike the Greek Moerae, who spun and apportioned the linear thread of fate for both humans and gods, the Norns and their cauldron gave us the great mystery of cyclic change.

So what about the eye of newt and toe of frog? Shakespeare's inspiration most likely came from the Medea story. Medea, a priestess of Hecate, was well acquainted with the cauldron arts. When her husband, Jason, begged her to restore youth to his aged father, she agreed to brew a spell that would cheat the Fates. She began by offering prayers and sacrifices to Hecate and Hades, then brewed within her cauldron magic herbs and seeds, sand from the seashore, hoarfrost gathered by moonlight, the heads of a screech owl and a crow, the entrails of a wolf, the liver of stags, and fragments of a tortoise shell. Where the cauldron boiled over, fresh new grass sprung up. The olive branch with which she stirred her magical brew leafed out and bore fruit. When the spell was completed, Medea cut the old man's throat and let out all his blood. Into his mouth, she poured her libation. The man's thin gray locks turned thick and black, his emaciated limbs resumed the muscle of his youth and he sprang to his feet, his vigor restored.

It goes without saying that modern Witches no longer use animal parts in their spellwork, but the system of casting spells is the same. Just as Medea used the parts of animals known for their virility or longevity, so we combine the magical properties of herb, crystal, and symbol to aid us with our magic work.

Shakespeare's Weird Sisters illustrate both properties of the cauldron: as a vessel for scrying or brewing and as a symbol whose shape suggests the Goddess's womb where life or possibility is born, matures, sickens, and then returns to be reborn again.

To gain a deeper understanding of the cauldron's use, we return to other ancient myths and the possible rituals they suggest to the modern Witch.

The Cauldron of Siris: Scrying

The cauldron has been associated with the goddesses of fate since the Bronze Age. One of these early myths comes from the Babylonians and their goddess, Siris, mother of the stars. This goddess of fate was said to have a cauldron named "Abyss." Made of lapis lazuli, the cauldron appeared as a vast blue sky sprinkled with stars. There seems an obvious connection between fate and the stars in her myth.

Your cauldron can become a valuable scrying tool as well. Fill the cauldron with fresh water and set it under the Full Moon. Once your water has been infused with moonlight,

it's ready to use. Some Witches place a crystal in the bottom of their cauldron. You might want to use a piece of lapis to work with. Lapis is said to subjugate the conscious mind to the psychic mind.

Prepare a surface with a black cloth and a new candle that is black, silver, or blue in color. The room in which you work must be completely quiet and dark. Cast your circle and light the candle. Sitting before the cauldron, allow the cares of the day to drop from you. When you feel you're ready, peer within the cauldron with an unfocused gaze. It will take a certain amount of time and patience for images or feelings to occur to you. As they do, you may wish to stay in this meditative state and ponder the meaning they have for you. Alternatively, you may wish to write about your impressions and their deeper meaning in your Book of Shadows.

Another means of scrying uses the energies of air. This is especially useful if your questions have to do with thoughts, communication, or inspiration—all provinces of the air element. Place a chunk of dry ice in a small bowl that fits inside your cauldron. The mists rising from the cauldron provides excellent images for scrying. As you open your magic circle, don't forget to thank Siris for your new insights.

The Cauldron of Cerridwen: Transformation and Wisdom

Cerridwen, the Welsh muse and goddess of transformation, had a son who was the ugliest boy in the world. Wishing to give the child some advantage, she obtained a spell that would make her son the wisest of all beings. The magician's spell required gathering a great quantity of herbs and magical ingredients, harvested at the most auspicious times according to their planetary properties. The spell was to be brewed in an enormous cauldron for a year and a day. While Cerridwen roamed the countryside gathering her ingredients, she charged her servant boy, Gwion, to stir the great cauldron.

One day as Gwion stood over the cauldron, three burning drops of the brew flew out of the cauldron and fell on his finger. He thrust the burnt finger in his mouth and immediately knew the thoughts of gods and man. In that moment, he realized that Cerridwen would murder him when she discovered that he'd inadvertently partaken of the mixture. Gwion fled and Cerridwen flew after him.

He transformed himself into a hare, she into a greyhound. He plunged into the river, changing into a fish; she changed herself into an otter. Gwion flew up in the air as a bird; she pursued him in the shape of a hawk. He plunged to the ground, shape-shifting into a grain of wheat; she transformed into a black hen and swallowed him.

Nine months later, Cerridwen gave birth to Gwion. At the sight of her beautiful baby, she no longer had the heart to destroy him, so she placed him in a leather bag and floated him out to sea. The baby Gwion was rescued some days later by a prince, who named the child Taliesen, meaning "fine value." Taliesen grew up to become the first bard of Ireland, famous for his wit and wisdom.

It is worth noting that Cerridwen's son, for whom the original spell was intended, took no part in the spell making. It was Cerridwen's own dedication to the spell that was important. An essential ingredient in all magic and endeavor is the work required to bring a goal from wishing to actualization. Thought and effort can truly bring about transformation.

Begin with a clear vision of what you seek to change in your life. Place small quantities of sage, vervain, mistletoe berries, sunflower, balm of gilead, caraway, eyebright, bodhi, and allspice in a jar and cover with a highly concentrated alcohol (I use Everclear, a 190-proof alcohol). Stir this mixture with your athame in a deosil (clockwise) motion. Cover the jar and place in a window for nine days. On the evening of the ninth day, pour the brew into your cauldron. With your intention held in mind and heart, light your magical brew.

Please use great caution during this particular spell, as this alcoholic mixture is highly flammable! Make certain that your cauldron is placed on a heat-proof surface.

I would also recommend that you not stand directly over your cauldron where you might breathe in the mixture's fumes, as some of these herbs can be toxic.

To invoke Cerridwen, recite these words from the Welsh poet Taliesin:

My verses from within the cauldron uttered,
By breath of maidens ninefold they were kindled.
I am a harmonious one; I am a clear singer.
I am steel; I am a druid.
I am an artificer; I am a scientific one.
I am a serpent; I am love.
I am a cell, I am a cleft, I am a restoration.

Another lesson from the myth of Cerridwen's cauldron is that a part of you dies and is reborn as you go through every major life change. So prepare to stand before the goddess with humility and great resolve. Over the next year and a day, you will see your life transformed.

The Cauldron of Dagda: Abundance

The Celtic father god, Dagda, provided for his followers from a bottomless cauldron. His cauldron was of such bounty that none would go away unsatisfied. The symbol of the inexhaustible cauldron is familiar in other mythologies and is similar to the horn of plenty. Many Witches fill their cauldrons with the fruits of harvest for Lammas and Mabon. You could also use your cauldron for an abundance spell.

For money, place a silver dollar in the bottom of your cauldron. Light a new green candle and allow the wax from the burning candle to drip on the coin. Secure your candle on top of the melted wax. Say:

Dagda, my good father
You have great bounty
I have great need
I pray to you for abundance.

As you watch the candle flame, reflect on all you have at this moment and be grateful. Then visualize our world as a place of great resources, a place where there is more than enough for all of us. Complete the visualization by imagining how you will feel when your current need is satisfied. Let the candle burn itself out.

The Cauldron of Branwen: Regeneration

Many versions of the Branwen story are told in myth. Whether she is represented as a powerful fairy queen; Babd (whose name means "boiling"), goddess of enlightenment; or the beautiful but hapless sister of Bran the Blessed, what remains consistent is that she owned the magical cauldron of regeneration. Many tales were told about this cauldron into which the slain were immersed and returned to life. It was this very cauldron that later became known as the Holy Grail.

Practitioners of magic know that in order to change or manifest something new in our lives, something else must be lost. Consider what change you wish to manifest in your life and what you are willing to give up to make room for this new way of being.

To cast this spell, fill your cauldron with pure water and add angelica, dragon's blood, and mistletoe. Heat this magical brew in your cauldron to the boiling point. Write on a slip of rice paper what must die away to make room for the new. Watch your old way of being dissolve within Branwen's regenerating cauldron.

Cauldron of the Old King: Sacrifice

Celtic myth relates how the king of the old year was drowned in a huge cauldron of beer during the feast of Samhain. At one time or another, many cultures practiced the cauldron sacrifice. Priestesses in ancient Denmark sacrificed men to their gods, catching their blood in sacred cauldrons. One such sacrificial cauldron was recovered from a Danish peat bog dating back to 100 BC. Thankfully, more swine than humans were sacrificed in cauldron rituals.

Modern Witches offer cauldron sacrifices of flowers in the spring and summer, and grain and vegetable sacrifices during the harvest. For a more traditional cauldron sacrifice, try a pork stew made in your cauldron.

Cerridwen's Cauldron Pork Stew

    2 tbsp. olive oil (for health and peace)
    1 ¼ lb. pork shoulder cut into ¾-inch cubes
        (pork is sacred to Cerridwen)
    3 tbsp. flour (for abundance)
    ¾ tsp. kosher salt (for grounding)
    ½ c. water (for creativity)
    ½ onion, coarsely chopped (for protection)
    2 garlic cloves, peeled (for protection)
    ½ tsp. dried summer savory (for mental powers)
    ½ tsp. coriander seeds (for love)
    ¼ tsp. turmeric (for purification)
    ¼ c. fresh cilantro, finely chopped (for protection)

Oil the inside of your cauldron. I've only used my cooking cauldron on the top of a barbeque, although it's possible to cook over a campfire. As you prepare this meal, be mindful of the magical properties of the various ingredients you're mixing together that eventually transform into something more than the sum of its parts.

Dredge the pork cubes in flour and ½ teaspoon salt; brown in oil. (It would probably be easier to do this part in a fry pan instead of your cauldron.) Once browned, place the meat in your cauldron with the water and heat. Sauté the chopped onion over a low heat and add to your stew.

Using a mortar and pestle, mash the garlic, savory, and remaining salt. Add this mixture into the stew. Using the mortar and pestle once more, mash the coriander seeds. Stir the coriander and turmeric into to the stew.

Once the stew is boiling, cover and cook over a very low heat until the meat is tender (about an hour). Stir occasionally. Remember to think of the magical properties of your ingredients as the foods transform into a stew.

Just before serving, stir in the cilantro. Serve your stew over mashed potatoes or noodles. If you make this stew for Mabon, sprinkle each serving with pomegranate seeds.

Halloween Cauldron of Abundance

by Janina Renée

The Halloween season is a good time to invoke and celebrate abundance, because at this time of year, the fruits of the ingathered harvest and the beauties of the world in autumn are truly golden. This is also a high-energy time, with children eagerly looking forward to costumes, parties, and treats—as well as a few of us planning a bit of magic and intrigue.

To prepare for this rite, fill a decorative cauldron (it could be a kettle or other cooking pot if you don't have anything more cauldronlike) until it is full to overflowing with symbolic seasonal items. A list of some meaningful items and what you could say as you present them will follow shortly. You can add to the ambience by ringing the cauldron with Halloween garlands, and setting it up on an altar-space decorated with autumn leaves, vegetables, fruits, and candles.

Be sure that there is more than enough of everything for everyone who is likely to be participating in order to underscore the intention of overflowing abundance. Also, allow for some extra goodies, so they can be offered to Mother Nature. If this ritual is being arranged by a group of friends, you may decide in advance what each person might bring to add to the cauldron; the more creative types might want to prepare some little treat bags or other special favors for this purpose.

On the other hand, if you will be performing this ritual at a party where you don't know all the people and can't talk to them in advance, encourage all of the bystanders to put something into the cauldron, even if only a penny. Later, everyone will be pulling things out of the cauldron, but it is also good for everyone to put something in, because such a gesture affirms that they are willing to engage the living universe in an exchange of energy. By contributing, they also affirm abundance in their lives, as well as their own magical potency as persons who have the power to give blessing.

When you are ready to begin the ritual, gather around the cauldron. The person chosen to lead the ritual should stand before the cauldron and declare:

At this season of All Hallowtide,
the cauldron of nature is overflowing:
Overflowing with the red and yellow and gold
of autumn leaves and apples and pumpkins.
Overflowing with the memories of childhoods past.
Overflowing with the magic of childhood's wonder.
Overflowing with the mystery of All Hallows Eve.

At this point, pause and ask everyone present to put their hands on the cauldron (if a small group), or to direct their hands toward the cauldron in an attitude of blessing, with the participants imaging themselves sending blessing energy to the cauldron. Continue:

And so, also, the cauldron of our lives:
Overflowing with abundance.
Overflowing with goodness.
Overflowing with blessings shared.
So it is, and so may it always be!

Say that final line with a flourish and a dramatic gesture of the hands, throwing a final burst of energy toward the cauldron; then, all drop their hands, and the leader continues:

And now, we all will share
in the cauldron of abundance.

Pass the cauldron around, directing each celebrant to take out different items in turn, as you explain their symbolic meanings.

Here are some examples of things that could be used in the cauldron and the things that you could say as each item is drawn out. These are just examples. You could put different things in your own cauldron (depending on what is available, meaningful, and convenient), and compose your own words to explain their significance. In the examples, here, the leader could say:

I bid each of you now
to take a packet of candy corn from the cauldron,
a token of childhood memories of Halloween fun.

As you hold the candy corn,
think back to your own childhood's delight,
as you gathered your Halloween treats.

After everyone has taken an item, set one aside on an offering plate, and repeat for the next item, saying something like:

> *I now bid you to take a box of raisins from the cauldron,*
> *symbolizing the autumnal harvest,*
> *and good health to carry you through winter.*

> *Now take a piece of dark chocolate from the cauldron:*
> *a treat to stimulate the pleasure centers of your brain,*
> *on these ever darkening nights.*

> *. . . take a hazelnut from the cauldron:*
> *the Celtic symbol of wisdom, for honoring this,*
> *the Celtic New Year.*

> *. . . take an apple from the cauldron:*
> *a token of the autumn harvest, just as it is also*
> *a symbol of the goddess Pomona,*
> *who was honored at this season,*
> *and the fruit of the Celtic otherworld.*

> *. . . take a crabapple from the cauldron:*
> *a token of the wild,*
> *reminding us that not everything is here to serve man—*
> *some things are here to serve themselves!*

The crabapple is also a symbol of the crone,
who speaks her mind and does what she pleases.

. . . take a miniature pumpkin from the cauldron:
this golden, globelike vegetable
is a symbol of golden abundance
and the fulfillment of harvest.

. . . take a penny from the cauldron,
to honor the circle of the year and the unity of life,
and affirm that we all deserve abundance.

. . . take [various toylike Halloween favor] *from the cauldron*
to invite the child within,
to enjoy this night of magic.

If someone has contributed a mixed bags of treats, you could say,

Now take the goodie bag [you can describe it],
which [name] *has prepared for us.*

Repeat for the items that each participant can take one of. There
might be some miscellaneous odd items left in the cauldron. In
this case, say:

To continue the circuit of blessings,
we will now pass the cauldron,
with each person taking something out.
We will stop when there are three items left,
and those we will dedicate to the spirit of nature.

This ends the ritual. Later, the offering plate will be set out in
some appropriate place outdoors. If there are any foodstuffs that
would be unsafe for animals to eat (like chocolate, which is dangerous for some animals), those items should be buried.

Magical Cleansing Reactions

by Calantirniel

When I worked in a New Age bookstore in Southern California as an intuitive consultant, I discovered that many customers had a hard time understanding how magic works. The old adage, "Be careful what you wish for," is certainly true, due to what I like to call "magical cleansing reactions"—anything unanticipated, jarring, or downright unpleasant that follows the launch of spellwork. It is the universe's way of clearing the path between where you are and where you wish to be, and it will do so with the least harm possible. Many people succumb to fear after these events and actually "cancel" their spell, hoping the unpleasant things won't happen anymore. But when a spell is canceled, you will not reach your original goal. Unexpected events just come with the territory.

As a certified Master Herbalist, I have observed a body in a state of *dis*-ease, where the goal is to get the body in a state of wholeness and wellness. The detoxification process can be excruciating, mostly consisting of painful withdrawal symptoms from unhealthy cravings of addictive substances. These substances range from sugar, dairy, meat and processed foods to coffee, cigarettes, and alcohol—even chemical "medicines" that mask pain but accumulate in the system and make health worse. During the process of consuming herbs; distilled water; and raw, cleansing, and nourishing foods, the body furiously pushes out the toxins in any way it can, which causes great discomfort. The farther away from health a person is, the longer and more difficult this cleansing process takes. However, when the body is arriving at a state of health, the process is entirely worth any pain and discomfort, due to the person's newfound health and rejuvenation. Their habits improve so that they do not experience such imbalance again.

It also works this way with magic. The further you are away from your intended goals, the more upset and discomfort you will experience before your wishes manifest. Luckily, it is not as hard as a physical detoxification most of the time! However, if you don't know this ahead of time (and many people do not), you might get the idea that your magic isn't working, when in fact it is! You may also think it is "messing up" your life, similar to the pain that is experienced when a person is physically detoxifying.

As an example, a woman came to our store to purchase supplies for a love spell because she wished to capture the romantic attention of a specific man. Without consulting us, she bought the supplies, performed her spell, and came back to the store complaining profusely that it didn't work. Upon asking for details, we explained the dangers of involving another person's will (and their karma) and that if she wanted love, she ought to send out a refinement of her intention—to allow her partnership to be an even better one. It is fine to notice things about a person that you find attractive, since it helps you define (and therefore recognize) your perfect partner when they arrive, but the universe is much wiser about how well that other person' energies would match yours—especially if you are healing and changing your energies so much and so fast that you literally change the "space" you are in. Your intended recipient may not be appropriate for you and could even keep you from evolving! Many people inadvertently bind themselves with their narrow intentions, and then want to know exactly how the universe will deliver their very limited wish!

The next thing we discovered was that the intended recipient of this spellwork had not only ignored her but had found an entirely different woman to date—one that she felt had much less to offer this man than she. Again, it only demonstrates that the spell worked perfectly, as it was obvious this man was entirely inappropriate for her and would have been a big problem had they become involved. However, it was quite an educational process relaying this to her. The most important thing to remember about magic is that YOU are the one that changes, not the outer circumstances, including other

people! However, that is where the true power lies: when you change, your circumstances and your entire universe automatically align with your intentions. After we talked to the lady for a while, she realized that she needed help learning how to know and love herself, learning how to truly receive, and extracting herself from the low self-esteem environments she was used to frequenting.

An astrological consultation helped her to understand herself even better than she could consciously know. She then began to appreciate things about herself that previously were not acknowledged, and thus began loving herself. When asking her what she liked to do, she said she loved to read and cook and also had fun with artistic exploration through drawing, painting, etc., as well as home decoration. I could see these things really fulfilled her, which was confirmed in her chart. When asking her where she was seeking a life partner, she said she went to the local bar. I asked if she had any alcohol issues, and she said she would maybe have a drink once a week and that was it, but her prior partner choices were always alcoholics. I then discovered alcoholism was in her family and that she was patterning herself after the non-drinking members of this dysfunction subconsciously, i.e., the ones who pick up all the pieces when everything falls apart. She likely did this to survive as a child in her family, but she didn't realize she was creating that situation again with a partnership. I then suggested she save her bar money and instead pay for classes about the things she liked to do, as this would be much better ground to meet someone who matched her new energy pattern.

In the meantime, she was to take flower essences for emotional education and begin correcting her chakras through meditation so energies would flow without blockage, with special attention on her yellow (solar plexus) chakra, having much to do with proper receiving and self-esteem. I relayed to her the differences between love and fear, giving and bribing, receiving and taking. We also taught her discernment (not judgment), or what others define as boundaries, so she could consciously choose her own experiences. When the experience is pleasant, she could continue, but when it was not, it was time to let it go. If questioned, we advised her to say, "I am not choosing such experiences anymore, and I don't have to justify it to anyone." I then said if a person who is usually pleasant begins to show traits that are unpleasant, she should tell them very clearly the problem <u>once</u>. If they continue, she should let them go, saying, "I'm making different choices now, and one of those choices is that the people in my life listen to me the first time." We advised her not to allow herself to be talked out of this decision. At first, this seemed harsh to her, but she soon realized how this could help keep her from getting involved in enabling situations.

She came back to the store to tell all of us that she hadn't met anyone yet (and she was really understanding the discernment techniques), but she loved the classes she was taking—the vibrancy really showed in her face. I then told her that because of her newfound happiness in herself, I saw her attracting a happy, available romantic interest in the near future. She said that would be great, but now she didn't care.

I told her: that is exactly why! Another month later, she was dating a wonderful man, and though I didn't see them again, I knew there was a marriage in their future! Her love spell did work after all—but not the way she thought it would. She had to emotionally detoxify and nurture herself first to become truly available. Then, she was able to attract an available and emotionally healthy person.

Another example of magical cleansing reaction often occurs when people wish for money or possessions without processing their existing poverty issues. I am not speaking of a temporary spell to get out of a financial bind (those spells tend to work very well in my experience) but am instead addressing people's wishes to be wealthy so they never have to work, or to own many material possessions, actually thinking such things would make them happy. Just like the woman who needed to learn to love herself in order to be loved, we need to feel deserving in order to be truly abundant. In fact, many of us need to define *abundance* as well as integrate abundant patterns. Unfortunately, many of us were raised with poverty consciousness, reflected in multiple forms we may not

recognize. When parents tell us to choose a "safe" career we know will make us miserable, or when we choose possessions only to make impressions upon others, these behavioral patterns are based on fear and limitation—they do not match truly abundant thinking.

Because of this way of thinking, we tend to mismanage the energies of money. If you need an example: most millionaire-plus lottery winners are at their original financial state or worse (even broke) within a short time of receiving their winnings! We need to examine what true wealth really is, and it starts on the inside. Is it measured with how much money and how many things you own (or that end up owning you)? Or is it measured by how much comfort and—most importantly— freedom you have in your life? Is the purpose of having things to impress people or is it to provide you a level of comfort so you can have the freedom to enjoy what you want to do, regardless of others' opinions? The idea is to bring in more income than you have in expenses so you can live at your chosen level of balance between comfort and freedom. It doesn't even have to be money, it can be through benefits, barter, or trade—abundant people are creative and think that way.

When casting spells, we also wish for the highest good and the highest expression of love possible, with no harm to ourselves or to others. If we ignore these rules, results can be mixed in a way you may not appreciate. For instance, someone who really wanted a $50,000 car at any consequence, solely to improve their image, ended up getting in an automobile accident where they sustained major permanent injuries and disabilities and nearly died. The payoff from the insurance company came and they bought their flashy car, but the additional price of lifelong pain and suffering (not to mention hospital costs) had clearly demonstrated the car was not worth it. And imagine what this did to their image! This particular example also shows us that health is indeed part of wealth. Please know that the universe always knows not only the most effective way, but also the least interruptive way to bring you your wishes. If the person had chosen instead to work on the reasons why they wanted such a car and resolved self-esteem issues, as well as any existing poverty-conscious issues, they may well be a healthy person today, and eventually would have had that car—not because they were trying to win popularity, but because they felt that car was of good quality and provided them comfort. See the difference? Or perhaps they would have realized they didn't want that car any longer and were happy with OR without it.

Checklist to Reduce Cleansing Reactions

I have come up with a checklist to help lessen and understand magical cleansing reactions. As you proceed with creating better magical intentions and as you grow into your practice, you will notice fewer of those unexpected events.

1. Always **align your intentions with the highest good**, bringing no harm to yourself or others, and exercise love over fear. This is accomplished by visualizing natural balance and the harmony of uninterrupted flow to achieve this, since the higher good always fluctuates. This is particularly useful in casting work toward solving the world's issues—many times we do not know what really is going on, but you can bet that the spirit does! No matter what you see or feel, only strive to achieve the natural balance and know that the spirit takes care of the rest.

2. Within the framework of the first step explained above, **create focused, crystal-clear magical intentions** to the extent possible. If results show you that you need to do a little more goal-refining, that is fine, but when your intentions are too vague, the universe may have trouble figuring out what it is you want. You may receive results that are not even close to those you seek. If these intentions are regarding another person, make sure everything you ask for is something you already do yourself. For instance, if you demand honesty and trust, make sure you are also honest and trustworthy and are able to trust others. Again, this is about seeking the natural balance. If an old issue keeps resurfacing, be diligent, do your healing work, and keep "sending it back," as the universe may

be testing you to see if you truly seek the change for which you are wishing.

3. Because we are human, we often cannot foresee the truly wonderful things the spirit desires for us. When we become focused on a wish, we might accidentally limit ourselves, and, unfortunately, the universe cannot deliver better than this. So, **add a "disclaimer" to your crystal-clear intentions** by telling the universe it has permission to deliver an even better outcome than you could ever imagine. Believe it or not, this very action can also help speed things up and lessen any cleansing reaction because the universe now has many more possibilities with which to work! Also, let go of your desire to control how the universe will deliver your intentions. If you did your job right in the second step, everything will take care of itself. The universe can also provide opportunities to heal known and unknown issues surrounding your intention. Be open to unforseen possibilities and work to manifest your desires.

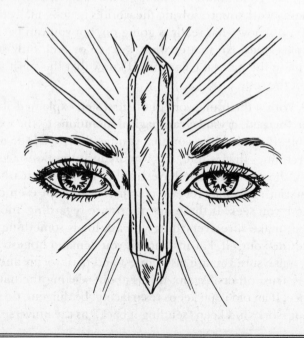

4. Remember: **Do not involve anyone else's free will**. This rule is particularly important to keep in mind with love spells, but also spells that involve unpleasant people or even enemies (see step five). If you find yourself attracted to someone, rather than placing a love spell on them, try to figure out what it is about them that you find so attractive. Add those qualities to the list when refining your intention in the second step. Since you will allow the universe to bring you even better things than you hope for, there is no harm in refining the qualities of your potential love interest as much as possible. Who knows? The universe may bring you that very person, but only if it is right for where you are and where they are. Otherwise, the universe will bring you an even better option. How can you possibly lose?

5. When dealing with an unpleasant person (maybe one who drains people with perpetual negativity), **do not wish the person away; wish instead the behavior and actions away**. And while you are at it, send the energy of love for them to learn! Often, we can find in ourselves (either by our similarity or difference) how we got into such a situation, so learn from it via balance. That person might not only "disappear" from your life, but also any others that match that energy pattern. If the person decides to change their energy pattern, their new pattern may bring them back to you, and you can proceed from there. However, be aware: most people do not change their energy, but they may lie because they are in a place of fear. You need to observe your intuitive messages and their actions, not their words! If the person does you harm and is combative, you have every right to protect yourself and others from this behavior. Besides making sure you are not in the wrong on the matter, a binding of their fear-based actions to immediately reflect back onto them is an ethical way to handle this. You may also visualize an action of justice that comes from the mundane (i.e. being arrested, etc.), but you should not attempt to control how the universe achieves the results. Again, the spirit knows the higher good better than any of us.

Along with a binding, I also like to add an extra dose of healing, loving energy, so that if the person ever does decide to learn to truly act from love rather than fear, the binding can fall away. In this way, there is no harm to others, and unpleasantness cannot karmically backfire. Always keep in mind that people act out of fear because they are in a fearful place and are likely in pain. It's their karma at work, but they haven't figured that out yet and may not for a long time. Be thankful that you learn, and give energy toward hoping that they also learn, while allowing that they might not. Similar to planting seeds, it is not our responsibility to determine which seeds grow and which ones do not. It is only our responsibility to plant them—nature wisely chooses which seeds are supposed to grow.

I hope you have enjoyed reading my cleansing reactions checklist and now have a better understanding of how magic works. The best way to really know, however, is through experience. It may be a bit bumpy at first, but as you learn more about yourself and more about magic and the universe, these results will get better and better, so don't give up. Good luck!

For Further Study

Frost, Gavin, Ph.D, D.D. and Yvonne Frost, D.D., *The Witch's Book of Magical Ritual*. Paramus, NJ: Reward Books, 2003.

Don't Fear the Reaper: The Reign of Saturn

by Raven Digitalis

He appears in a long, black, hooded cloak. Sickle in hand, his influence is that of reaping the harvest, declaring reign on the fruitful land by taking its life to the underworld. He is Saturn, Kronos, Azræl, the Grim Reaper. He is the archetype of the dying year. He is Death.

As deities of life, light, and fertility exist, they must also have their necessary counterparts. Without death there would be no life, and this often maligned force of nature demands equal observation. All pantheistic structures include one or more representatives of the vibration or occurrence of death, be it the death of the land or the death of humans and animals. This deity had no option but to manifest as an enigma, for death is a grand mystery.

Mythology

The ancient Greeks recognized the deity Kronos as the first-born Titan. His name is also spelled Cronus or Kronus, and should not be confused with the deity Chronos, who is the personification of time (though Kronos does have some reign over the time as marked by cycles of seasons and harvests). The Titans were the mythological offspring of the primordial deities Gaea and Uranus. Because of his divine associations—which are comparative to that of Horus, the son of Isis and Osiris in Egyptian mythology—Kronos was especially honored during antiquity's Golden Age, and continued to be celebrated in Græco-Roman harvest festivals.

The Roman agricultural deity Saturn (or Saturnus) was aligned with Kronos as the Greek and Roman cultures merged. Saturn was the father of Ceres, Veritas, and Jupiter. In mythology, Saturn overthrew and castrated his father, Uranus. Later, because of a prediction that one of Saturn's sons would in turn overthrow him as universal sovereign, Saturn devoured his children as a preventative measure (much as the Egyptian sky goddess Nuit "devours" her children, the Sun and the stars, each night).

However, Saturn's mother, Ops, hid her sixth child, Jupiter, on the Mediterranean island of Crete. Later, Jupiter overthrew Saturn and the other Titans. Note that in Greek mythology, Jupiter is equivalent to Zeus, and Ops to Rhea.

Saturnalia was the Roman festival associated with Saturn, and it took place around the time of the Winter Solstice as a festival of the harvest. Saturnalia was a celebration of Earth's bounty, as well as a time to feast. Fascinatingly, common culture went topsy-turvy during the holiday, as the slaves and lower-caste individuals were allowed to "turn the tables on their masters" and were free to do as they pleased.

Later in history, as the experience of death was anthropomorphized into a deity, associations were drawn between the folkloric Grim Reaper and Kronos/Saturn. Azræl, the archangel of death in Islamic belief, has also been associated with these deities, though he seems to have a livelier, less corpselike depiction.

In Hinduism, one of the nine planets (Navagrahas) is Sani (or Shani), which corresponds to our Saturn, the deity who is the Karmic judge.

Some modern Wiccan traditions draw associations between the Saturnine archetype and the Holly King, who rules the dying year. The common Wiccan imagery of the Oak King and Holly King is derived from *The White Goddess* by Robert Graves, which is itself a poetic account of ancient histories interwoven with modern myth. Indeed, the archetype of death is a universal phenomenon because death is life's doppelgänger.

Astrology

Before the discovery of the outermost planets, Saturn was thought to be the furthest planet from the Sun, earning it metaphysical associations with death and the cycle of life. Naturally, mythological deities representing death and the overarching life cycle were ascribed and aligned to its properties.

Astrologically, Saturn rules the zodiac signs Capricorn and Aquarius (though modern astrology often recognizes Uranus as ruling Aquarius). Saturn is exalted in Libra and represents the following traits:

- Magic
- Challenges
- Limitations
- Melancholy
- Life Lessons
- Mortality
- The Hidden
- Structure
- Karma
- Death
- Fasting and Self-Sacrifice
- Wisdom
- Aging
- Fear
- Doubt
- Self-Discipline
- Career
- Heaviness
- Ambition
- Seriousness
- Order
- Power
- Prestige
- Maturity
- Accomplishment
- Self-Examination

These characteristics are essential to keep in mind when you're performing any magic or meditation concerned with Saturn.

According to Western esoteric sects of the Jewish mystical tradition called Kabbalah, Saturn rules the sephiroth (sphere) Binah on the Tree of Life. In Hermetic alchemy, the planet Saturn represents lead and the "black phase" of what is called the Great Work. The astrological phrase "Saturn return" refers to the full circle of Saturn in one's natal chart (just like everyone's birthday is a "solar return"). It takes Saturn roughly thirty Earth years to make a full orbit around the Sun. Saturn returns usually occur twice or thrice in a person's life cycle, and each cycle signifies a rite of passage or spiritual maturation.

In a Neopagan or Wiccan sense, the first (approximately) thirty years of a person's life can be viewed as the "Maiden" or

"Son" phase, the second thirty years as the "Mother" or "Father" phase, and the final years as the "Crone" or "Sage" phase of the life cycle.

The Planet

As for the physical planet itself, Saturn is the second largest planet in the solar system (after Jupiter), and is the sixth planet from the Sun. Also, following Jupiter's Ganymede, Saturn's Titan is the second largest moon in the solar system. Curiously, Titan even has all the proper elements and components to develop into a planet similar to Earth, though this never happened due to its location. Saturn actually has thirty-five named moons, and their cyclical rotation around the planet represent, in a sense, a miniature Saturnine solar system in and of itself.

Saturn has a number of rings surrounding it, which were first observed by Galileo Galilei in 1610. These rings are made of billions of ice and dust particles, average 150 feet thick, and may be a result of a moon or comet that shattered hundreds of millions of years ago.

Saturn is made up of the element hydrogen, has a 75,000-mile diameter, and could encompass more than 700 Earths. Also, a day on Saturn lasts approximately eleven Earth hours. The name *Saturday* is an English carryover of the Roman name signifying the planetary rulership for that day of the week.

Ritually Connecting to Saturn

The following is a ritual designed to connect to Saturnine energy. It should be performed on a Satur(n)day at 3:00 am or 11:00 pm. The time you choose should be the time that you emerge from the cleansing water preceding the ritual.

As with all non-ceremonial rituals, keep in mind that this is simply an outline; it is your choice to either follow it to the letter or modify it slightly for your own purposes.

You will need:
- One black candle with the symbol of Saturn inscribed on it
- One piece of obsidian or onyx
- Any combination of the herbs alder, bistort, boneset, comfrey, cypress, elm, hemp, ivy, kava-kava, mullein, patchouli, poplar, skullcap, or slippery elm

- One rose
- One whole beet (not pickled!)
- A towel or blanket (preferably black)
- Black body paint, greasepaint, or a body marker

Before this ritual, it is essential to shower, bathe, or otherwise physically cleanse your body. I would also highly recommend listening to an album by the darkwave band Sopor Aeternus and the Ensemble of Shadows before this ritual. Anna-Varney Cantodea, the musical project's creator, references Saturn, occultism, and emotional darkness like no other artist. This gorgeous, atmospheric music is perfect for setting a Saturnine mood. Perhaps you would like to listen to it in a candlelit bath beforehand. Additionally, it is essential to be surrounded by as much darkness as reasonably possible before and during this rite. The color of Saturn is black.

After bathing or showering, dry yourself and remain naked. Look at yourself in the mirror, connect your eyes with their reflection, and take three very deep breaths to center your energy. These breaths should be taken in through your nose and out through your mouth.

The symbol of Saturn represents the deity's sickle. With the body paint or marker, draw a large symbol of Saturn on your chest. Take some time to perfect this design. Make it thick and visible, painted with the "cross up" and "tail down." If you

♄

The symbol
of Saturn

are a more seasoned occultist, draw the Seal of Saturn on the back of each hand. To continue attuning to Saturnine vibration, draw the Saturn-aligned numbers 3, 6, 9, 11, 15, 30, and 45 on various places on your body, such as the arms, legs, and belly. Whether or not you understand the numerological correspondences of these numbers is unimportant (though doing serious studies into the associations could be of great benefit).

Grab your black towel or blanket. Wrap it around yourself, concealing your nudity. With your other tools on hand, journey outside to an area where you can be undisturbed in nature, even if you have to drive to get there.

Once you are in a good spot, unwrap the blanket or towel, standing nude in the outdoors and "symbolized." Looking up at

the night sky, take three more long, slow, deep breaths, filling your body with the energy all around you.

At this point, ignite the black candle and set it in a secure spot. Lie with your back flat on the ground, your flesh touching the ground. Cover yourself from the neck down with the blanket and sprinkle the herbal mixture atop. Finally, lay the rose across your chest to, in a sense, symbolize death. Once again, take three deep breaths to center your energy and feel yourself in this symbolic ritual setting.

Once you feel that you are appropriately grounded, either whisper or roar (depending on how you feel or how vocally conducive the setting is) three times: "Saturnus . . . Saturnus . . . Saturnus! Great Reaper and Lord of Karma, he who oversees time and the death of all things great and small. Great Saturnus, great Kronos, great angel Azræl, I connect with you now on this most sacred night of Saturn. I invite you to surround me, to deliver messages that I must hear, and to hear my prayers. Saturnus . . . Saturnus . . . Saturnus!"

At this point, close your eyes and "see" yourself surrounded in darkness. Open your psychic and perceptive channels to see if you receive any messages from the archetypal deities of life and death. You may receive messages having to do with qualities or properties that Saturn represents.

When you feel this meditation has continued for as long as is beneficial to you, speak aloud any personal prayers you have to Saturnus, Kronos, or Azræl. When finished, keep your eyes closed and pluck the rose from atop your body. Hold it high above you and say "Great Saturnus! With the severing of life in this rose, I too ask you to sever and break issues in my life that no longer serve me. Great Lord of Karma, and Bestower of Divine

Justice, I ask you to assist me in harvesting that which restricts my development, that it may fall before me to analyze, understand, and banish. Saturnus, with your mighty sickle, I ask you now to oversee this rite."

Break the rose in two, either in the middle or at the top of the stem. With a piece in either hand, let your arms fall, hitting the ground with force. Close your eyes and slip into meditation. Again, allow any visions to fill you, and simply be in the presence of the energy at hand.

When you are finished, re-enter your normal waking state of consciousness, get up, shake the herbs off the blanket, and throw the flower pieces in opposing directions. Snub the candle in the ground, declaring "So mote it be." End by thanking the deities, bowing to each direction, and leaving the beet as an offering.

For Further Study

Douthitt, Bill. "Saturn As You've Never Seen It." *National Geographic Magazine*, December 2006.

Greer, John Michael. *The New Encyclopedia of the Occult.* St. Paul, MN: Llewellyn, 2003.

Harris, Stephen L. and Gloria Platzner. *Classical Mythology: Images & Insights.* Mountain View, CA: Mayfield Publishing, 1995.

Tresidder, Jack, ed. *The Complete Dictionary of Symbols.* San Francisco, CA: Chronicle Books, 2004.

Wikipedia contributors, "Cronus," *Wikipedia, The Free Encyclopedia,* http://en.wikipedia.org/w/index.php?title=Cronus&oldid=155600951.

Witch, Heal Thyself: A Guide for Your Magical Energy System

by Mickie Mueller

Ok my dear Witch: you've been working your magical fingers to the bone. You've been really busy in both your mundane life and in your magical life, as well. You know, work, family, errands, a healing spell for your cat, the solstice is coming up, your friend's coming by for a tarot reading later. . . . Now you feel drained. So what's wrong? Well, let's see, you're a magical practitioner and you work with energy all the time, right? When was the last time you gave your energy field an overhaul? It's one of your most valuable magical tools, and you use it every time you do magic. You're probably using it even when you don't know it.

Magical practitioners open up themselves naturally to powerful input and work closely with their own energy fields and, therefore, are naturally more sensitive to the changes in it. Your aural body is your personal energy field and is made up of several layers of your spirit self. When you're projecting yourself into your environment as a vivacious person and you feel like the world is in the palm of your hands, your aura extends out several feet from your physical body, surrounding it with its spiritual light. When you're feeling tired, drained, weak, or ill, your aura is weak and pulls in tightly to your body in order to conserve energy. When you are working magic, sending energy, or shielding, it's your aural body that you are using. In order to be a healthy, happy person and an effective and powerful Witch, you need to keep it clean and in good working order.

Lots of outside factors can negatively affect our energy fields, such as EMFs (electromagnetic fields) from power lines, appliances, or other electrical equipment. Another one is the general "psychic sludge" that we can pick up just from being around people sending out negativity. Our own negative thoughts and feelings may also become lodged within our aura, weighing us down and draining us of energy. But there is good news: as Witches, we also have the tools to heal ourselves! Remember, if you don't take care of yourself first, you can't help anyone else.

Cleansing Your Aura

The first step to cleansing your aural body is to find a quiet place to work. It should be a place where you can sit and relax for at least twenty to thirty minutes uninterrupted, clear of clutter, quiet, and peaceful.

You may sit comfortably or lie down, whichever you prefer. Close your eyes and begin breathing in through your nose, out through your mouth. Begin relaxing your feet, then ankles, and then calves, working your way slowly up your physical body. Become very aware of each part of your body as you go, tighten it, and then completely relax it until you reach the top of your head. Once you have reached a deep relaxed state, envision a white mist forming several feet above your body. Once you see it clearly in your mind's eye, visualize the mist beginning to rain liquid light down upon you. It feels warm and sparkles as it falls on you. You feel the liquid light flowing down, down, and as it moves over you, it also moves through you. It begins to wash away black specks that you now notice in your aural body, pushing them down through the floor and into Earth, where it will be neutralized. Nothing is stronger than the liquid light and its power to heal. As the liquid light rains down on you, it washes all the black specks away, and your aural body begins to pulse and glow with strength now that the specks no longer block your personal shining light. Your aura flows about you, naturally healing itself of any holes or nicks. Now the liquid light has stopped flowing, and the mist that it flowed from dissipates.

You may remain in a meditative state as long as you wish, enjoying the feeling of your cleared and healed aural body.

Before you finish, visualize your aural body forming a shield of light, like clear armor, that no negative energy can penetrate. See it in your mind's eye. Anytime in the future you are in a situation when you feel you need extra protection from negativity, visualize that light again and allow your aural body to form a tight shield around you.

When you feel you are ready, slowly open your eyes. Drink lots of water over the next few days as that will help flush any built-up toxins your physical body might have been storing due with the negative energy. If you feel tired a few days afterward, repeat the exercise, as body toxins can release into your aural system and it may need to be cleansed again. If you begin to perform this exercise regularly, at least once a month, you'll begin to feel your personal energy grow stronger on a regular basis.

Cure for the Magic Hangover

Have you ever had a "magic hangover?" After that big spell, you feel really lousy the next day, drained perhaps? That's a magic hangover, and it's not uncommon when you do a lot of magical workings. What's happened is that you have spent too much of your personal energy for your spellwork; as when you donate blood, it takes time for your body to produce more and allow you to bounce back. The above exercise can really help you recover from a magic hangover, but are there any ways to prevent that feeling? You bet! The key is to not expend all your personal energy on the spell, but to build up *extra* energy during spellwork and then allow your aural body to direct it, but don't spend the energy you need to keep yourself going. It's really easy to get caught up in the trap of spending all your energy for a spell, but in the long run, you really don't have to do that—so don't! A powerful and wise Witch needs to keep their personal energy strong all the time.

Techniques for raising energy can include chanting, dancing, singing, and humming. I have even done it by whispering intently. But doing these things alone is not enough. As you do them you need to visualize the energy coming up from Earth and the natural elements, building around you inside the circle you have cast. Program this energy with your intent. This is the energy you will send, not your personal energy. See it with your third eye, swirling about, sparkling, feel it crackling on your skin, or perhaps you feel the pressure of it building. However you sense it is fine, but be aware of it. Then, when the energy seems to be at its pinnacle, direct it with your will and intent toward your goal. If you do this properly, you'll send lots of energy for your magic *and* keep your personal energy field intact. Practice makes perfect, so make sure you take the time to raise energy every time you do spellwork. You'll get great results with no magic hangover!

Chakras: Wheels of Light

Chakras are very important to the practicing Witch's energy. In fact, they're important to every living being. Just as we use our aural body, we also use our chakras for magic. Without a properly running energy network, it is very hard to raise the energy needed to perform magic. The human body contains a network of hundreds of locations for focused and concentrated energy, but here we'll focus on the seven major chakras. *Chakra* is a Sanskrit word that roughly means "wheel of light." They are energy vortexes within our aural bodies. They process energetic input and translate mind, body, spirit connections. When chakras are operating properly, they keep the spiritual energy properly flowing through our bodies. When they are blocked or imbalanced, our mind, body, and spirit can be adversely affected.

Seven Chakra Correspondences

Listed here are the chakras—location, color, energies processed by the chakra, and crystal correspondences, in that order. There are many books on the subject that go more in depth, but these will get you started:

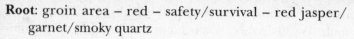

Root: groin area – red – safety/survival – red jasper/ garnet/smoky quartz

Sacral: below the naval – orange – sexual reproduction – carnelian/orange calcite

Solar Plexus: 2 inches above naval – yellow – personal power – citrine/topaz

Heart: center of the chest – green – love/compassion – rose quartz/emerald

Throat: base of throat – blue – communication/creativity – turquoise/lapis

Third Eye: middle of forehead – indigo – intuition/visions – amethyst/purple fluorite

Crown: top of head – violet/white – connection to higher realms and deity – quartz crystal

Crystal Chakra Balancing

You'll need one of the tumbled stones from each chakra category above and a small bag to keep them in. Your chosen stones are now your set of chakra stones and will be used only for chakra work.

Cleanse the stones under running water; visualize all unwanted energy pouring out of the stones. Hold each stone, one at a time, and charge them with the intent that they'll assist you to balance and heal your chakras. Lay down in a comfortable place where you won't be disturbed. Beginning at your root chakra and working your way up, lay each stone on your body with the corresponding chakra location. The quartz should go right at the crown of your head; it won't be laying on your head, but just get it as close to the top of your head as you can.

Now close your eyes and, starting with the root chakra, visualize a white beam of spiritual light coming from the sky, down into your root chakra. Feel it merge with that chakra, and visualize the chakra spinning and glowing red and vibrant.

When the chakra is free of all blockages and running smoothly, the white light will vanish. Move on to the sacral chakra and visualize the same thing, only this time it is glowing orange. Continue up the chakra system in this manner all the way to the crown. When you're done, you can remove the stones. Your chakra system should be free of blockages and running smoothly. Feel free to repeat this exercise anytime you wish to re-balance your chakras.

Grounding and Centering

Here is a simple technique for grounding and centering that is useful to use before doing magic, or anytime you need it. Close your eyes and pull your aural body in as tight as you can, focusing on your solar plexus chakra—your personal energy center. Allow it to align with that chakra, now gently release your aura back out to its original expansion, seeing it aligning properly with each chakra and your physical body as it goes. You are now centered.

In order to ground—that is, to connect with the energy of Earth—stand or sit in a cross-legged position. Allow roots to

grow down from the place where your body meets the floor. Those roots grow down, deeper and deeper and begin to form a deep connection with Earth. Now an exchange takes place: all the negative and unhealthy energy you may be storing flows down the roots into Earth to be neutralized, and you may draw up fresh Earth energy. Feel it filling you until it flows up to the sky. You are connected to the higher and lower realms, and you are grounded. Now you are ready for anything, magical or mundane!

When a magical practitioner takes the time to work on their personal energy system, they are doing something very important by healing themselves. Once you have taken good care of yourself, you have confirmed your own power and its importance in your life and in your magic. Without a properly working energy system, magic can't take place and manifest the changes that you are working toward in your life. Therefore, before you even begin thinking about bringing about the things you want to see in your life, the first step, my Witch, is to heal yourself.

Retiring Ritual Tools

by A. C. Fisher Aldag

What do you do with a worn-out wand, a tired old talisman, an athame that's lost its ambiance? You've likely invested years of time and loads of magical energy into your special ritual tools. Yet some of them may not "work" for you any longer. You might have a drawer full of implements that have outlived their usefulness. An amulet may have kept you safe from numerous negative situations, but as a consequence, it is beyond cleansing. You don't have the heart to just pitch your old ritual tools into the garbage. Besides, that wouldn't be good for the environment—or the custodial worker who has to handle your "dirty" energies. So what do you do?

My favorite *Robin Wood Tarot* deck is literally falling apart. The poor thing is more than twelve years old, and has survived flooded campsites and grubby-fingered students. It provided thousands of accurate readings. Yet, my deck has had its day. I received a new *Robin Wood Tarot* for Mother's Day, so it's time to stop using the old one. This gave me the idea to share suggestions for retiring ritual tools.

First, I'll discuss some philosophies on the use of magical implements. These beliefs are neither right nor wrong; the use of ritual objects is completely up to the individual magician. I suggest that you practice awhile and find the magical philosophy that is perfect for *you*.

Types of Tools

Personal Tools: Some people believe that ritual tools are very personal and should not be shared with anyone else. These individuals do not like others to handle their magic items, as energy may be transferred from a person to an object. Some Witches can sense the aura of a person who has touched an item, and this interferes with their magical process. They'd be horrified at the notion of using a pre-owned ritual tool. They may charge their magical objects with their own energies and cleanse them after each use.

Coven or Family Tools: Some magical objects are shared by all the people in a group or all members of a family. These items may contain the energies of all individuals who have handled them. The implements might gain strength and power after each use. They may be heirloom objects, such as great-grandma's onyx necklace or the high priestess's original chalice. Magical items that are coven property may be cleansed at specific times—during the waning Moon or after a highly charged working, like healing a soldier who has just returned from active combat. All the people in the group may aid in the cleansing ritual, or one individual may be responsible for ritual tool maintenance, such as the matriarch of the family or the priest of the coven.

Everybody's Tools: These are items handled by many people. They can include public objects, such as an outdoor statue. Other items may have been purchased at a garage sale or previously owned by a famous magician. Some magical implements are displayed at a Pagan Pride event, passed around a large ritual circle during a festival, or used for divination by a professional reader. Students can practice with them. (This is why I don't own very many glass magical tools!) Ritual items used by many people can accumulate strong levels of energy and be used as "magic banks" to store power. Psychically speaking, they can also get quite dirty. After a while, some well-used ritual tools may need to be seriously cleansed, retired, or discarded.

Have you ever touched a magical tool that just seemed, well, polluted? This feeling is quite different than lifting Lady Rowan's athame, and intuitively knowing that it belongs exclusively to *her*. A "dirty" ritual object might give you a negative mental image or an emotional reaction, such as anxiety or revulsion. The item may have a slimy texture that only you can feel, or it could even psychically "burn" you. This is a magical object that needs intensive cleansing. It might even need to be destroyed.

Other items might simply be worn out or inappropriate to your current situation. Perhaps in college, you adored your purple robe with dramatic silver moons and stars, but that was twenty years (and twenty pounds) ago. Or, like my cherished tarot deck, your object might be bedraggled from years of hard use. Yet, you still have a profound emotional attachment to your tools—they were always there when you needed them!

Retiring Techniques

Here are some techniques and guidelines for cleansing, retiring, or otherwise getting rid of used ritual implements:

Cleansing

The following suggestions are meant to be used with tools that may contain residual energy, which is perceived as negative or harmful, or just overly "busy" with psychic vibrations. Before beginning any purification rite, take precautions to shield yourself from any possible baleful influences. Some traditions cast a circle, others use wards or images of protection, such as a bubble of pure white light. Many individuals perform a self-blessing ceremony before a working such as this. Numerous methods of psychic protection can be found in Llewellyn books about Wicca, Paganism, and ceremonial magic. Of course, if an object is the property of your coven or group, be sure to gain a consensus before performing any magical act with the object, such as cleansing or re-charging.

The following purification rituals work on items that are sturdily constructed of metal, stone, wood, leather, or heavy fabric. Using clean running water, such as stream water or rainwater, immerse the item three times while you visualize washing away any harmful energies. If the item will stand up to rough treatment, bury it for a short period, preferably in sandy soil outdoors. This works especially well if the buried item is rained on or experiences a light snowfall. Don't bury badly contaminated objects in flowerpots, near your garden or water supply, or under a threshold. If your magical object is inflammable, pass it briefly through a flame (optimally during the sacred fire of a sabbat). Use a candle color that you associate with purification: white, yellow, or even black, which absorbs negativity. The wind has cleansing properties, so you might hang a magical item in a tree for period of time. Be certain to verbally request that any negative energies dissipate, while causing no harm to anyone. Use words like *remove, cleanse, heal, dispel,* or *banish* rather than *cast forth, scatter,* or *change.* You want the harmful influences to be truly vanquished.

Magical objects of a more delicate nature—paper, cloth, or feathers—require gentler treatment. Smudge the item using strong incense with purifying qualities, such as frankincense, Nag Champa, sage, cedar, or sweetgrass. Sweep the smoke counterclockwise over the object with a white feather, a bundle of oak leaves, or a broom. Caution: do this in a well-ventilated area, and don't breathe the fumes! Sprinkle uncured tobacco or powdered nettle leaf over the object, then brush the used herbs onto the ground. Place the item in a sunny windowsill or under the light of the New Moon. Some cultures anoint ritual tools with consecrated oil, cornmeal, salt water, or pollen. Others place an egg on top of the object, asking that any negative powers be absorbed through the eggshell. They then discard the egg.

A magical tool that contains seriously baneful influences may require a longer period of cleansing. It may need to be buried in fallow ground during the winter, or sit undisturbed in the sunshine all summer long. Some items might need two or three purification ceremonies to truly "chase" them clean. Other objects can be purified by combining several ritual techniques. One enterprising Witch washes her healing crystals under the lawn sprinkler on a sunny afternoon. The combination of sunlight and running water effectively clears the stones of any lingering malevolent energy. Calling upon deities, spirit guides, or elementals can also aide the magical cleansing process.

After completing one or more of these ceremonies, you may wish to re-charge or re-consecrate your magical objects. Appropriate rituals for cleansing, dedicating, and consecrating tools can be found in many Llewellyn books designed for beginners and experienced Witches alike.

Sharing
Some individuals may be uncomfortable with this concept. If the notion of handling other's ritual items bothers you—or the idea of recycling your old tarnished pentacle fills you with dismay—don't do it. It's your stuff, after all. However, if an implement has been gently used, and still has a good "vibe", you may feel it best to pass it on for others to use. Of course, you'll want to cleanse everything first.

Tool swap: That crystal ball might not work for you, but it could be an invaluable divination tool for someone else. That aforementioned purple robe might look fantastic on the new dedicant, and it could help her feel especially magical. Or, if it has threadbare spots, it might make a nice altar cloth. If you experimented with Egyptian rituals, then found that the Celtic pantheon works better for you, you might swap your Eye of Horus wand for a "new" oaken staff.

Garage sale: We've raised funds for our regional Pagan Pride event with a sale of slightly used items, both

magical and mundane. When advertised in local bookstores and online lists, our former possessions were quickly sold to proud new owners. Of course, if your neighbors will have a conniption when they see your pentagram wind chimes, then you might wish to sell them at a flea market, consignment shop, or through an online auction service instead.

Donate to a teaching coven: If one of your students drops the slightly chipped ceramic candelabra on the cement floor, it won't be a complete disaster. If your tarot set is missing a card, a beginner can still use the deck to learn. You may have underlined all the best parts of *Buckland's Complete Book of Witchcraft*, yet the coven library will still find it useful.

Recycling: Okay, the item won't be used for magic ever again, but it might see a new life as fiberglass insulation, an automobile bumper, or a newspaper. If something has negative energies stored within, you will want to cleanse it prior to hauling it to the recycle center.

Retiring an Object

This applies to magical items that have given you good service and are still humming with positive energy, but are old and worn. You can save the object to use as a house-blessing talisman, secreting it under the floor, in the rafters, or inside a wall. If the item is made of paper, you can use it for a scrapbook or Book of Shadows. For example, I have a lot of plans for my now-shabby tarot cards. Once I transfer their power for accurate divination to my new deck, the old cards can serve as bookmarks, altar decorations, a collage-style journal cover, and several protective talismans—such as placing the Chariot card in the glove compartment of my car. Magical objects can be used to safeguard your locker at school or your workstation, or they may be hidden in that special place where you keep your childhood treasures. Nonperishable ritual items can decorate your garden, flowerpot, or outdoor altar. Perhaps the children can make a "fairy shrine," filling it with pretty stones, glass beads, and other things that just don't fit your lifestyle any longer. Please be certain to verbally re-charge or consecrate the item to its new purpose.

You may wish to draw the good feelings and beneficial magic out of your old power object, and transfer the energy to a new ritual tool. The optimal time for this type of ceremony is a "cusp" situation (dawn, sunset, or midnight) and location (in a doorway, on a bridge, or at a crossroads). If this is not possible, you might simply put the old object on the left side of your altar and the new item on the right. Solstices and equinoxes are good days for this sort of magic, as is the waning time right before the New Moon or the waxing Moon right before it's full. You may also wish to use astrology to determine an optimal day. Llewellyn's almanacs (including this one!) can help you to find the most beneficial periods for transferal rituals. For instance, I will reassign energy to my new *Robin Wood Tarot* when the Moon is in the air sign of Libra, symbolizing both communication and balance.

Standing with the old power object in your weaker hand and the new item in your stronger hand, state your intent for the old object and your wishes for the new. Thank your retired tool for its help and service and request that it bequeath its power to the new implement. Visualize the energy flowing from the old object into the new. You may see the magic as colored mist, hear it as a static sound, or simply feel it flowing from one location to the other. If you wish, you can prepare a "conduit," such as a wand between the two objects, asking that the reserve of magical power flow from the old item to the new tool. Once the ceremony has been enacted, the power can naturally drain or transfer, as long as the implements remain undisturbed. You may then wish to re-consecrate both the old and new magic items for their current purpose. After you're finished, thank any entities you summoned to help you.

Ritually Destroying an Object

This is for magical items that are completely ruined. They are physically ragged and psychically spent, or so filled with "bad vibrations" that they can never be used again. Some readers may remember my article on car spells, and the story about the talisman that helped my husband to survive a wreck. That particular magical object looked as though it had been burned to a crisp. Objects that have absorbed massive amounts of negative energy, or tools that remind someone of their abusive ex-spouse, or magical implements that protected you from a truly harrowing experience—war, a fire, cancer surgery—are just not salvageable.

I don't usually deal in absolutes, because each individual will know what is right for them. But in this case, I insist that destroying a ruined magical tool is a must. Do *not* give it away to the charity rummage sale. Do *not* hand it down to your grandchildren. Things like our crispy talisman should never, *ever* be used again. Even if it's still pretty, get rid of it.

Burn it: This is a different type of magic from burning an offering, which sends energy with the smoke for the purpose of giving a tribute to a deity, or making a sacrifice to increase magical power. Because a votive offering can create more of the same type of energy, you must be certain to convey that you are performing a banishing ritual rather than a sacrifice. You don't want more negativity brought into your life; your objective is for any baneful energies to be removed from this plane. Make it a point to use very precise words of power to cleanse, vanquish, and destroy harmful influences. Obey local fire laws and follow safety precautions when ceremonially burning any object.

Bury it: Bury the implement in a location where it is not likely to be dug up for a long period of time, and where there is little foot traffic. Again, ensure that the object will not create more negativity, that it has not been "planted" like a seed, but buried to disintegrate and be gone. Let the item rot in the ground or snow. Give it a symbolic funeral. Other ways to ritually bury an object include casting it into deep water or immersing it in salt. The Biblical practice of "seeding the ground with salt" was likely a ceremony to banish negative energy.

Break it: Many ancient shrines contained broken objects. The items may have been broken to make a votive offering—or it may have been a method to get rid of a particular implement's harmful effects. Some were bent then cast into a stream or sacred well or dropped into a cave. Ensure that this will not pollute the environment or cause a hazard for anyone who might find the object.

Do *not* discard dirty magic items by flushing them down the toilet or washing them down the sink. Or, for pity's sake, down the garbage disposal. Often, when I caution folks about what *not* to do, it is something that I've learned the hard way. I've practiced magic for more than twenty-five years and facilitated many classes. Yet, I can still make some pretty awful mistakes—like taking an old protective talisman filled with harmful energies and tossing it into my indoor wood-burning stove. Take it from me, if you wish to dispose of something that contains negative power, don't use household utilities, such as your plumbing system or furnace. Your insurance company won't appreciate it.

Optimal times for banishing magic are the distinct endings of seasons, such as Samhain or the final day of the waning Moon. Black, gray, white, yellow, or dark-blue candles, stones, and altar cloths symbolize the removal of negativity. Politely ask your guides, deities, and elementals for assistance. Use the same techniques as for cleansing, including sprinkling with salt, smudging with a sage bundle, washing in pure water, and so forth. Herbs of purification include hyssop, nettle, mistletoe, pine, and rowan flower. Immersing a spent ritual tool in liquid pine cleaner can be an effective way of destroying harmful influences.

Discarding your worn-out ritual tools gives you an excuse to purchase new magical items! Blessings, and good luck!

Transforming the Magical Self for the Twenty-First Century

by Abby Willowroot

Magical thinking, being, and living is growing rapidly among people of all ages. Many young people are discovering the Pagan and Wiccan paths for the first time. Some older seekers are returning to ideas, first discovered in their youth, that they did not fully understand until now. Some of us are reinventing ourselves based on our beliefs about what is sacred and natural. All of us share one thing: we are moving into the future along paths that are metaphysical, spiritual, and powerful.

Sacred Transformation is the magical act of stepping into a future that you are creating by your thoughts, actions, and beliefs. It is shedding the old and creating the new with positive intent and visions of a different future. The past may have served you well, but the future that will serve you best is an unwritten one, an unexplored one. A vibrant future that reflects and honors your new perceptions, insights, and visions is what you are able to create now, if you so choose. Knowing and understanding that who you were yesterday is only a single facet, a small part, of who you will become tomorrow allows you to expand your power and vision as you move forward.

Joseph Campbell said, "When we talk about settling the world's problems, we're barking up the wrong tree. The world is perfect. It is a mess. It has always been a mess. We are not going to change it. Our job is to straighten out our own lives."

In changing our own lives, we *do* change the world, more than we could ever imagine! Our lives are an affirmation of our beliefs, desires, and dreams, and we create it daily.

Magic and magical opportunities and changes are all around us, we have only to look to see that what was hidden from us yesterday is possible today. Our spiritual rituals and practices have expanded our awareness of Earth's messages. Spiritual connections between people are expanding, and our magical beliefs are shared by more people every day. Long-held Pagan, Wiccan, Indigenous, Heathen, and Earth Spirit beliefs are gaining popularity and are beginning to change the world's thinking in positive ways. What unites us is greater than the diverse rituals, customs, and trappings that separate us. The ancient wisdom of Earth's people is emerging from the shackles of Colonialism and forced Christian conversion and suppression. We are being joined by the enlightened—Christians, Jews, Hindus, Buddhists, Muslims, Atheists, and others—who understand that the way forward must be based on respect for Earth.

Individually, we each must decide how to best advance these positive changes using our own unique magical skills and gifts. Finding your own special place in a magical future is sometimes scary, but it is also exciting and empowering. The challenge is to decide what path we want to walk as magical people. Finding the right path for yourself begins with asking yourself two questions: What is important to me? What is meaningful for me? The things that intrigue you, inspire you, and bring you a sense of accomplishment and joy are the things you need to move toward and add to your daily life.

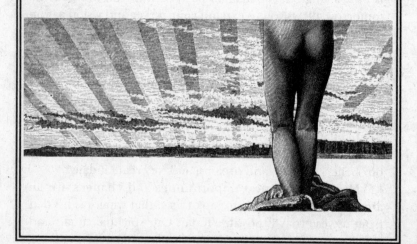

Living Magically

In our modern culture, it is easy to fall into a kind of automatic sleepwalking, an unconscious living. This hypnotized way of life becomes deadening over time. We can awaken ourselves by integrating blessings, rituals, divination, sacred silence, and eco-friendly habits into our daily lives. It may seem challenging at first, but these practices soon become natural and automatic as we establish new, more magical ways of being. Another favorite quote from Joseph Campbell is, "Reality is repetition and participation." What we think, value, and do is what we will become and what we create in the world.

Each day, it is important to focus on doing things that move us closer to our true selves, our most magical selves. "BE MAGICAL," is a mantra you can live daily to transform yourself in powerful and healing ways. Doing these few simple things every day will put your feet firmly on a positive spiritual path: Bless, Eco-live, Move, Awaken, Gratitude, Inspire, Chant, Act, and Learn.

B*less yourself and others daily in invocations, rituals, and prayers*
E*co-live and be conscious of your impact on Earth*
M*ove and celebrate your body in dance and movement*
A*waken yourself to being really alive with yoga or meditation*
G*ratitude expands joy and promotes sharing and understanding*
I*nspire others with your words, actions, and spirit every day*
C*hant, sing, celebrate, and create something every day*
A*ct consciously on your beliefs in some way every day*
L*earn something new and teach something every day*

Silence is rare in our world—the din and sounds of the modern world are all around us. We are overloaded with input. It is essential that we take some time each day to sit silently and listen to the sounds and rhythms of Earth and Mother Nature. It is in this silence that our spirit finds itself and recharges, but it is very easy to get caught up and forget to take this vital time for refreshment. Silence means no multitasking. This does not mean sit silently and text, draw, write, or exercise. It does not mean sleep, it does not mean eat. It means sit silently with NO function. Adding other kinds of meditation, yoga, or contemplation (at other times) is beneficial, but the act of simply "being quiet" for at least fifteen minutes a day is essential for a healthy spirit and expanding consciousness.

Another important aspect of living magically is learning to simplify your needs and wants. Magical regalia is an important part of our spiritual practice, but do you really need five ritual cloaks? Eight different pentacle pendants? Or five different magic wands? In the West, we have become accustomed to too much, too much of everything! We often buy it, use it, and dispose of it with little thought or consciousness. While there is nothing wrong with collecting an item, we need to be mindful of what we are doing and how we are using our abundance. It is fine to collect any of these things, but it is a bit greedy and wasteful to collect all of them and more, simply for the pleasure of having them. This kind of thinking is so nineteenth century that it's surprising people still cling to it, and it is an attitude whose time has long since passed.

Accumulating lots of possessions and magical trinkets is no proof of your spiritual or magical powers. Your ritual tools can be ornate or simple, common everyday items, purchased or homemade—the power they carry comes from how you use them. What magical tools should not be is a way for you to feel better than, or cooler than, those around you are. Sacred tools are just that: tools. The power they hold is the power within you, amplified by repeated use. Remember, "Reality is repetition and participation." We become magical by using our magic daily. Moving into the future, it is time we all consider lightening our baggage a bit.

Flowing with the many changes the future brings requires flexibility and a willingness to expand our perceptions of possibility. Exciting and challenging changes are coming, and the stronger our connection to our spiritual essence, the more easily we will be able to happily experience those changes. These are exciting times, and who we choose to be as we move forward will impact our world for generations to come.

This century is bringing robotics, nano everything, radically new medical treatments, revolutionary gene therapies, Earth changes, stronger global interactions, and many things most of us cannot even imagine yet. These things will drastically change our day-to-day lives. Some changes will be universally celebrated, some will challenge us, and others will be vilified and feared. Whatever the changes, the stronger and more spiritually centered we are, the better prepared we will be to deal with them. As the world becomes more complex, our own human natures will hunger for simplicity.

There need not be a disconnect between complexity and simplicity, as they are both necessary facets of modern life. We are grateful for modern medical complexity when we are sick or injured; we are grateful for simplicity when we hunger for relaxation and personal connections. Both have their place and purpose in our lives. The trick is to maintain our spiritual centers through all these shifts and changes.

Cultures around the world are changing quickly. Many "foreign" traditional customs and practices are becoming part of our own lives, and the globalization is cultural as well as

economic. While megacorporations are focusing on the economic changes, people are focusing on the cultural, social, and human changes. With all this new input, the sheer information avalanche will soon overwhelm us if we don't do a bit of paring down now to make room for all the new things we'll be learning.

Today, traditional Western magical practices mingle with distant indigenous and shamanic beliefs. These different metaphysical systems are being drawn together and are blending into each other more rapidly each day, creating rich new traditions and beliefs. Prejudices against magic are still present in many cultures, and persecution exists in some places, while magic and metaphysics flourishes in others. We are being touched by the blending of beliefs in both subtle and profound ways. Modern books on Wicca and magic are finding their way into cultures that traditionally feared and persecuted Witches. Thanks to publishers such as Llewellyn, Wicca, metaphysics, and their teachings are spreading around the world rapidly.

These are exciting times; we are reclaiming the many Earth-oriented faiths of our ancestors and adding the wisdom of all human history to that of our own genetic memories. Generations of shamans and healers of the Andes, Himalayas, Alps, Urals, and Rocky Mountains speak to each other through us. The ancestors of the plains, forests, islands, deserts, hills, and seashores share their wisdom through us. We are a sacred conduit to the future. As magical people, we are each of us the sacred keepers of ancient truths and Earth wisdom.

This is a time of power, possibility, and hope. We're in a unique position. Never before have we had access to the diverse ancestor wisdom and practices available to us today. What we will do with these many millennia of sacred knowledge and guidance remains to be seen. However, one thing is sure: the more prepared we are individually and as a sacred, Earth-honoring people, the more powerfully we will use the gifts of our ancestors as we move forward into the future.

Creating a Foundation for Your Spiritual Beliefs & Practices

Eager to blaze your own Wiccan spiritual trail? Ready to express your own form of Divinity by crafting a tradition that's all your own? Raven Grimassi's comprehensive guide will help you merge your core Wiccan beliefs into a cohesive and transformative spiritual practice—a personalized path to the Divine.

Handpick a pantheon of harmonious deities. Customize your own rules and rituals. Incorporate existing myths or create your own. Perform magick? Choose a patron deity? Work with egregores? Keep a traditional Book of Shadows? It's up to you! Grimassi explores all modes of Wiccan worship and maps out key elements—Gods and Goddesses, ritual structure, religious / philosophical views, magical practices, coven structures, training, laws—to guide you through this soul-searching process.

CRAFTING WICCAN TRADITIONS
288 pp. • 6 × 9
ISBN 978-0-7387-1108-9 • U.S. $15.95 Can. $18.50
To order call 1-877-NEW-WRLD

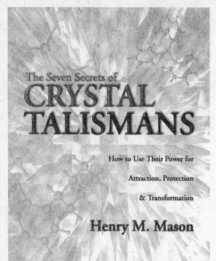